I0432275

Reading list
07.02

LANDSCAPE PROFESSIONAL PRACTICE

Second Edition

LANDSCAPE PROFESSIONAL PRACTICE

A Guide to Legislation, Conduct, Appointments,
Practice and Contract Procedures

Second Edition

Hugh Clamp

Gower

First edition published 1988 by Gower Technical Press Ltd.

This edition published by
Gower Publishing Limited
Gower House
Croft Road
Aldershot
Hampshire GU11 3HR
England

Gower
Old Post Road
Brookfield
Vermont 05036
USA

Hugh Clamp has asserted his right under the Copyright, Designs and Patents Act 1988 to be identified as the author of this work.

British Library Cataloguing in Publication Data
Clamp, Hugh, 1927–
    Landscape professional practice. – 2nd ed.
    1. Landscape architecture 2. Landscape architects
    I. Title
    712.3

    ISBN 0 566 08071 0

Library of Congress Cataloging-in-Publication Data
Clamp, Hugh.
    Landscape professional practice: a guide to legislation, conduct,
appointment practices and contract procedures/Hugh Clamp. — 2nd ed.
        p.   cm.
    Includes index.
    ISBN 0–566–08071–0 (hardback)
    1. Landscape architects—Legal status, laws, etc.—Great Britain.
    2. Landscape protection—Law and legislation—Great Britain.
    3. Landscape architecture—Contracts and specifications—Great
Britain.   I. Title.
KD2990.L37C55   1999
343.42'078712—DC21   98–38680
                                                                 CIP

Typeset in Century Schoolbook by Bournemouth Colour Press and printed in Great Britain at the University Press, Cambridge.

CONTENTS

LIST OF FIGURES AND TABLES

Figures

Tables

PREFACE TO THE FIRST EDITION

Landscape architects, managers and scientists need, in addition to their academic qualifications and practical experience, to have acquired the necessary minimum standards of professional competence in:

professional conduct and legal responsibilities; a knowledge of both common and statute law in matters affecting the environment; and the efficient management and administration of their projects.

Those who require their services either as a consultant or an employee can then be confident that their interests will be safeguarded and that the work will be competently and expeditiously executed.

This book covers the above aspects of landscape practice in detail and sets out clearly and in a logical sequence the necessary information and procedures. Practical examples for those concerned with the design, management and scientific sides of landscape projects are also given.

Hugh Clamp
Richmond 1988

PREFACE TO THE SECOND EDITION

Since this book was first published there have been a number of significant changes in professional practice affecting landscape consultants, not to mention the award of chartered status to members of the Landscape Institute, who are now required to have:

O   an understanding of the legal and professional obligations of a landscape consultant in relation to clients, the profession, fellow consultants and society in general;

O   an understanding of the organization, administration and management of landscape practice including client relationships and professional charges;

O   an awareness of the extent and application of law and legislation relating to land and the landscape;

O   a sound knowledge of the legal and contractual aspects of implementing landscape work.

The second edition of this book has therefore to take account of the Landscape Institute Code of Professional Conduct and the new Landscape Consultant's Appointment; the Value Added Tax Regulations affecting landscape work and the Construction (Design and Management) (CDM) Regulations 1994; the implementation of the Latham Report on the Building Industry leading to the imposition of new procedures for interim payments and the obligatory adjudication scheme for all construction contracts incorporated in the Housing Grants, Construction and Regeneration Act and the Arbitration Act, both dated 1996; and the Environmental Assessments being demanded by planning authorities exercising their powers under the 1990 Planning Act over a wider range of medium-sized projects than those laid down in the EC Directive, not to mention the 1997 Hedgerow Regulations (SI 97/1160). The JCLI contract has been amended six times since the first edition of this book, and a new library of National Landscape Specification Clauses has been published by the NBS. All these innovations and their implications have been taken into account in this present edition.

The Landscape Consultant's Appointment and the Forms reproduced in the Appendices at the end of this book are the copyright of the Landscape Institute and are reproduced with their permission.

Hugh Clamp
Yetminster 1998

THE CODE OF CONDUCT AND THE LANDSCAPE CONSULTANT'S APPOINTMENT

 THE LANDSCAPE INSTITUTE CODE OF PROFESSIONAL CONDUCT

Landscape professional practice is no different from the other professions in that, as distinct from any other occupation, the professional is trusted to put his or her client's interests before any financial gain to themselves. In spite of the fact that the longer a doctor's patient is sick, a lawyer's client's litigation continues, the financial affairs of an accountant's client take to finalize or the value of an engineering project rises, the greater the financial reward, the professionals involved in each of these respective areas must nevertheless be relied on to cure or finalize the affairs of their clients at the earliest possible moment and at the minimum cost.

So it is with landscape architects, managers and scientists. Whether they are remunerated by salary, or on a time or percentage basis, they also are entrusted with ensuring that all the projects on which they are engaged are completed in both the minimum time and the minimum cost commensurate with the client's particular requirements.

Earlier professional codes of conduct were drafted as much for the protection of the members of the respective professional institutes as for their clients. There were mandatory minimum scales of charges, but no minimum standards of competence. Professionals were prohibited from advertising their existence or special expertise, except in the most oblique and subtle manner, and certainly did not compete with a fellow member for the same client.

Now, under the threat of legal proceedings from the Office of Fair Trading, all that has been swept away. Fee scales may only be 'recommended', members are encouraged to advertise their services and no one can expect another job from the same client however well the previous one was executed. Landscape consultants no longer compete with their fellow professionals by attempting to offer a better service for the same fee as their competitors. Now they must submit tenders of fees for a professional service, the quality of which is almost impossible to define in writing, on projects the scope of which by their very nature must be unknown at the outset of the commission except in the most general of terms.

It must not be thought that as a consequence codes of professional conduct for those who work in the landscape business have disappeared. On the contrary, the need for firmly controlled professional standards of conduct is still as strong as ever. The Landscape Institute's Code of Professional Conduct (see Appendix 1) contains nine undertakings covering such standards, but while under Clause 3 members are still required to act impartially and to interpret the conditions of contract fairly between client and contractor, the acceptance of their primary allegiance to their client is undisputed. Not since 1974 have they mistakenly been thought of as acting as 'quasi-arbitrators' in the exercise of their landscape contractual duties – unless the latter are disputed by the contractor (in which case another consultant is appointed as arbitrator) – and as a consequence they are no longer immune from charges of professional negligence.

While the Code insists on the observance of the highest standards of professional conduct and self-discipline, the landscape consultant is expected to devote all his or her energies in the best interests of the client. It is quite possible, therefore, for two landscape consultants at a public inquiry each to put forward diametrically opposed but equally valid viewpoints on behalf of their respective clients.

Although there is no restriction on the framework within which members practise their profession – whether salaried or self-employed, in partnership, as a company (limited or unlimited), as a contractor or as a consultant – any conflict of interest with their client or their shareholders must always have been previously disclosed in writing, so that in the event of their advice turning out to be not as impartial as might at first have been thought, any conflict of interest has been previously made clear.

By permitting landscape consultants to advertise – that is, to offer their services directly to a potential but previously unknown client – the Code allows them to 'tout' for work provided that it is done discreetly (see Figure 1.1).

As a consequence this also means that they may well be approaching a client who is already using the services of a landscape consultant on another project. In effect (although many may not realize it) consultants are now permitted to 'poach' another's client, again of course provided it is done discreetly and not in a proactive manner. It is

Dear Sir

Mr .... has suggested in a letter to us of .... that we write to you concerning the proposals to .... and we understand that he has kindly put our name forward for consideration in the appointment of a landscape consultant.

Our practice was established in .... and we presently employ .... qualified landscape architects and town planners, ... senior assistants, ... technicians and .... students.

I am pleased to enclose details of the practice and hope you will not hesitate to contact us if you require further details. If appropriate, we shall be pleased to attend an interview and to arrange for you to inspect our offices.

Yours faithfully

Figure 1.1   Pro forma of a letter from a landscape consultant in response to an enquiry from a potential client

also important to remember that Clause 8 of the Code only requires a landscape consultant to notify a fellow member of the fact of their having been approached to proceed with work on which to their knowledge another has already been employed. The obligation is only to 'notify' – the consent of the former landscape consultant is not required. However, when taking advantage of this right it is always prudent to ascertain that no outstanding fees are due to the former consultant, just to make sure that this is not the sole reason for the client's wishing to make such a change! As in any divorce, both sides are rarely blameless and it is wise to remember this fact and to take particular care to ensure that the same thing that happened to the former consultant does not happen again with their replacement.

Equally, while advertising is no longer prohibited and those seeking the services of a landscape consultant need no longer rely on personal recommendation – provided of course they knew who to go to for such a recommendation in the first place – members of the Landscape Institute, in paying for such an advertisement, must not 'mislead those for whom they carry out professional services as to their capabilities and skills'.

This also raises the question of reaching the right markets. While it is always gratifying to see one's work illustrated in the pages of *Landscape Design* or *Horticulture Weekly*, this is less likely to bring in new commissions than publication in the *Architect's Journal*, *The Local Government News*, the *Estates Gazette* or *Country Life*, depending on which market or area of possible future demand for one's services one is aiming at.

 ## FORMS OF PRACTICE

Having qualified, landscape architects, managers and scientists have the choice of working in the public or private sector as an employee or in the private sector in a self-employed capacity. Most choose to work as an employee, at least initially until they have consolidated their academic learning and gained further experience.

CONTRACTS OF EMPLOYMENT

Contracts of employment are now required by law to comply with the Employment Rights Act, all subsequent EC directives and UK legislation, covering *inter alia* at least:

1. The name of the firm and the employee.
2. The starting date of employment.
3. Any probationary period (and salary?).
4. Job description, alternative location of employment, obligations and responsibilities.
5. Basic salary, working hours, overtime, bonus, salary increases and any other remuneration.
6. Holiday entitlement dependent on number of years employed and restrictions as to accruments, duration and time of year.
7. Any group staff pension, health insurance and retirement provisions.
8. Sick leave entitlement, duration and statutory sick payment and deduction provisions.
9. Entitlement to reimbursement of travelling, subsistence and hotel expenses.
10. Trades union rights.
11. Time off and Continuous Professional Development (CPD) obligations.
12. Restrictions on spare-time work and entry into architectural competitions.

13. Retention of copyright by the practice of work undertaken on its behalf.
14. Confidentiality of work undertaken by the practice and its clients.
15. The obligation of employees to notify any matters likely to give rise to a claim for professional negligence, and the obligation of the practice to abrogate claims for professional negligence by its insurers against employees.
16. Provisions for the termination of employment and the restrictions on location of offices and enticement of employees and clients of the practice by former employees setting up in business on their own account.
17. Grievance and disciplinary procedures, termination of employment in the event of contravention of the Landscape Institute Code of Professional Conduct, misconduct or conviction of a relevant criminal offence.
18. Any other conditions.

All employers are required to deduct from any payments and salaries due to staff the tax for which they are liable and forward it to the Inland Revenue. Detailed guidance is given in the Department of Employment booklets Nos 1–16.

PUBLIC SECTOR

The technical work of a landscape consultant, either as a principal or an employee, is no different in the public sector than it is in the private sector. The conditions under which the work is carried out do, however, differ in a few respects. In the public sector the services of landscape architects, managers and scientists are required in central government offices, in the statutory authorities such as the health authorities, in development corporations, and in local government at both county council and district council level.

In the latter case chief officers are responsible to committees of elected members who lay down priorities, allocate funds and whose approval is necessary on all schemes before the work is put in hand. These committees and the staff in their respective departments have to comply with established council procedures and standing orders, particularly those affecting the invitation and acceptance of tenders, with alternatives and limits dependent on the amount of the expenditure involved (private consultants engaged by the council also have to follow the same procedures). The various committees – for example planning, housing, recreation, highways, and so forth – are therefore the 'client', professional advice being provided either by employees working within the department concerned or more usually by a technical services department that comprises architects, engineers and quantity surveyors working either in single or multidisciplinary teams.

It is usually assumed that public sector projects are for the good of the community as a whole, free of individual and commercial interests, and – because of the relevant authority's responsibility for the subsequent upkeep and maintenance of the work carried out – designed with due regard to both capital and revenue running costs.

PRIVATE SECTOR

If and when employees – from either public sector or private sector offices – manage to acquire sufficient continuity of private work to enable them to go into practice as self-employed landscape consultants, they have a choice of six ways of practice.

As a sole practitioner

This is the only option available to aspiring freelance consultants in cases where there is unlikely to be enough income generated to support more than one individual. The difficulty inherent in this arrangement (although initially there is often no alternative) is that due to fluctuations in workload or the postponement of projects there may well be long periods of inactivity which can only be overcome by taking in work subcontracted from other more busy practices, with the accompanying legal problems that may arise as a consequence of this, not least of which is the question of professional indemnity insurance.

There are, however, considerable tax advantages to being a sole practitioner, in the form of the greater tax-deductible expenses and allowances available to the self-employed (even when one works from home using only the kitchen table). Working on a self-employed, full- or even part-time basis does not necessarily have to start from the beginning of the fiscal year in April, and the advice of a tax consultant is always advisable, even on this point alone, as it is often advantageous to start later in the year.

Practice as a partnership

To even out the peaks and troughs in workload and to take advantage of the tax concessions available to them, most consultants arrange to practise, as soon as they can, with others as a 'partnership'. This is defined in the Partnership Act 1890 as: 'the relationship which subsists between two or more persons carrying on a business in common with a view to profit'. This is not to say that they must *make* a profit; indeed, it is not unknown, unfortunately, for some partnerships from time to time to make a loss and still continue in business. The only legal requirement is the *intention* to make a profit.

There are other defining characteristics and requirements to being in partnership. Sharing an office or staff does not necessarily constitute a partnership. Practising in partnership with another, or others, who do not necessarily have to have the same qualifications or disciplines is also possible (provided they are not activities incompatible with individual codes of professional conduct) and enables a practice to provide a more comprehensive service. Partners' liabilities in law, however, are total and apply to the full extent of their financial assets, property and homes without restriction of the limits of their liability individually or collectively in any way, it being considered that this 'concentrates the mind' in respect of their proper duty of care.

The main advantages of a partnership over practising as an individual are:

1. Financial liabilities are spread over more than one individual.
2. Peaks and troughs in individual workloads can be evened out and executed more economically.
3. Accommodation, equipment, technical and secretarial resources can be shared.
4. Greater capital can be provided for work in progress and to minimize overdraft requirements.
5. The costs of 'practice promotion' can be shared.
6. Different skills and abilities can be incorporated into the practice at partnership level.

Partners cannot by definition draw a salary but must rely for remuneration on a share of the profits, which does not have to be on an equal basis and which may or may not be directly related to the capital they have invested in the firm. Often new partners joining an existing practice may agree to leave a proportion of their share of the profits in the firm so as to build up any capital they may have put in initially until they have gained parity with the existing partners, after which they become entitled to an equal share of the profits; however, this is not always necessary.

Only when the capital of individual partners in the firm is unequal is it normal for it to attract interest.

Salaried associates, even if entitled to a bonus or share of the profits by definition if receiving any salary, are not in law 'partners' even as 'junior' partners, the phrase 'salaried partner' being a legal contradiction in terms.

When the names of associates are included in the partnership's letterhead, to give due recognition of their status they must be identified separately. The same stricture applies to any consultants whose services the partnership may make use of – these are often retired partners who receive a retainer or smaller share of the profit, and who are no longer legally liable for the actions of the partnership subsequent to their departure. Retired partners are, however, still liable for any actions by the partnership prior to their departure and so 'run-off' professional indemnity insurance must be maintained either by themselves or by the partnership to cover any claims that may subsequently be made against them.

If the names of all the partners are not included in the name of the partnership it is advisable but no longer obligatory for the name of the practice to be registered as a business name.

Like any other contract, partnership agreements should – if for no other reason than to establish their existence with the Inspector of Taxes – but do not have to, be in writing and should cover *inter alia*:

1. The name of the firm.
2. The place (or places) of business.
3. The date of the commencement of the partnership.
4. Its minimum period of duration and earlier dissolution in event of disagreement.
5. Initial provision of working capital by each partner, payment of interest, payments on death and settlement of accounts on dissolution.
6. Arrangements for property belonging to the firm, that which is co-owned and that individually owned but used by the firm.
7. Mutual rights and duties if differentiated – for example holidays, illness, sabbaticals, work introduced, and so on.
8. Miscellaneous earnings from other activities – for example lectures, journalism, honoraria or teaching.
9. Profits and losses and subdivision by partners if not equally, including a minimum share for any individual(s).
10. The bankers to the partnership and arrangements for authorized signatures and names and numbers of signatories for sums over a certain limit.
11. The partnership's accountants, whose opinion is final and binding and if not to whom the dispute is to be referred.
12. Provision for changes in the constitution of the firm, including new partners.
13. Arrangements for pensions and retirement at a certain age, after fixed term, notice required, consultancy payments, repayment of capital or current accounts on retirement or death.

14. Dissolution of the practice, resignation of partners, exclusion of goodwill from practice assets to minimize tax liabilities.
15. Restrictions on practice in locality, with existing staff and/or clients, by resigning partners or after dissolution of the practice.
16. Insurance against liability of surviving partners for dead partner's share.
17. Arbitration procedures in the event of dispute between partners.

Cooperatives

Similar in most respects to partnerships, cooperatives (which by definition are effectively made up of all members of the firm, either including or excluding secretarial staff) would seem to offer advantages in encouraging individual identification with the financial prosperity of the practice, but in fact are difficult although not impossible to put into practice. There are a number of practical problems involved in such arrangements – for example size, requirements for capital distribution of profits, professional liability and indemnity insurance, and so on – but for those who value equal ownership, control and job satisfaction above the size of earnings and output, the effort to overcome these difficulties is often worthwhile.

Cooperatives are of two types. The first is made up of those cooperatives that are based on 'common' ownership principles where no one can build up any equity in the enterprise which they can sell or take away when they leave. These are the most common form and are usually based on the Industrial Common Ownership Movement (ICOM) model rules.

The second type of cooperative are those run under 'co-ownership' principles in which members acquire shares which earn a dividend but without earning additional voting rights and which members can sell back when they leave. Model rules have been produced by the Co-operative Development Agency (CDA) and Job Ownership Ltd (JOL) in which shareholdings can alter in value.

Both types of cooperative can be legalized by registering with the Registrar of Friendly Societies under the Industrial and Provident Societies Acts or with the Registrar of Companies as a company limited by guarantee of £1 per member (or if appropriate by shares). Both types of cooperative provide limitation or liability protection.

Group practices and consortia

Similar advantages in sharing economies in accommodation and administrative costs, sometimes by setting up a separate company solely for this purpose, are achieved by group practices and consortia.

In this kind of working arrangement each practice retains its individual identity and thus does not enjoy the advantages (or suffer the disadvantages!) of sharing profits and workload. Members of the Landscape Institute must not, however, misrepresent themselves as being qualified to perform the work of another division or grade of the Institute. Consortia are usually formed from practices of different disciplines – for example landscape consultants, architects, engineers and surveyors – for a single project or series of similar projects, each practice retaining its separate identity and practising as such from separate addresses in order to provide the client with a wider range of disciplines but with a single responsibility in the event of something going wrong, and for a single fee. In both cases meticulous care is necessary in the clarification of responsibilities in respect of professional indemnity insurance.

Practice as a company

Architects, solicitors and accountants have always been able to practise as a private company but until recently they have been prohibited from limiting their liability to their shareholding. The increasing number and cost of professional indemnity claims, together with the enactment of the Civil Liability (Contribution) Act 1978 and the Latent Damage Act 1986, has resulted in many consultants giving serious consideration to practising as a limited liability company in the UK, in a similar way to that which has always been permitted overseas. Practising as a limited liability company does not, however, give automatic immunity from claims, a company still being liable to the full extent of its assets and individual directors still being personally liable if they can be identified (not difficult in the case of a professional practice).

There are, however, other advantages to such a way of practising one's profession (although there are an equal number of disadvantages); one such benefit is that changing a partnership into a company is relatively easy (the corollary, unfortunately, is that reversing the process is often time-consuming and painful!). It is advisable for companies to be registered under the Companies Act 1985 and its subsequent revisions. Companies are distinct and separate entities which must submit their annual accounts to the Registrar and which are entirely separate from their directors, who are paid a salary, usually fixed by themselves, subject to PAYE. Not surprisingly they are responsible to their shareholders who, in the case of a private company, are limited to the directors themselves, each director being responsible to the extent of his or her own individual shareholding. This may be less than £100 but in the case of a landscape 'company' is usually equivalent to its capital, rarely less than £10 000 and often in excess of £50 000.

The main advantage of all this to a landscape practice is that when operating as a company it does not have to distribute all its profits to its directors (who would then be obliged to pay tax on them). It does, however, have to pay corporation tax on undistributed profits. Set against the undoubted tax advantages that registering as a limited company brings is the fact that, when simply operating as a partnership, practices have to include in their accounts an amount for the estimated value of 'work in progress'; in certain circumstances this can achieve the same effect of evening out the peaks and troughs of annual fee income as that gained by practising as a company.

The actual management of a practice run as a company will probably be little different from that of one run as a partnership. Monthly meetings of the partners, chaired by a senior partner, are replaced by monthly board meetings of the directors under the chairperson, assisted by a 'company secretary', with an annual general meeting of shareholders in accordance with the Companies Act.

Whether a practice is run as a partnership or a company, its respective partners or directors are usually working partners or executive directors and rarely are decisions made on the basis of voting rights, it being usual to rely on a consensus view.

It is unlikely that the ability to practise as a limited company, with non-executive directors and shareholders providing capital from the listed or unlisted securities market, will arise in the landscape professions for all but the largest practices (as is beginning to occur with architects) for some years to come.

Simultaneous practice

Members of the Landscape Institute, while always being permitted to work – either on a salaried basis or as consultants on a fee basis – for landscape contractors, may now also be directors of a contracting company without loss of professional status or membership, provided always that they 'inform clients in writing at the outset of the full extent of their interest'. This means that they can at the same time be both landscape consultants and directors of a company or organization trading, for example, as landscape contractors (particularly those offering a design and build service) or nurserymen. Since their names and professional qualifications can also, and sometimes must, appear on the headed notepaper of each of the respective businesses with which they are involved, it is considered advisable for there to be two quite separate notepapers so that the client is fully aware without any possible doubt of the particular responsibilities and loyalties of the person with whom he or she is dealing at any one time.

PRACTICE PROMOTION

Landscape consultants have always been able to make the work of their offices more widely known by sending unsolicited articles and details of work in progress and recently completed jobs to the technical press, provided no payment is made to the journal concerned. The relaxation of the prohibition against advertising has given rise to illustrated professional directories circulated free of charge by the publishers to potential clients. A charge is made for inclusion in such directories. This is a convenient way of ensuring that illustrations of one's work, together with that of one's professional colleagues and competitors, are well publicized, but it should be used with discretion in view of the cost involved.

Professional-standard photographs of all completed jobs carried out by the practice are therefore essential and should always be readily available, in black and white and in colour. With modern processing techniques it is no longer necessary to hold large stocks of enlargements of each job and one or two shots enlarged to A4 or A5 with an accompanying description filed separately in the practice's library will usually suffice. 35mm colour slides are sometimes an advantage but take time to copy and are not essential.

Printed single sheets containing a number of photographs of a particular project or type of project are helpful to potential clients, as are printed practice information sheets and CVs of the partners. Copies of objective and unbiased articles in the press, including those describing either the general work of the practice or individual jobs, are always of interest to new clients. An illustrated summary of recently completed work, prepared on a regular basis and sent not only to existing clients but also to potential ones, is also useful.

'Entertaining' clients is often counter-productive, particularly when dealing with those in the public sector, but the discussion of mutual problems before or after a meeting in congenial but not ostentatious surroundings – perhaps over a meal – can sometimes be helpful.

While in a similar way it could be seen to be clearly undesirable for consultants to have business connections with certain individuals, this no longer applies to having connections with or involvement in the landscape-contracting and plant-producing side of the industry. Landscape architects, managers and scientists have always been able to work within these sectors of the industry provided it was on a salaried or consultancy basis. Now they can be shareholders or directors of such businesses, participating directly in the profitability of the organization resulting from their own individual efforts. This injection of professional expertise at board level can only be of benefit to the industry, *provided that* – as the Landscape Institute's Code makes clear – anyone engaging in such simultaneous professional practice observes the basic precaution of disclosing the fact to clients, so as to eliminate any conflict of interests.

Irrespective of any mandatory codes of conduct, however, the basic principle of acting with integrity – whether as a consultant in the public or private sector, or as a director or employee of a landscape contractor or nurseryman – must still apply. To act fairly, even without the protection from legal actions on the grounds of negligence, must always be the essential obligation of the landscape practitioner.

 ## THE LANDSCAPE CONSULTANT'S APPOINTMENT

The essential ingredient of any landscape project is the existence of an atmosphere of trust and goodwill, without which any scheme is doomed to failure. Like other professional codes of conduct, which lay down standards of behaviour without specifying details of compliance, the landscape professional conditions of engagement list the duties of landscape architects, managers and scientists but not how these duties are to be carried out. The conditions are totally silent on the manner in which the work is undertaken and the quality, resources, effort and skills required for any particular project. These are matters which at present depend entirely on the individual concerned and for this reason alone make the present arrangements for fee tendering totally ineffectual unless supplemented with supporting information. One cannot therefore proceed without first agreeing in writing with the client exactly what is to be undertaken. Even today, two hundred years after the consultancy services offered by Capability Brown, many, if not most, clients (except perhaps those in the public sector and fellow professionals) are unaware of the scope of the services that are available or the quality necessary for any particular project. It is essential to confirm the terms and conditions of the services they are providing in writing at the outset of a commission. Most litigation between a client and a landscape consultant arises from a lack of a clear understanding between the parties, each thinking the other knew what he or she themselves expected of the other, whereas in fact the other party in turn thought they were required to undertake something quite different and as a result the item in question was never done by either. Had the details been put down in writing beforehand the situation would never have occurred.

Landscape projects are often complex, involve a number of different individuals and disciplines, and may extend over a long period of time, due to seasonal planting requirements which usually have to take precedence over the needs and wishes of the various individuals concerned; as a result, changed circumstances often involve other changes not envisaged at the outset. It is therefore essential that all agreements make provision for the resolution of such problems.

The Landscape Institute has therefore prepared a standard document – the Landscape Consultant's Appointment (see Appendix 2) – registered with the Office of Fair Trading and setting out and defining in detail the scope of the service to be provided by the landscape consultant, the responsibilities and obligations of both the client and the consultant together with any limitation of liability, the fee to be charged, the method of payment, and provisions for the settlement by adjudication or arbitration of any dispute that may subsequently arise between client and consultant.

The document is set out in the following three related parts:

○ *Part 1* – describes and defines the preliminary and basic work stages to be provided by the consultant in the design, construction, planting and management processes normally required on all projects large or small, under 11 work stages.

○ *Part 2* – covers other additional services which by prior agreement are thought to be necessary for a particular project, such as site surveys, cost estimating, negotiations with planning authorities, litigation, and any administrative or design services additional to the normal preliminary and basic service, including also the work of other consultants in connection with the 1994 Construction (Design and Management) Regulations (CDM).

○ *Part 3* – details the obligation of the consultant to use reasonable skill, care and diligence, the duties of the client in respect of fees and payment terms, the responsibilities of the contractor, site inspection, copyright and dispute resolution.

The document also includes as its Appendices a Memorandum of Agreement and a Schedule of Services and Fees summarizing the services agreed to be provided and remuneration, either on a percentage, lump sum or time basis.

 PART 1 – LANDSCAPE CONSULTANT'S PRELIMINARY AND BASIC SERVICES

Most projects proceed in the following 11 clearly defined work stages and landscape consultants should never proceed to the next stage without notifying the client accordingly so that there will be no dispute in the future when the appropriate fees become due. The 11 work stages, each with the relevant subsection identification numbers that relate to its position in the Landscape Consultant's Appointment document, are described below.

PRELIMINARY SERVICES

Work Stage A: Inception (1.2)

The assessment of a client's requirements – that is, his or her true needs as distinct from what they think they want – can be a lengthy and time-consuming business, as can be reconciling the often irreconcilable conflict between the cost of meeting these needs and the amount of money available. Obtaining information on site ownership, boundaries, access and underground services also takes time, as does discussing the timescale and advising on the need for other consultants and specialist advice. Consequently this work, particularly when complex or involved, should almost always be charged on a time basis (see p. 25).

Work Stage B: Feasibility studies (1.3)

Having ascertained the client's requirements before outline proposals can be prepared, there follows consideration of their feasibility and alternative ways of meeting them, the consequential technical and financial implications and the need for planning and other statutory consents. This work is also usually charged on a time basis.

BASIC SERVICES

Work Stage C: Outline proposals (1.4)

Once the client's requirements have been ascertained, the site and its constraints and potential identified and the financial cost limits laid down, the way is clear for the landscape consultant to prepare his or her outline proposals with an approximation of their cost, in order to secure the client's approval and instructions to proceed to the next stage. These proposals can be in written form but usually involve drawn material as well.

Additionally, in performing the duties of the designer as defined in the CDM Regulations, the consultant should cooperate with the Health and Safety Planning Supervisor, if one has to be appointed, and pass to him or her the relevant information for the Health and Safety File.

Work Stage D: Sketch scheme proposals (1.5)

The key factors at this stage are that the consultant should have developed the outline proposals so that they include cost estimates and a programme for the project and 'indicate the size and character of the project in sufficient detail to enable the client to agree the spatial arrangements, materials and appearance'. It must therefore be obvious at this stage that there must be a considerable input of drawn material. It is also important to emphasize to the client that once approved at this stage, the design becomes frozen and no further changes can be incorporated without delaying the programme and incurring additional fees, not only on the part of the landscape consultant but also for any other consultants who may be involved. For this reason discussions with the planning and other statutory authorities are essential at this stage, with possibly the submission of an outline planning application, if appropriate.

Work Stage E: Detailed proposals (1.6)

Further detailed design involving selecting the precise materials and standards of workmanship to be used and coordinating the proposals of other consultants and specialist contractors or suppliers, including obtaining quotations and cost checks, is involved at this stage, with further approvals from the client and detailed applications for approvals under planning legislation, building regulations and other such statutory consents as are necessary.

Work Stages F and G: Production information and bills of quantities (1.7)

At this stage working drawings, schedules and a detailed specification of workmanship and materials are required (all to be in sufficient detail for the preparation of bills of quantities by a quantity surveyor if necessary) to enable a contract to be negotiated or competitive tenders invited. It is absolutely essential to allow sufficient time for this stage to be carried out carefully and with meticulous attention to the necessary detail required.

Work Stages H and J: Tender action and contract preparation (1.8)

Having decided the appropriate type of contract for the particular project – for example lump sum, cost plus, and so on – and whether tenders are to be negotiated or invited from a specially selected list, it is necessary to discuss and agree with the client the contractors to be involved. Once this has been done, tenders are invited or negotiated, appraised and finally reported with recommendations to the client. Once approval to proceed is received, the responsibilities of the client, the contractor and the landscape consultant must be explained (and not taken for granted) to all concerned and any further information provided to enable work to start on site.

Work Stage K: Operations on site during construction and subsequent maintenance (1.9)

The administration of the contract on site by the landscape consultant is time-consuming but it is important that it is carried out properly. Although the contract quite clearly states the contractor's obligation to execute the work in accordance with the contract documents, the landscape consultant has an equally clear obligation under the terms of his or her agreement with the client to 'monitor' the progress and quality of the work against the contract documents. It is for this obligation to the client, in addition to that of inspecting progress, issuing Interim Certificates for payment, and instructing and valuing variations, that the consultant receives almost one third of his or her total fee for this stage when remunerated on a percentage basis.

Work Stage L: Completion (1.10)

Giving guidance on maintenance, certifying when practical completion has been achieved, ascertaining when defects have been made good and preparing the final account constitute the last of the landscape consultant's work stages.

 ## PART 2 – OTHER SERVICES

There are a number of other services that the landscape consultant may be, and often is, called on to perform. In the days before the profession had any involvement with the Office of Fair Trading and fee tendering, these services were often included with the basic service for no extra fee. Unfortunately those days are no more, since it is clearly unrealistic for a client to receive both a reduced fee and additional services at no extra cost.

Examples of the additional services that may be necessary are given below.

SURVEYS AND INVESTIGATIONS (2.2)

1. *Site evaluation:* The selection of sites, advice on their suitability and acquisition are additional to the preliminary and basic services.
2. *Measured surveys:* The costs of measuring sites and existing buildings, taking levels and drawing them out, whether carried out by the consultant or by specialist surveyors, are recoverable as an additional expense.
3. *Site investigation:* Preparing reports on the nature and conditions of the site's vegetation, soil and other features is an additional service.
4. *Maintenance and management:* Cost in use studies, management and site maintenance studies are not included in the preliminary and basic services.
5. *Environmental Impact Assessment studies:* The assessment of the impact on the environment of development proposals is now obligatory for certain schemes in order to comply with the EC directives or local authority requirements.
6. *Development plans:* Where only part of the site will be developed initially, but that part must be designed to take into account future development, the design of the future part merits an additional fee.
7. *Demolition and clearance:* Services in connection with demolition work are not included in the basic service.
8. *Special drawings and models:* Any materials of a graphic design nature prepared for use in connection with applications for planning consents, approvals or negotiations with authorities, mortgages, conveyancing or other legal services attract an additional fee.
9. *Prototype:* If designed for repetitive use and agreed beforehand, prototype proposals can be covered on a royalty basis.
10. *Site furniture and equipment:* Design and advice on the selection, inspecting during fabrication, trials and instructions on the use of such material provisions are not included in the basic service.
11. *Multidisciplinary meetings:* Although coordination of the proposals of other consultants is included in the basic service, provision is also made for extra fees to be charged for attending multidisciplinary meetings.
12. *Public meetings:* The often time-consuming work of preparing material and attending public meetings to hear and/or give evidence is additional to the basic service.
13. *Works of art:* Any advice required on the selection, commissioning and installation of works of art are chargeable separately.

14. *Scientific development:* If research or trials are necessary to overcome problems where traditional systems are inadequate, this is considered as additional to the basic service.
15. *Visits to nurseries:* The cost of visiting nurseries to check on the quality, size and health of plants, when time permits, is always well worth while and is a recoverable extra.

COST ESTIMATING AND FINANCIAL ADVISORY SERVICES (2.3)

While financial cost checks and approximate estimates are included in the basic service as a means of ensuring the cost of a project remains within the authorized expenditure, any detailed cost planning and cash flow analyses are not, neither are the preparation of schedules, bills of quantities or the remeasurement of work executed. The inspection of damage, negotiation of claims for the cost of reinstatement, and making grant applications are all considered to be extra to the basic service.

PLANNING NEGOTIATIONS (2.4)

Any exceptionally prolonged, unforeseen or detailed planning negotiations and all work in connection with the preparation and submission of appeals, including submission of proofs of evidence and appearing as an expert witness, are not part of the basic service, nor are submissions to other organizations such as the Royal Fine Art Commission, negotiating proposals with ground landlords, liaising with, submitting plans to or conducting negotiations with statutory bodies such as education or highway authorities or statutory undertakers, or advising on other matters such as those affecting rights of way, support and wayleaves.

ADDITIONAL ADMINISTRATION OF PROJECTS (2.5)

While the work involved in advising the client on progress and compliance with the contract documents, issuing certificates, instructing and valuing variations is included in the basic service, frequent or constant attendance on site, the administration of other than lump sum contracts and the preparation of 'record' drawings and landscape management plans are not, nor are assisting a client's legal advisers in preparing and giving evidence, attending on solicitors, counsel and the courts in connection with litigation and arbitration, providing or recruiting site staff, administering and inspecting aftercare and maintenance work after the end of the defects liability period, or work restarting after suspension. Where the consultant is required under the 1994 Construction (Design and Management) Regulations to appoint a Planning Supervisor, prepare a pre-tender Health and Safety Plan, notify the Health and Safety Executive of the project, or assemble the Health and Safety File and prepare 'as built' drawings for the file, these also justify a fee additional to the basic service.

Where the consultant is required to provide the services of a Health and Safety Planning Supervisor under the CDM Regulations, the terms and fee for this service should be agreed under a separate appointment.

SERVICES NORMALLY PROVIDED BY OTHER CONSULTANTS (2.6)

Landscape consultants' services are frequently included alongside those of other professions, such as architects, engineers and quantity surveyors; in such cases it is important to ensure that, where these other services are provided from within the same landscape office or firm, the fees charged are in accordance with those recommended by the relevant professional body.

In the past many of these additional services would have been provided by the landscape consultant at no extra cost to the client, in accordance with the obligation to follow the mandatory minimum fee scales. Today, in order to comply with the mistaken belief of the Office of Fair Trading that these minimum rates were not in the public interest and therefore should be no more than 'recommended', together with the insistence of some authorities that fees must be tendered in competition with other consultants, it is essential that whenever the need for any of these additional services arises, or is thought likely to arise, this fact is pointed out to the client and a proper basis of remuneration agreed before the work is put in hand.

ADDITIONAL DESIGN SERVICES (2.7)

This covers the alteration or modification of any design, specification, drawing or other document as a result of new instructions from the client.

PART 3 – CONDITIONS OF APPOINTMENT

The fact that the Landscape Consultant's Appointment document's Conditions of Appointment section runs to over thirty clauses, setting out the conditions under which a landscape consultant is engaged and describing what (but not how) he or she is to perform the work and how he or she is to be paid, emphasizes the importance of getting these matters clearly understood and agreed at the outset.

PROFESSIONAL NEGLIGENCE

It used to be thought that provided consultants exercised reasonable skill, care and diligence in accordance with the normal standards of the profession and in compliance with their conditions of appointment, they would be able to practise in the confident belief that they would be free of any action for professional negligence. Sadly this seems to be no longer the case, with the courts apparently upholding the public belief that in the event of an accident, whatever the circumstances, the recipient should not suffer the financial consequences and someone, preferably with insurance cover, should be found to bear the cost. The final straw was the Civil Liability (Contribution) Act 1978, which entitles a plaintiff to recover the whole of their loss from a number of defendants and which lays down that, if one or more of the defendants is without the means to pay, possibly if he or she has conveniently 'ceased trading', the remaining defendants must share the whole of the cost of the loss themselves.

For this reason the Landscape Institute requires registered practices to take out professional indemnity insurance, as do government departments and most statutory and local authorities: this ensures that consultants have sufficient funds to meet their financial obligations should a case of professional negligence be found against them. In the current climate of public opinion, however, it no longer seems necessary for a lack of a duty of care to be proven against a practice, and landscape consultants now seem likely to be held liable for any single mistake or error of judgement on their part, however carefully they had considered the matter before coming to a decision.

The incidence of claims for 'mistakes', irrespective of the reasonable skill, care and diligence exercised by consultants, has resulted in enormously increased insurance premiums, often in excess of 10 per cent of gross fee income. This is not helped by some authorities requiring from their consultants proof of insurance cover of an amount equivalent to double the fee income of the individual or practice concerned.

To reduce the risk of allegations of professional negligence it is therefore essential to keep the client fully informed – in writing – at all times, particularly when making economies below what would otherwise seem prudent or when instructed by a client on a course of action against one's better judgement, and to obtain the client's authority before initiating or proceeding to another stage of the work.

For the same reason approved proposals should never be altered without the client's consent nor any variations instructed, particularly those affecting the authorized expenditure or contract period.

OTHER CONSULTANTS

While a landscape consultant must neither assign his or her commission nor subcontract it in whole or part without notifying and obtaining the consent of the client, consultants from other professional disciplines may be employed either by the landscape consultant or directly by the client, provided their respective divisions of responsibility are clearly defined. Under these circumstances each must be solely responsible for his or her own sphere of the work (and suitably insured against their own professional negligence), notwithstanding any authority the landscape consultant may have to coordinate and integrate the others' work into his or her own. Should any design work be required of a specialist subcontractor or supplier, the latter must bear the burden of responsibility for its efficacy and satisfactory performance to the client, not the landscape consultant, and the extent of such responsibility must also be clearly defined.

CONTRACTOR'S OBLIGATIONS

It cannot be too often repeated that, quite apart from the similar requirements placed on the landscape consultant, the landscape contractor also has a clear obligation 'with due diligence in a good and workmanlike manner to carry out and complete the works in accordance with the contract documents'. While the landscape contractor is also responsible for his or her own operational methods, the landscape consultant is equally contractually responsible under his or her own quite separate agreement with the client generally 'to monitor the progress and quality of the works against the contract documents'. If therefore the quality of the works is not in accordance with the contract documents the client can, and often does, either jointly or severally sue both the landscape consultant and the landscape contractor for breach of their contracts with the client.

QUALITY CONTROL

To reduce the chances of being sued two things can be done. First, the contract documents may include clauses requiring the contractor to report when certain stages of the work are completed, so that they can be inspected before they are covered up and the work proceeds to the next stage. Secondly, the client may agree to the appointment of, and pay for, either professional staff and/or a clerk of works to be employed permanently on the site. While this will relieve neither the contractor nor the consultant of their responsibilities, it does at least reduce, but not eliminate, the chances of mistakes occurring during the progress of the work. It cannot of course cover deliberate or fraudulent concealment of errors or omissions. It also helps if instructions from the client are received from only one individual acting on his or her behalf and, equally essentially, if instructions to the landscape contractor are passed to him or her only by the landscape consultant.

COPYRIGHT

Copyright of the designs in all drawings and documents (unless otherwise agreed) always remains with the landscape consultant. It is common practice, however, for the client to be able to make use of them *provided that* they are used only for the same site or part of the site for which they were originally prepared – for example when they are used for subsequent maintenance or management. The law on copyright of drawings begins with the Fine Arts Copyright Act 1842, followed by the Berne Convention 1908 and the Copyright Act 1911, which included under the definition of 'Artistic Works' 'any building or structure having artistic character or design or any model of such building or structure'. Today, in any case involving infringement of copyright, reliance is placed on the Copyright Act 1988 which includes, 'irrespective of artistic quality', drawings:

O   reproducing the work of art in any material form;
O   publishing the work of art; and
O   including the work in a television broadcast.

Drawings are defined as including 'any diagram, map, chart or plan', and works as either 'buildings (including any structure) or models'.

Ownership

The ownership of copyright of a drawing resides with the person who drew the plan (or whose employee drew it), and, after his or her death, to his or her personal representatives including partners, inheritors or next of kin, unless previously assigned. As far as drawings are concerned the ownership of the paper on which they are drawn passes to the client on payment of his or her fee, but the 'design' remains with the 'artist', who may wish to use the same details on another project. Photographs, paintings, drawings or engravings of the project, particularly those used subsequently by contractors who had worked on the project in advertisements for their own businesses, do not involve infringement of copyright, nor do photographs or films of the project used in a television broadcast, but copying of the 'artist's' drawings themselves, for whatever purpose, does (unless it is for the purpose of construction of the design). Under the 1988 Copyright Act, however, the Crown is entitled to the copyright in all artistic work 'made by or under the direction or control of Her Majesty or a government department'.

Infringement

Infringement of copyright occurs when the work copied is known to the copier – in other words, ignorance of the existence of that which was copied is a valid defence. As one might expect, the reproduction of a drawing into a building or landscape project does not involve infringement of the copyright of the drawing.

In *Meikle* v. *Maufe* (1941) – a case that arose when Maufe extended the existing Heals building in Tottenham Court Road in 1935 to match the adjoining building built to the design of Smith and Brewer in 1912 (the ownership of this design had by then passed to Meikle) – a claim by Meikle that his copyright had been infringed was upheld. It was considered that there could be no implied consent by Smith and Brewer to the reproduction of their design because they had not known of the possibility of an extension at the outset.

Copyright of partial services

If the client makes it clear at the outset that all he or she requires of the consultant are drawings to obtain a statutory consent, and the client then pays for these drawings, they would be considered as valueless unless the client could then use them to construct the project (even if it had started as a full commission). The client therefore has an implied licence to issue the drawings to a contractor to complete the project as designed.

In *Blair* v. *Osborne and Tompkins* (1971) the architect was instructed to acquire, and obtained, a detailed planning consent for two semi-detached houses at the bottom of Blair's garden, but nothing more. It was held that the client had therefore an implied licence 'to use whatever plans had been prepared at the appropriate stage' for all purposes for which they would normally be used, namely all purposes connected with the erection of the building to which they were related.

Stovin Bradford v. *Volpoint Properties* (1971) concerned the modification of a refused application prepared by their own office for the conversion of an existing warehouse and the erection of six others. The original design included a distinctive diamond design feature in the elevations, and when the building was built, in accordance with a revised planning application (granted on appeal), it was held that in view of the 'agreed nominal fee' there had been an infringement of copyright and no implied licence had arisen, as a result of which £500 damages were awarded.

The landscape consultant's appointment should, as a consequence, ensure that the client has an express licence to use the drawings solely for the purpose for which they were prepared and that drawings prepared to obtain a planning consent should not be used to construct the works except with the consultant's express consent.

Injunctions cannot be granted after the construction of the building has started nor can they require the building to be demolished.

SUSPENSION OF THE PROJECT

The Landscape Institute's Conditions of Appointment provide for the client to suspend the appointment of the landscape consultant, having given reasonable notice of his or her intention to do so, on receipt of which it is prudent for the consultant to ensure that the work has been completed to a clearly defined work stage. Equally, should circumstances arise which make it impracticable for the consultant to continue with the work, he or she must notify the client and agree the future course of action. If after six months and in response to a request for instructions the consultant has received no instructions within a further 30 days, the project is considered terminated. If the consultant has died or become incapacitated, the client may be entitled to use all the drawings and documents prepared that far, provided all outstanding fees have been paid.

DISPUTES BETWEEN CLIENT AND CONSULTANT

Should a dispute occur – and regrettably they sometimes do – and it cannot be resolved by mutual agreement, there are, in addition to recourse to the courts, three options open to both client and landscape consultant.

First, an agreed joint statement of undisputed facts may be submitted to the President of the Landscape Institute for his or her ruling, which is accepted as final and binding. Secondly, an adjudicator agreed between the disputing parties as being a suitable person and by whose opinion they both agree to abide may be appointed, either by the parties themselves or by the President of the Landscape Institute.

Thirdly, an arbitrator may be appointed under the Arbitration Acts 1950, 1979 and 1996, whose decision is binding and enforceable by law without the right of appeal, unless the existence of a 'serious irregularity' by the arbitrator can be proved. These options are discussed in more detail in Chapter 8.

 ## GUIDANCE FOR CLIENTS ON FEES AND ENGAGING A LANDSCAPE CONSULTANT

Guidance on the completion of Appendices I and II of the Landscape Consultant's Appointment is contained in the Landscape Institute booklet *Engaging a Landscape Consultant: Guidance for Clients on Fees*, first published in August 1996 and based on a September 1994 RIBA publication of a similar name.

The Landscape Institute's Landscape Consultant's Appointment Parts 1, 2 and 3 are silent on the fee to be charged, the basis on which it is to be calculated and the stages at which it becomes due. Information on this is to be provided in Appendices I and II, guidance for the completion of which is contained within the booklet.

There are only three ways of remunerating a self-employed landscape consultant:

1.   On a percentage basis based on the cost of the works.
2.   On a time basis.
3.   On a lump sum basis.

See Figure 1.2 for an example of a letter from a landscape consultant to a client providing confirmation in writing of the consultant's appointment and fees. (This letter gives a good illustration of the kind of confirmation appropriate for small projects, as an alternative to that given in more detail in Appendix I of the Landscape Consultant's Appointment.)

Dear Mr ....

Following our meeting yesterday I/we are writing to confirm that I/we shall be very pleased to accept the appointment as your landscape consultant(s) for the above project.

(A)   As I/we mentioned our fee will be on a percentage basis in accordance with section 3 of the enclosed LI Conditions of Appointment. In this instance the contract coefficient being .... and the job coefficient being .... the combined coefficient is .... and on an authorized expenditure of £........... the percentage will be .... x .... x .... = %.

(B)   As I/we mentioned our fee (for post-contract services) will be charged on a time basis in accordance with section 2. Accounts will be rendered monthly/quarterly in accordance with section 8.1.

Principals' time will be charged at £........... per hour in accordance with section 7, and VAT at the rate prevailing at the time.

Expenses and disbursements plus .... % will be charged including mileage at ... per mile.

Yours sincerely

Figure 1.2 Pro forma of a letter from a landscape consultant to a client confirming his or her appointment and fees

PERCENTAGE BASIS

In the case of lump sum and prime cost contracts where landscape consultants are responsible for the work from inception to completion, remuneration is traditionally on a percentage basis, the fee being based on the total cost of the work carried out under the consultant's direction. If any work or materials are supplied to the contractor without charge, then their value (as are increased costs if allowable) is added to the contract sum for the purposes of evaluating the sum on which the percentage fee is based. However, the Landscape Institute recommends fees should be recalculated when the Final Certificate stating the total construction cost has been issued. When the fee is paid in stages – as for example based on the work stages in the basic service – it is becoming common practice for the fee to be fixed and based on the estimated value at that stage and not readjusted at the end when the final account has been completed. Under this arrangement, therefore, the fee at tender stage is based on the lowest tender and only that part of the fee due for post-contract services is based on the final account. The reason for this arrangement arose at a period of high inflation when it seemed unreasonable for landscape consultants' fees for the preparation of tender documents to be increased for no extra work, by basing them not on the contract sum but on the final account enhanced by the value of the increased cost of labour and materials. The only advantage to the landscape consultant of this method is that it reduces the chances of overlooking fees due for landscape services for work designed and detailed but not carried out. Fees are not chargeable on any value added tax recoverable by the contractor from the client.

Should any part of the work be considered to involve sufficient repetition to justify a reduction in the fee for the design and detailing of that part of the work, then the amount of any abatement must always be by prior written agreement, as should be the fee for any work carried out on a site other than that for which it was designed, when some form of royalty basis might then be appropriate.

Classification of different types of work

It is generally accepted that some types of work are more complicated and time-consuming than others yet do not entail a corresponding increase in the cost of the work, and therefore different percentage fees are appropriate for different categories of work. Landscape work involving alterations is more complicated than new work and private gardens more complicated than industrial estates. These differences must be taken into account by the landscape consultant when agreeing with his or her client a percentage fee based on the cost of the work carried out.

Landscape consultancy today involves an infinite variety of work of differing complexity, and consequently there is a difference in the amount and levels of service required to ensure a satisfactory completion of the project and a corresponding differential in the fee to provide the necessary resources. Projects such as urban rehabilitation and the restoration of historic gardens clearly involve more input at all stages than do car parks in rural areas or hedgerow renewal. The Landscape Institute's guide therefore includes the classification of 30 types of landscape work into four categories of ascending order of complexity (see Table 1.1).

WORK TYPE	COMPLEXITY RATING			
	1	2	3	4
Planting Design and Implementation Services for:				
Golf Courses and Rural Sports Projects	✓			
Rural Roads and Parking	✓			
Country Parks and Estates	✓			
Rural Recreational Areas	✓			
Afforestation/Shelter Belt Planting/Hedgerow Renewal	✓			
Rural Amenity Schemes	✓			
Comprehensive Design and Implementation Services for:				
Agricultural Improvement and Estate Enhancements		✓		
Coastal Defence and River Catchment Schemes		✓		
Camping and Caravan Sites, Tourist Facilities		✓		
Cemeteries, Crematoria and Gardens of Remembrance		✓		
Industrial, Commercial and Research and Development Sites		✓		
Roads and Roadside Facilities and Parking Schemes		✓		
Coastal Marinas and Water Recreation and Sports Schemes		✓		
Inland Marinas, Canal, River and Lakeside Schemes		✓		
Rural Recreational and Pursuits Centres		✓		
Infrastructure, Parking and Access for Major Projects			✓	
College and University Campuses			✓	
Defence Establishments			✓	
Hospital Grounds			✓	
New Housing			✓	
School Grounds and Playing Fields			✓	
Sports Stadia and Multi Sports Facilities			✓	
Golf Courses and Recreational Properties			✓	
Urban Offices and Commercial Properties			✓	
Public Parks, Exhibition Sites and Urban Recreation Areas			✓	
Mineral Workings and Landfill Sites			✓	
Reclamation of Contaminated or Derelict Land				✓
Urban Rehabilitation, Pedestrianization, Renewal				✓
Urban Environmental Improvements				✓
Garden Design Historic, Restoration or Conservation				✓

Table 1.1 Classification of landscape work according to complexity

See Notes to table on page 30.

Notes to Table 1.1

1   Work in Column 1 is classified as normal, whereas columns 2, 3 and 4 list work of increasing complexity. These classifications are shown on the fee graph in Table 1.2.
2   Where the landscape work is not listed above but falls within or between complexity ratings, the client and landscape consultant may decide to interpolate an appropriate complexity rating and fee graph curve.
3   Environmental Assessments, Landscape Appraisals, Siting Studies and Development, Conservation and other Environmental Strategy Planning Studies are normally remunerated on a time or lump sum basis.

The fee graph

As the cost of a landscape consultant's services does not increase directly in proportion to the cost of the work, the percentage charge should be greater for the smaller contract and decrease as the cost of the works increases for contracts of £20 000 and above. Fees for projects below the £20 000 threshold should be agreed on a time charge or lump sum fee basis. For projects above £20 000 the reduction in percentage for the larger contract is shown graphically in Table 1.2, based on June 1995 contract sums, with correspondingly lower percentages as the cost rises for each of the four different classifications of landscape works each levelling off at £1.5m.

TIME BASIS

For all classes of landscape work, particularly consultancy and advisory work of some magnitude or intermittent work spread over long periods, fees based on the actual time taken are often the most appropriate.

It is essential to keep accurate records for inspection by the client when this method is used, with the grade of staff, dates and time involved clearly identifiable. The hourly rate is normally 18p per £100 of gross annual salary: thus the hourly rate for an assistant earning £17 500 net plus £500 emoluments (£18 000 gross) would be £32.40. The gross annual salary of the individual concerned, including bonus, national insurance, pension, medical schemes and other emoluments, is charged irrespective of the type of work on which he or she has been engaged.

A partner's time is normally excluded from this arrangement and is a matter of separate negotiation, rates of £50–£75 being normal in 1997 for the smaller practice and £75–£100 for the larger practice with higher overheads, dependent on the experience and qualifications of the partner concerned and the type of work on which he or she will be engaged.

Table 1.2   The fee graph

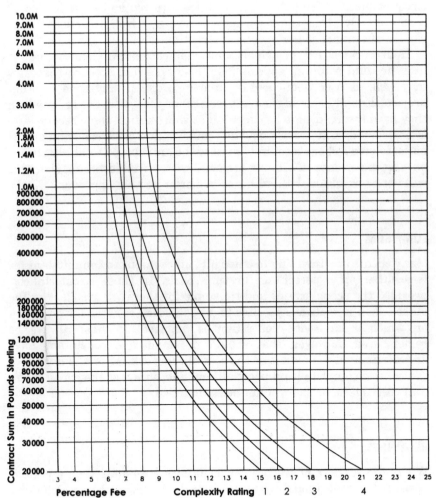

If staff are engaged through an agency then their rates should be agreed separately, as should those of resident site staff when hotel and subsistence allowances may or may not be involved. Secretarial and administrative staff time is not normally charged.

Travelling time during office hours is charged at the same rate. Charging for travelling time out of office hours depends on the circumstances, office policy and distance involved and must be agreed separately. Overtime is not normally recoverable from the client unless carried out on his or her express instructions.

Hourly rates for principals and staff attending lengthy public inquiries and planning appeals must also take into account that they may well, as a consequence, be unable to devote any time to other projects. Equally, should the requirement for their attendance for which they have reserved time be cancelled at short notice, some recompense is normally due. It is normal, when undertaking work solely on a time basis, to give a client a ceiling figure of the anticipated total cost, based on past experience of similar projects, with an undertaking that this will not be exceeded without his or her prior written approval.

LUMP SUM

Many clients are unwilling to enter into an open-ended commitment for fees either on a percentage or time basis. In these circumstances, provided the scope, extent and timetable for the work are clear at the outset, then it is always possible to agree a lump sum fee for any work on which a landscape consultant is engaged. It must always be remembered, however, that should the landscape consultant have underestimated the extent or the cost of the work, he or she must still continue to complete it properly, although it is then at the consultant's own cost and he or she will not be reimbursed.

RETAINERS

Where the services of landscape consultants are required on a regular basis, either continuously or intermittently, on projects for which there may or may not be an identifiable 'cost of the works', a retainer is often the most appropriate form of remuneration, either on a lump sum or time basis. When the fee is on a lump sum basis it will be paid at monthly, quarterly or annual intervals irrespective of the work required. On a time basis, accounts are rendered when the work has been completed, or at similar agreed intervals, for the actual work involved.

PARTIAL SERVICES

For a variety of reasons, including the uncertainty of future funding arrangements, an increasing number of landscape commissions are let on a partial service basis, with either some earlier previously completed or later post-contract stages omitted. Under these circumstances special care is necessary to clarify such aspects as copyright, financial and other professional liabilities for work which may have been carried out by others beforehand or in the future. In such cases when the work is carried out on a percentage basis the work stages to be undertaken and fees to be paid are usually an adequate indication of those parts of the work for which the landscape consultant is responsible and liable. When the consultant's work is to be carried out on a time basis – for example, Work Stage K, involving operations on site – clarification of the responsibilities of the succeeding consultant for a design undertaken by a previous consultant (and errors within that design) and for inspection by the subsequent consultant are particularly important.

STAGE PAYMENT OF FEES

Whereas Clause 3.6 of the Conditions of Appointment of the Landscape Consultant's Appointment details the obligations of the client in such matters as the prompt payment of fee applications, disputed fees and payments on the termination or suspension of a consultant's appointment, it is left to the Schedule of Services and Fees in Appendix II to be completed in respect of interim payments to be made either on a periodic basis, monthly, quarterly or half-yearly. Many clients and their consultants prefer to pay fees by predetermined regular instalments to ease any cash flow problems.

Instead of requiring the payment of equal regular instalments with an adjusted final payment on completion of the work, however, fees can be agreed as becoming due on the completion of each basic service work stage, the percentage proportions being comparable with the relative amount of work incurred by the consultant at each stage. (An apportionment is given in Table 1.3.) This method of remuneration – the stage payment of fees – differs from that of other means of payment in that it attempts to provide the consultant with adequate financial resourcing at each stage, without 'front loading' the early stages and thus running the consequent danger of providing insufficient fees for the later work stages due to having overspent earlier on in the project or on other projects.

Table 1.3   Guide to stage payments of fees, relevant fee basis and proportion of fee applicable to lump sum and percentage fee basis (*details of preliminary, basic and other services are set out in detail in the Landscape Consultant's Appointment*)

WORK STAGE		RELEVANT FEE BASIS			PROPORTION OF FEE	
		Time	Lump	Percentage	Proportion of fee	Total
Preliminary Services						
A	Inception	✓	✓	N/A	N/A	N/A
B	Feasibility	✓	✓	N/A	N/A	N/A
Basic Services						
C	Outline Proposals	✓	✓	✓	15%	15%
D	Sketch Scheme Proposals	✓	✓	✓	10%	25%
E	Detailed Proposals	✓	✓	✓	15%	40%
F, G	Production Information and Bills of Quantities	✓	✓	✓	20%	60%
H, J	Tender Action and Contract Preparation	✓	✓	✓	5%	65%
K	Operations on Site	✓	✓	✓	30%	95%
L	Completion	✓	✓	✓	5%	100%
Other Services		✓	✓	N/A		

Timing of Fee Payments

Percentage fees are normally paid at the end of each work stage. Time-based fees are normally paid at monthly intervals. Lump sum fees are normally paid at intervals by agreement. Retainer or term commission fees are normally paid in advance, for predetermined periods of service.

SUSPENSION, RESUMPTION AND TERMINATION

Should a landscape consultant's commission be suspended, fees are charged on a partial services basis for work completed up to that time and for all expenses and disbursements incurred while work is stopped. After six months or if the appointment is terminated, fees, expenses and disbursements are due on all work completed to date.

Should the work be resumed within six months the fees previously received are considered to be payments on account.

EXPENSES AND DISBURSEMENTS

All expenses and disbursements properly incurred by the consultant, to which he or she may add an administrative charge, are normally recoverable. Those commonly involved are as follows:

Printing

The cost of printing and copying of all drawings and documents provided by the consultant for the project, including those provided free to the contractor, are recoverable from the client including any necessary maps, models and photographs.

Subsistence and hotel expenses

Expenses necessarily incurred by principals and staff while away from the office are recovered from the client either on the basis of the actual expenditure incurred or by an agreed lump sum. The option selected must be agreed with the client beforehand and is not necessarily the same as that paid to the staff involved – in other words, while staff may be reimbursed the actual cost, clients may require a fixed allowance or rate.

Travelling

Clients will normally require public transport to be used particularly for return journeys in excess of 100 miles. However, when this involves uneconomically long travelling times, the cost of journeys by private cars is usually allowed on an appropriate mileage basis, arrived at by calculating the petrol costs plus a suitable allowance for insurance, road tax, repairs and depreciation.

Postage and telephone

These are usually allowable as recoverable expenses but it is rare to charge for postage costs of less than £1 and for telephone charges other than trunk calls. Air freight and courier costs are, however, normally identified and are fully recoverable from the client.

Miscellaneous charges

Charges for items such as the cost of models, site progress and aerial photographs, special drawings and perspectives must be agreed with the client before they are incurred. Fees for planning and building regulation applications, if not paid by the client direct, are also recoverable.

Compounding expenses

Expenses and disbursements may be estimated, added and included within the lump sum or percentage fees. Even so they are never 'free' as far as the consultant is concerned.

ADDITIONAL WORK

Fees for additional work arising for reasons which could not have been envisaged at the outset or which are beyond the consultant's control are always recoverable from the client on an agreed basis: for example, the need to revise drawings and other documents arising from changes in statutory regulations or the client's requirements; delays or changes for which the contractor, subcontractor or suppliers are responsible, and the cost to the landscape consultant of any work arising from claims from the contractor for extension of the contract period or for the reimbursement of direct loss and expenses, particularly when these are rejected, are recoverable also.

Fees for all work other than that included in the basic services, including site surveys, visits to nurseries, quantity surveying, resident site staff and responsibility for the services of other disciplines, on the basis of the scales of the profession concerned are always chargeable.

VALUE ADDED TAX ON FEES

All fees for professional services for work carried out in the United Kingdom, irrespective of the origin of the client, are subject to the surcharge of value added tax, levied under the Finance Act 1972, except for those consultants whose total fee income is less than the current limit of exemption.

PAYMENT

Landscape consultants' fees become payable at agreed intervals or stages and are considered to be instalments as interim payments on account (see Figure 1.3). If any item is disputed or questioned by the client, payment of only the disputed item should be withheld and the remainder settled in full, if interest on the balance outstanding is not to be charged.

WORKING WITH RELATED PROFESSIONS

Landscape projects often involve working with other disciplines, such as architects, engineers and surveyors. Their work has then to be integrated with other programmes, timetables, work stages and priorities and it should not be forgotten that these are not necessarily the same as those of the landscape consultant. The fees for one profession are often quite different from that of another discipline at the same work stage. Great care is necessary to ensure that problems are not left unresolved, either because each of the parties thinks that one of the others is aware of the problem and taking responsibility for its resolution or, even more serious, because the one in whose sphere of responsibility the problem arises does not appreciate that the problem exists – for example, a highways engineer might be quite unaware of the effect on the landscape caused by lighting a motorway intersection in the middle of the countryside. Tact and diplomacy are always necessary when a change or a solution is required which may well involve a different discipline in additional work, for reasons which they themselves do not think justified. This is particularly relevant when the other discipline considers rightly or wrongly that they are the 'lead' consultants.

```
                              INVOICE
To:    ............................................................
       ............................................................
Your ref:
Our ref:
Date:
Dr to  ............................................................
```

Interim/Final	To professional services in connection
STATEMENT	with ....
....................199......	
....................199......	To fees in accordance with LI

Landscape Consultant's
Appointment as agreed .../.../...
*with complexity rating 1/2/3/4

(a) ...% on amount of est. cost/
     lowest tender/contract/value
     of work executed of £...........   £_____

     ...% due on completion of Stage... £
(b) Time basis as attached

     Statement   £
     less previously received
     on Account dated .../.../.../
     (exclusive of value added tax) £

(c) Additional services   £_____

Balance now due   £_____

Out of pocket expenses
(period .... to ....)   £
(exclusive of value added tax)
as per attached statement
     Printing   £
     Travelling   £
     Copying   £
     Miscellaneous   £_____

Balance fees and expenses now
claimed   £
Plus VAT @ ... %   £
Disbursements ....   £_____

TOTAL NOW DUE   £_____

Please note this is not a tax invoice. An authenticated
tax receipt will be forwarded on payment of this account
in accordance with HM Customs and Excise Note 708 for
Construction Services Supplied under a Contract, which
provides for periodic payments.

                                    With compliments

Note: Complexity ratings to establish percentage fees may
not be necessary if these have been previously confirmed
with the employer and have not been subsequently varied.

* Delete complexity ratings not applicable.

_____

Figure 1.3   Pro forma of a model fee invoice

WORK OVERSEAS

It is important to remember when engaged on or seeking work overseas for either a UK- or foreign-based client that professional practice, procedures and codes of conduct in other countries are rarely the same as those in the UK. Different economic conditions and ethics create different codes and procedures. It is essential to spell out in great detail the service being offered, and how it is to be provided, in order to eliminate any future misunderstandings, particularly those with regard to payment. The tender and contract conditions to be adopted in the country in question must be ascertained beforehand, and also whether there are any stipulations as to where the consultant's work is to be carried out. Are the fees to be subject to any local taxes and what arrangements are necessary for them to be transferred to the UK in pounds sterling? What are the arrangements for the reimbursement of travelling expenses and hotel accommodation? When undertaking work for overseas clients, membership and advice from the British Consultants Bureau (5 Westminster Palace Gardens, Artillery Row, London SW1) is often useful.

 ## GUIDE TO COMPETITIVE FEE TENDERING PROCEDURES

The relationship between a landscape consultant and his or her client, depending as it does on the need for mutual trust and goodwill between them, and without which any project is doomed from the start, makes the task for the client of choosing the right consultant for the project a matter of crucial importance and one not to be rushed into nor based on the use of a pin and the Yellow Pages.

The traditional method of selection, based on the client having one or two consultants personally recommended to them, followed by an interview in their offices, is by far the best; having then decided which is the most suitable consultant for the project, the client can then begin to negotiate an appropriate fee with them.

When, however, an innovative design solution is the most important requirement, then consideration has to be given to a limited or open competition in accordance with the established procedures advised by the Landscape Institute on either a local or national scale.

If the client has reason to believe that a simple negotiation of fees with the selected consultant (instead of the candidates competing on the grounds of standards of service, with fixed fees) would not achieve the necessary climate of competition in the case of a consultant to be chosen by a limited design competition, a 'two-envelope' system as developed in the USA (the Brooks Method or QBS) has been recommended whereby each shortlisted consultant submits a design or technical proposal together with a separate sealed fee tender which is only opened when the choice of the shortlisted consultant has been made. If the fee is considered acceptable the commission is awarded accordingly. Only if the fee is unacceptable is the fee envelope of the second-choice consultant opened.

Government preference for the choice of shortlisted consultants to be made on the basis of competitive fee tenders led to the creation of the Compulsory Competitive Tendering (CCT) Regulations. These required local authority and government departments to invite competitive tenders for all services including their own, whether it was for school meals, hospital cleaning, landscape maintenance or the legal and professional services within their own organizations.

In order to overcome the difficulties of specifying the quality of service required and thereby ensure the comparability of tenders, and notwithstanding the encouragement to obtain Quality Assurance Certification in accordance with BS 5750 (ISO 9000), detailed guidance to those inviting tenders was clearly necessary. The first was HM Treasury Public Competition and Purchasing Unit Guidance CUP 13 (*The Selection and Appointment of Works Consultants*) 1991 followed in July 1992 by the Landscape Institute's *Guide to Procedures for Competitive Tendering*. This guidance covers the pre-tender selection of landscape consultants; the factors to be taken into account in making the initial selections and the need to see examples of a candidate's previous work; details of all the tender information required and the brief to be provided to tenderers including a full description of the proposed project; background information, and full details of the client's requirement in the matter of both the project and the consultant's service to be provided. Tender procedures must be given in detail including those to be adopted when tenders are qualified, the assessment of tenders, notification of results and the withdrawal of tenders before acceptance.

The Landscape Institute's guide also includes a standard Form of Tender, together with the standard Memorandum of Agreement and the Schedule of Services and Fees with Appendices I and II of the Landscape Consultant's Appointment; all three are for use at all times and need to be amended only in exceptional circumstances.

2

COMMON LAW RELATING TO LANDSCAPE PROFESSIONAL PRACTICE

 COMMON LAW

THE GENERAL PRINCIPLES OF LAW AND LEGAL CONCEPTS

English law has its origins in a combination of Saxon and Norman law (as distinct from the law in France and Scotland which is derived from Roman law). 'Common law' has never been written down or enacted, but following the Norman Conquest in 1066 it derived from a system developed by Henry II for the whole country. It was based on the judicial decisions of itinerant judges and, where common law was inapplicable, the concept of equity was applied through the use of rules requiring a specific performance of a remedy in cases where the payment of damages would not result in an adequate solution to the problem – in other words, to achieve an 'equitable solution'. Both common law and equity are still applicable today although there are no longer different courts for each, and the judgments of both are based on previous decisions of the courts – that is, 'case' law.

Changes in the basis on which these judgments are made can, however, be brought about by enabling Acts of Parliament, which may lay down general principles leaving the meaning of the words they contain to be interpreted where necessary by the courts – who, however, do not have the power to change the words themselves. The English courts work on the basis of contestorial procedures and do not themselves conduct an inquiry to ascertain the facts. Everyone is subject to the same laws.

Criminal offences are offences against the state, whether damage has arisen or not, and involve prosecution and punishment by fine or imprisonment, to be decided by a magistrate or Crown Court judge with or without a jury depending on the severity of the alleged offence. *Civil cases*, on the other hand, affect an individual whose rights have been infringed and whose claim following the issue of a writ may result in his or her receiving such compensation as the county, Crown or High Court may decide he or she is entitled to. In some cases, there may be a right of appeal to the Court of Appeal and the House of Lords.

The law relating to *personal property* only affects goods, the possession of which can be proof of ownership, whereas *real property* involves land of which possession is not prima-facie proof of ownership, and which may involve intangible interests such as a right of way.

Easement interests, may, however, be acquired by an easement, either orally or in writing, covering, for example, such items as drain runs, footpaths and daylight over another's land (but not views or privacy), any infringement of which constitutes a nuisance and can be remedied by an application to the courts for an injunction restraining the offender. Conversely the establishment of an interest can be prevented by restrictions under a covenant, which once entered into can rarely be easily set aside.

NATURAL RIGHTS

Common law recognizes three natural rights protecting the land against nuisance: 1) the right to support from neighbouring land, 2) the right to prevent interference with the supply of water by either pollution or excessive extraction and 3) the right to light. All three types of natural rights are dealt with below.

The right to support

The right to support includes the restriction on loss of support from adjoining land including that arising from excavation, recontouring or the laying of the foundations of adjoining buildings, although this does not extend to loads imposed by a new building – in other words, while support of the land from an adjoining site is protected, that from an adjoining building is not, neither can there be any restriction on an alteration to the existing water-table by pumping. These restrictions, however, refer only to natural rights which are always subject to amendments by mutually agreed easements permitting the limited use of another's land without actually owning part of it.

This question of the right of support was considered in the recent case of *Holbeck Hall Hotel and others* v. *Scarborough Borough Council* (CILL 1307 Oct 97) concerning the collapse of a large part of the hotel on the clifftop due to subsidence caused by erosion by the sea below. Judge Hicks, sitting as a High Court Official Referee, extended the duty of care imposed by *Rylands* v. *Fletcher* in 1868 that owners could not remove the support of the adjoining land nor permit the escape of 'dangerous things' on to or under the land adjoining, and ruled that, subject to an appeal, the Borough Council, as 'downhill' owners of the land between the hotel garden and the sea, were responsible for the demolition of the hotel due to their failure to exercise the necessary common law duty of care to remove or reduce the hazard of the erosion of soil by the sea at the base of the cliff below.

Rights to water

Rights to water are protected provided such water runs in a defined channel, otherwise a landowner can extract as much as he or she requires for ordinary purposes (provided he or she returns the same quantity and quality) irrespective of the effect on adjoining land. Rights of water are, however, often modified by statutes imposed by Acts of Parliament such as the Rivers Act 1951 and the Water Resources Act 1963. This inevitably affects such activities as horticultural irrigation and to a lesser degree water cooling, but not uses such as electrical generation.

The right to light

A landowner cannot normally prevent the erection of buildings which overlook his or her property or spoil the view. These can only be secured by a covenant, and to prevent the owners of the new buildings from acquiring their own right to light the landowner must now register an objection under the Rights of Light Act 1959, instead of erecting a screen as was previously necessary. In any case an adjoining owner is only entitled to sufficient uninterrupted light such as that which is required for the ordinary purposes of inhabitants or any business of the tenement according to the ordinary notions of mankind (*Colls* v. *Home and Colonial Stores*, 1906). In similar circumstances (*Allen* v. *Greenwood*, 1980) a neighbour was required to remove a caravan and a closeboarded fence which blocked the light to a greenhouse in an adjoining owner's garden in Rochdale.

NUISANCE

This, whether public, private or statutory, involves an 'indirect' interference to people's rights or property.

Public nuisance is a criminal offence and 'has to involve a sufficient number of persons to constitute a class of the public' (Lord Denning), when either the Attorney General, local authority or an individual can bring proceedings provided they can prove that the nuisance was foreseeable.

Private nuisance covers the effect on the reasonable enjoyment of the land of a single individual from nuisances from another individual, such as smell, noise, or the vibrations from an industrial process, a nearby disco or shop. The court will decide if the nuisance is unreasonable and, if appropriate, what compensation is due.

Statutory nuisance arises when the alleged offence is controlled by statute – for example the Public Health Act 1936, the Clean Air Acts 1956 and 1968 and the Control of Pollution Act 1974. Again the action can be brought by the Crown or an individual, but it is more usually instigated by the local authority.

TRESPASS

This arises if the interference with the rights of an individual is *direct* – that is, actual entry or an encroachment – and involves direct *injury* to people, their goods, or more usually land. The act of intrusion must be done intentionally, even if in the mistaken belief that no trespass was involved and no actual harm has been caused. Dumping rubbish, encroachment of a building over a boundary, leaning a ladder against another's building, growing a creeper on another's wall, fixing something to that wall or painting it are all examples of trespass. Trespass through one's tree or shrub branches growing over an adjoining owner's boundary or roots growing under it causes special problems in that the adjoining owner may cut off the offending branches or roots without prior reference to the first owner providing he or she does not go on to the first owner's land without permission.

An interesting example of trespass resulting in damage to an adjoining owner's property arising from tree roots, and the establishment of legal responsibility for this intrusion, is that of Mr Greenwood (see Figure 2.1). Mr Greenwood bought his house in 1971; after the dry summer of 1975, 5mm cracks appeared in the walls, and following the dry winter and a further dry summer in 1976, these cracks increased to 10mm. This damage resulted in the need for remedial works to the foundations costing £11 382, which were carried out in 1979. Mr Greenwood had a 3m-high thuja tree growing 2.7m from his house, but the adjoining owner, who had lived there since 1965, had an 8m-high beech tree growing 5m away from the house. Unknown to both of them, there was a layer of shrinkable clay 1m beneath the surface of the ground.

The case came before Judge Fallon in the High Court in Bristol in 1985, who, having accepted evidence, ruled that because of the thuja

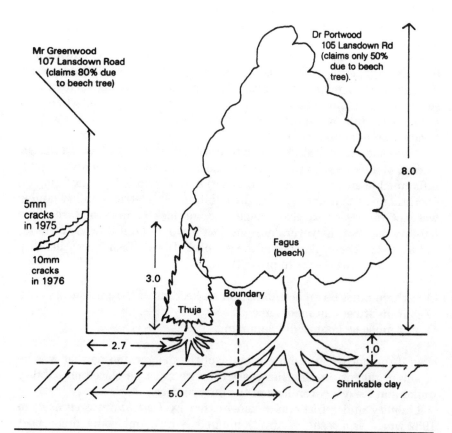

Figure 2.1   Trespass by tree roots

only 50 per cent of the damage was due to the Fagus (beech) and that because there was no way in which either of the owners could have known of the risk, there was therefore no reason for any of them to have taken any precautions to prevent the damage that occurred. Under the circumstances, therefore, the respective insurance companies involved should share the cost of the necessary repairs to the foundations equally between them.

NEGLIGENCE

Contractual negligence can only arise when damage can be proven as a consequence of the breach of a contractual duty of care. The obligations of a landscape consultant and a landscape contractor under contract, written or oral, are relatively simple, being covered by the meaning of the words expressly stated or implied in the contract concerned, or occasionally the meaning behind them or arising from common usage.

Tortious negligence arises as a civil wrong covering a legal duty owed to people generally. The position under 'tort' is complicated, being derived from principles going back many years, and is enshrined in a series of cases starting with *Rylands* v. *Fletcher* in 1868, when two Lancashire mill owners had a reservoir built and the water escaped, flooding an adjoining colliery.

It was then held that if it could be established first, that there was an 'escape of a dangerous thing' on to another's land (such as water, spoil, inflammable substances and vibration) and secondly, that the thing or operation was man-made, then the liability was a 'strict liability' and it was not necessary to prove negligence or lack of duty of care. This liability was not, however, 'absolute' as it would be if it arose from an Act of God or the negligence of the plaintiff. To establish 'strict' liability it is therefore necessary to prove that:

O   there must be an accumulation and escape of the nuisance;
O   it must be man-made; and
O   it must be potentially damaging,

even if the perpetrator did not know of the danger and neither was he or she negligent. In all other cases reliance must be placed on liability under statute or proven lack of the duty of care.

Liability under tort was taken further by *Donohue* v. *Stevenson* in 1932 when, as a result of Mrs Donohue having drunk some ginger beer made by Stevenson in Paisley, from a bottle with a decomposed snail in it, it was held that everyone owes a duty to take all reasonable precautions to ensure the safety of anyone else who might be likely to be affected by his or her actions whether they were involved in a contractual relationship or not.

The responsibility for negligent acts was extended in 1964 when, notwithstanding an express disclaimer of responsibility in *Hedley Byrne* v. *Heller*, a firm of merchant bankers, Heller, was held to be responsible to a firm of advertising agents, Hedley Byrne, for the economic loss caused not only by a negligent act, but by careless advice as well.

The responsibility of local authorities for compliance with building regulations was established in 1971 with *Dutton* v. *Bognor Regis* when Mrs Dutton, the second purchaser of a house built on a rubbish tip, not being therefore able to sue in contract, sued Bognor Regis Council in tort for defective foundations which they themselves had inspected and approved for a previous owner, both on the plans and on site. This was confirmed in the House of Lords in 1977 by *Anns* v. *LB of Merton*, but may now be less certain in view of the opinion expressed in *Sir Lindsay*

Parkinson v. *Peabody* (1985) that a building inspector employed by a local authority has only a duty of care to the occupant and not to an absentee building owner. The case of *IBA* v. *EMI Electronics and BICC* (1980), in an appeal to the House of Lords, established that there was an implied responsibility on the main contractor (EMI) for the provision of the complete structure, including the design, of a television mast which had been built and designed by a subcontractor (BICC) and which had subsequently collapsed in a storm. This was confirmed a year later in 1981 by Judge Newey in *Holland, Hannen and Cubitt* v. *WHTO* with regard to defective windows, where the ruling was passed that 'there were implied terms of the contract that the building work should be carried out in a good and workmanlike manner with proper skill and care, with materials reasonably fit for their purpose'.

In the case between *Junior Books Ltd* v. *Veitchi CI Ltd* (1982), a specialist flooring contractor, who had laid a floor in a book factory in Grangemouth in 1970 and which broke up after two years, was held to be liable in tort to Junior Books Ltd, since although there was no direct contract between them they were sufficiently close and there was no limitation of liability in existence. It was also established that in spite of there being no physical harm to anyone, Junior Books were entitled to any economic loss they could prove they had suffered.

LIMITATION

There is no limitation on the right of action in tort or contract law, but it may be raised by a defendant. The Limitation Act 1980 provides that an action on a simple contract must be brought within six years, and under seal within 12 years, from the date on which the breach of contract occurred (three years in the case of personal injury).

Pirelli v. *Oscar Faber* in 1982 covered a different, if not more important aspect, when a factory chimney designed and erected 13 years previously in 1969 was found to be defective. The House of Lords held that an action in tort was statute barred because more than six years had elapsed since the defects had occurred in 1970, notwithstanding the fact that they had not been discovered until 1978, a further eight years later.

The cause of action arises not from the date when the contractor finished the defective work nor from the date on which the owner became aware or ought to have become aware of damage, but the date on which the damage came into existence. However, having come to this decision the courts considered it to be unsatisfactory and enacted the Latent Damage Act 1986.

Latent Damage Act 1986

Although stated as intended to cover all forms of latent damage, it was clear from the examples used during the parliamentary debates about this new legislation, both in the House of Commons and the House of Lords, that the primary intention of the Act was to cover the construction industry. Under this Act, for claims that cannot be made under contract, claimants now have a longstop of 15 years in which to claim, from the date of discovery of the breach of the duty of care (not completion of the works), while defendants now have the protection of the limitation of six years from the date of damage and three years from the date of discovery of a latent defect.

RESTRICTIVE COVENANTS

Restrictive covenants occur when the owner of one piece of land or building agrees (covenants) that it will not now or in the future be used for particular purposes, the restriction being for the benefit of those who own or occupy another piece of land or building in the vicinity. For instance, in the transfer or conveyance of a house, the covenant might state that the owner might not carry out any business in a private residence, not put up a shed in the garden without consent, nor park a car, caravan or boat in the front garden, restrictions which might not be covered by existing planning legislation. Restrictive covenants do not become incorporated in the title of a property and are principally only an agreement between the vendor and present and future purchasers. As such, covenants may be removed by agreement, for which a 'consideration' may be given, but it is necessary to establish that the restrictions are no longer applicable or relevant. This is often difficult and the originators are often difficult to trace. It has therefore now become common practice to insure against the risk of a subsequent action at some future date by a beneficiary unexpectedly appearing and attempting to enforce the covenant or demand compensation.

CHAPTER

3

STATUTE LAW RELATING TO THE PROTECTION OF THE ENVIRONMENT

In addition to a working knowledge of the fundamental general principles of common law and statute law relevant to town and country planning, highways, value added tax legislation, tree preservation, the Building Regulations and the Construction (Design and Management) Regulations, landscape consultants are also expected to be aware of other statutory Acts, Regulations and procedures laid down by the government which regulate the use of land, such as those relating to planning consents, countryside protection access and its management.

In addition to Acts of Parliament, the government also strengthens this legislation with Statutory Instruments – Regulations/Orders – Circulars and Policy Guidance Notes clarifying, amplifying and laying down the procedures necessary to implement it.

 ACTS

The following Acts cover those areas of whose existence, significance and application landscape consultants should be aware – while not necessarily being required to know the details – should they become relevant to a particular project on which consultants may be engaged. Recent Statutory Instruments, DETR Circulars and Planning Policy Guidance Notes (particularly relevant to planning appeals) are listed in Appendix 7.

NATIONAL PARKS AND ACCESS TO THE COUNTRYSIDE ACT 1949

National Parks only came into existence as recently as 1949 with the National Parks and Access to the Countryside Act 1949, creating a

National Parks Commission (now the Countryside Commission) to be chaired by a person appointed by the Secretary of State for the Environment. It is responsible for extensive tracts of country in England and Wales designated for their natural beauty and the opportunities which they offer for public open air recreation – having regard both to their character and their position in relation to centres of population.

The first National Park was designated in the Peak District in 1950, followed by the Brecon Beacons in 1955. As the British National Parks remain largely in private hands the Commission exercises its responsibilities by stricter planning controls (changes of use authorized by SI 71/289 are not allowed) and by access arrangements. In 1981 these were strengthened by SI 246 restricting height and volumes. Part IV of the Act makes provision for the creation of long-distance recreational routes and Part V for public access to open country consisting wholly or predominantly of mountain, moor, heath, down, cliff or foreshore including any banks, barriers, dune, flat or other land adjacent to the foreshore and for which the authority must prepare maps.

Under section 60, agreements and orders can be made permitting the public to enter the land concerned without the owner being as responsible as he or she would be for other authorized visitors and who become liable for trespass only if they damage walls, fences, hedges, gates or engage in activities which would harm livestock, wild animals or plants, deposit rubbish, light fires or drive vehicles on to the owner's land.

Areas of outstanding natural beauty (AONBs)

Section 87 of the Act also authorized AONBs and as a consequence large areas of the countryside – for example the Chilterns, the Cotswolds, and much of Dorset and the Norfolk Broads – were so designated, much to the irritation of local farmers. Section 87 provides similar restrictions on development and similar management agreements to control farming methods to those involved in the setting up and running of the National Parks. Local and county authorities are required also to consult the Countryside Commission before preparing development plans which cover any of the areas designated.

CIVIC AMENITIES ACT 1967

Listed buildings

Part I of the Civic Amenities Act 1967 provided for the listing of buildings of special historic or amenity value built before 1939. This was provided for in section 54(1) of the 1971 Town and Country Planning (T&CP) Act and further elaborated by the T&CP Listed Buildings and Buildings in Conservation Areas Regulations: SI 72/1362. This prevented any work being done to the interior or exterior of a building so listed which would affect its character, without prior consent, and involved a special separate application to the local authority (except for work of purely maintenance, repair and reinstatement and buildings in use for ecclesiastical purposes).

The lists were revised in 1986 and now include over 360 000 buildings in three grades. Grade I covers buildings of exceptional interest (about 2 per cent of those listed), Grade II* those of particular importance and more than of special interest (about 4 per cent) and the balance are listed as Grade II and are considered as being of special interest and as warranting every effort being made to preserve them. All buildings built before 1700, most of those before 1840 and some of those built before 1914 which are of definite quality and character are included.

Special regard has to be paid not only to the building, but its setting also. Planning officers must therefore be consulted before making any alteration including landscape work within the curtilage (that is, the site) of a listed building. Buildings are listed for architectural, planning, social and economic or historic reasons, because of technical innovation, or because of their group value.

Conservation areas

The Civic Amenities Act 1967 also provided for the establishment of 'areas of special architectural or historic interest the character of which it is desirable to preserve or enhance'. This was incorporated in section 277 of the 1971 Town and Country Planning Act and requires permission to be applied for to demolish buildings in such areas. Provision is also made in article 4 for the exclusion of permitted development in conservation areas if the planning authority so decides. This is normally done in consultation with local amenity societies and residents, the latter often being understandably reluctant to accept the restriction on their freedom to alter the colour of their front doors, park cars in their front gardens and convert their roof spaces into extra bedrooms.

Tree preservation orders

Part II of the 1967 Civic Amenities Act provided also for the protection of trees against 'cutting down, topping, lopping, wilfully damaging or destroying' and later 'uprooting' a tree or permitting such an action unless the authority had been notified in writing six weeks previously and had then raised no objection. This enabled an authority to initiate procedures to protect a tree by making a tree preservation order. If, however, a tree was indicated as to be removed on a drawing included in a planning application in a conservation area then the removal of the tree is deemed to be granted also.

Detailed procedures were set out in SI 69/17 (T&CP Tree Preservation Order Regulations) and excluded fruit trees (is a walnut tree – *Juglans regia* – a fruit tree?) and those whose main stem is less than 75mm in diameter when measured 1m above the ground. Breach of a tree preservation order is dealt with as a criminal offence summarily or on indictment. This was included in section 60 of the 1971 Town and Country Planning Act and subsequently in the 1990 Act permitting local authorities to make tree preservation orders on individual trees, groups of trees or woodlands in the interests of amenity. No consent is needed, however, for work on dying, dead or dangerous protected trees or for work necessary to prevent or relieve a nuisance. It must be appreciated, however, that what an applicant considers to be a nuisance may not be considered in the same way by the local authority.

Landscape consultants are particularly vulnerable to criminal prosecution under this Act if, notwithstanding any contract clauses protecting listed trees, they subsequently condone or permit such damage by a contractor – which includes damage to tree roots as well as branches. It must be remembered that tree roots extend at least to the diameter of the crown and trees can be damaged irreparably by trenching for service pipes or cables injudiciously located on the drawings to be beneath them.

An example of a local authority's tree preservation order can be seen in Figure 3.1.

TOWN AND COUNTRY PLANNING ACTS 1971–1990

Although there has been planning legislation in existence in the UK since 1947 and subsequent Acts were passed in 1959, 1962, 1968 and 1971, current legislation is covered by the 1990 Town and Country Planning Act, which is a consolidation and repealing of the 1971 Act together with those provisions listed in the Planning Consequential

Town and Country Planning Act 1990

TREE PRESERVATION ORDER, 19

THE COUNCIL OF THE CITY AND DISTRICT OF
in this Order called "the authority", in pursuance of the powers conferred in that behalf by sections 198 and 199 [[and] 201*] [and] [300] of the Town and Country Planning Act 1990, and subject to the provisions of the Forestry Acts 1967 and 1979, hereby make the following Order:—

1. In this Order:—

"the Act" means the Town and Country Planning Act 1990;

"owner" means the owner in fee simple, either in possession or who has granted a lease or tenancy of which the unexpired portion is less than three years; lessee (including a sub-lessee) or tenant in possession, the unexpired portion of whose lease or tenancy is three years or more; and a mortgagee in possession; and

"the Secretary of State" means the [Secretary of State for the Environment] [Secretary of State for Wales].

2.—Subject to the provisions of this Order and to the exemptions specified in the Second Schedule hereto, no person shall, except with the consent of the authority and in accordance with the conditions, if any, imposed on such consent, cut down, top, lop, uproot, wilfully damage or wilfully destroy or cause or permit the cutting down, topping, lopping, uprooting, wilful damage or wilful destruction of any tree specified in the First Schedule hereto or comprised in a group of trees or in a woodland therein specified, the position of which trees, groups of trees and woodlands is defined in the manner indicated in the said First Schedule on the map annexed hereto‡ which map shall, for the purpose of such definition as aforesaid, prevail where any ambiguity arises between it and the specification in the said First Schedule.

3.—An application for consent made to the authority¶ under Article 2 of this Order shall be in writing stating the reasons for making the application, and shall by reference if necessary to a plan specify the trees to which the application relates, and the operations for the carrying out of which consent is required.

4.—(1) Where an application for consent is made to the authority under this Order, the authority may grant such consent either unconditionally, or subject to such conditions (including conditions requiring the replacement of any tree by one or more trees on the site or in the immediate vicinity thereof), as the authority may think fit, or may refuse consent:

Provided that where the application relates to any woodland specified in the First Schedule to this Order the authority shall grant consent so far as accords with the principles of good forestry, except where, in the opinion of the authority, it is necessary in the interests of amenity to maintain the special character of the woodland or the woodland character of the area, and shall not impose conditions on such consent requiring replacement or replanting.

NOTE: Where appropriate this Order has been updated to reflect statutory amendments which have resulted in the need to show substitutions or repeals of the prescribed form.

* Include only where Order contains a direction under section 201 of the Act.

‡ Map to be to a scale of not less than 25 inches to one mile (1:2500), except in the case of large woodlands when the scale shall be 6 inches to one mile (1:10000 or 1:10560).

¶ NOTE: If it is proposed to fell any of the trees included in this Order and the felling requires a licence under the Forestry Act 1967, an application should be made in the first place to the Forestry Commission.

Figure 3.1   Proforma of TPO for use by local authorities

Provisions Act of the same year, with most of the provisions of the 1971 Act incorporated in the 1990 Act.

The 1990 Act repealed and restated the provisions of the 1974, 1971 and earlier Acts requiring consent to be sought for any operations on or change of 16 classes of use specified in a DoE Circular 13/87 that were considered to be development. Part VIII of the 1990 Act also made provision for the preservation of trees or groups of trees, it being a criminal offence to 'cut down, top, lop, uproot, wilfully damage or wilfully destroy or cause or permit the cutting down, topping, lopping, uprooting, wilful damage or wilful destruction of any tree specified' without consent unless in the interest of public safety.

The Act also empowered the Secretary of State to make regulations to restrict or regulate the display of advertisements in the interest of amenity or public safety, including their size, appearance, position and fixing.

The Act continued the ability of authorities to impose conditions to the consent; the kind of conditions most often used and most affecting landscape consultants are those such as proposed by DoE Circular 1/85, requiring submission and approval of proposals for landscaping and its maintenance before a development is completed.

Permission is required for any development of land, development being defined in draconian terms as:

1   the carrying out of building operations, engineering operations, mining operations or other operations in, or over, or under land; or

2   making any material change in use of any buildings or other land.

Building operations are defined as including 'rebuilding operations, structural alterations to buildings and other operations normally undertaken by a person carrying on business as a builder' and a building as including 'any structure or erection and any part of a building but does not include plant or machinery'.

Under such definitions, it can be seen that there is little work that can be undertaken on buildings or land without the necessity of a planning application for consent for development.

Building operations

Certain building operations within a building do not constitute development: for instance, those that are internal and do not affect the exterior of a building or buildings within the curtilage (that is, site boundaries) of a dwelling house; those that are incidental to the enjoyment of the building, such as outdoor provisions for pets, a car or a caravan in the garden, or a room used as an office; or restrictions on the use of land for agriculture or forestry, including the use of any buildings for such purposes. Therefore erecting a 16-foot coal hopper on wheels; repairs and maintenance such as repointing, retiling and repainting; and the removal of cornices and garden ornaments (with certain exceptions) are not building operations, but laying tarmac on a forecourt, erecting a flagpole or building a model village have been held to be.

Engineering operations (other than the formation or laying out of means of access to highways) are not defined, but any works involving large-scale earth moving, such as are involved in golf courses and water features, are clearly included, as was that of the Georgian ha-ha in Richmond Old Deer Park in 1957; widening an existing access a few inches by 'shifting a few cubic yards of soil with a digger and a lorry' was not (Lord Pearson, *Coleshill District Investments* v. *MOHLG*, 1969). Mining operations are not defined other than to exclude peat, but topsoil, gravel, sand, clay and stone extraction are considered to be development, as are excavations from old tips, slag heaps and railway embankments.

Enforcement proceedings to stop unauthorized operations must be brought by the planning authority within four years, but there is no such immunity for material change of use except where the change involves a single dwelling house.

Material change of use

Section 22 of the 1990 Act lists three instances of a material change of use: 1) if a building is used as two or more separate dwelling houses; 2) if the deposit of refuse or waste material on land already used for that purpose covers more of the surface area or increases the height above that of the land adjoining the site, and 3) to display advertisements on any external part of a building not normally used for that purpose.

In 1972 the Use Classes Order (SI 72/1385) was brought into effect classifying into 18 different categories the various uses of buildings and land to which they could be put, and within which changes could be made without the need for planning consent, unless as the result of an application the authority restricted its use to one particular activity. These use classes were revised in 1987 to provide more flexibility in the use of business premises in industrial and commercial areas, with new provisions for snack bars, cafes and 'take-aways' and regulating the use of open land.

It was left to the planning authorities to decide if the change of use was material or not as a question of fact; namely, if there was:

○   a physical change in the use of the land;
○   a significant alteration in the quantity or quality of the activity; or
○   a change relevant from the viewpoint of planning.

This covered not only a physical alteration in site boundaries but also a significant intensification of use in proportion to the site as a whole and the period of time involved.

Permitted development

De minimis non curat lex – the law does not concern itself with trifles. To reduce the burden on planning authorities, the government introduced a General Development Order, SI 77/289 (Permitted Development). This set out development which was to be permitted without the necessity for a formal application for planning and consent, such as:

○   limited enlargement or improvement of a dwelling house;
○   forming, laying out and constructing a means of access to a highway; or
○   painting the exterior of any building or work other than for the purposes of advertisement, announcement or direction,

followed by 23 different classes of work, including:

Class I: Development within the curtilage of a dwelling house of not more than 50m³ which does not increase the size above 115m³, the height above the highest part of the roof and does not project beyond the front wall facing the highway. This includes a garage, stable, loose box, coach house and a building for domestic poultry, bees, pets, animals, birds and other livestock not more than 3 metres high or 4 metres to the ridge, porches not more than 2m² not less than 2 metres from the front boundary, a hardstanding for vehicles and oil storage tanks less than 3 metres high and containing less than 3500 litres.

Class II: Sundry minor operations covering new gates, fences, walls and other means of enclosure not more than 1 metre high adjoining a vehicular highway and 2 metres high elsewhere; the maintenance, improvement or alteration of other gates, fences, walls and means of enclosure, provided they do not increase the height above that which is appropriate.

The remaining permitted 21 classes cover certain changes of use for temporary buildings, recreational organizations, agricultural buildings, industrial development, repairs to private roads and services, war-damaged buildings, local authority and private Acts, drainage, highway, water, sewerage authorities and statutory undertakers, mineral workings, the National Coal Board, aerodromes and caravan sites.

Development plans

It is sometimes unkindly said that the activities of planning authorities are entirely negative. This is certainly untrue in the case of their obligation to produce a structure plan laying down their policy and strategy for an area and their ability to prepare local plans to show development proposals for any part of that area. These do not, however, have to be followed slavishly and planning authorities have the discretion to diverge from the plan if circumstances change or they consider there are good planning reasons for so doing.

The preparation of structure plans began in 1971, and 14 years later, in 1985, county and district authorities had completed plans for less than 10 per cent of the country. The DETR has since suggested that structure plans should now be abolished and sole responsibility for both structure and local plans be transferred to the district councils.

Planning applications

Applications for permission to develop land are made on a prescribed form provided by the planning authority. Since the Local Government Planning and Land Act 1980 this must be accompanied by a fee calculated in accordance with Town and Country Planning (Fees for Applications and Deemed Applications) Regulations 1985 (SI 85/1182), the period within which a decision must be given not starting to run until the correct amount has been paid. Planning authorities then have eight weeks in which to approve or reject the application, in the absence of which applicants may 'deem the application refused' and appeal to the Secretary of State for the Environment, Transport and the Regions to decide on the application instead of the planning authority. Once this has been done, the matter is taken out of the hands of the planning authority, who are not then allowed to issue a consent even if they would otherwise have done so. (To overcome this constraint it is not unknown for developers to submit (and pay for) two identical applications so that, if consent is refused on the one, the second application can continue to be negotiated with the local authority while the appeal for the first is being prepared.) Applicants may, however, agree to the period being extended, if so requested by the planning authority, and in practice planning authorities usually assume this to be the case unless they are told otherwise by the applicant.

Planning applications may be made either in full or in outline. In the case of the latter the application for consent is for the principle only, leaving aspects such as siting, design, landscaping, external appearance or means of access to be considered as 'reserved matters', the consent being granted subject to the condition that these are subsequently submitted for approval before the development is completed. Once a planning consent has been granted the benefit attaches to the land and any subsequent owners, but the development must usually be started within five years unless other time limits are laid down.

Planning conditions

DoE Circular 1/85 provides guidance to planning authorities on reserved matters and gives standard conditions for use in such instances including clauses 20 and 21, dealing specifically with landscape matters. Should the applicant object to any of the conditions or to a refusal by the planning authority to approve any reserved matters subsequently submitted to discharge a condition imposed, the applicant may appeal to the Secretary of State in the same way as he or she can appeal against the refusal of consent. Conditions must not be unreasonable and, to be enforceable, the applicant must have the power to comply with them. Authorities may, however, enter into special statutory covenants to cover items for which they cannot impose conditions within the consent. Provision for such an agreement is covered in section 106 of the 1990 Planning Act, and such arrangements are therefore commonly known as 'Section 106 Agreements'!

Appeals

Appeals against the refusal of an application or the imposition of conditions must be made to the Secretary of State within six months. He or she then considers the whole application as if it had been submitted directly to him or her in the first place, and it is open to the Secretary of State to attach an entirely different set of conditions if he or she so chooses. The Secretary of State, who has a separate department within the Department of the Environment, Transport and the Regions to deal with appeals, immediately after receiving an appeal form appoints an inspector who issues directions for a public or private hearing, or for written representations only if after consultation with the parties it is considered these will suffice. The rules for the conduct of the appeals are laid down in SI 71/419 and SI 71/420. These provide for any interested party to give evidence in support of or against the application if they so wish. After the hearing the inspector visits the sites, accompanied by the parties, who can then draw only his or her attention to facts and are not permitted at that stage to express an opinion, after which the inspector then makes a recommendation to the Secretary of State, who either confirms or rejects the recommendation and publishes his or her decision accordingly. Appeals take up to six months for a decision depending on the complexity of the case, and the decision itself is final and binding save only for an appeal to the High Court on a point of law.

FINANCE ACT (VALUE ADDED TAX) 1972

When value added tax (VAT) was introduced into the United Kingdom by the Finance Act 1972 it zero-rated all construction work except for repairs and such items as domestic loose furniture, electrical white goods and professional services, all of which were taxed at the standard rate of 8 per cent.

In June 1975 a VAT Order was issued excluding from zero-rating civil engineering works in the grounds or garden of a private residence, including 'site restoration, clearing rubble, levelling the land, applying topsoil, laying grass and simple paths, planting trees or shrubs or elaborate ornamental works', all of which were to be taxed at the standard rate. In June 1979 the standard rate was increased to 15 per cent.

The Value Added Tax Act 1983, introduced in October 1983, consolidated the earlier statutory provisions; subsequently, in the budget in June 1984, the Chancellor announced that all alterations and 'secondary' buildings (detached garages, greenhouses, garden sheds and similar buildings) in the grounds or gardens of private residences and all home extensions, fitted kitchens, loft conversions, double glazing and central heating installations would be liable for tax at the full standard rate; as a concession, however, alterations for the handicapped and alterations to listed buildings (but not repairs) were zero-rated.

The Finance Act 1989 made all construction work standard-rated (by now $17^1/_2$ per cent) except for new housing, including nine categories of residential buildings, such as old people's homes, school dormitories and buildings intended for non-business use by charities, such as church halls.

A further VAT Act in 1994 consolidated the regulations in respect of caravan parks, listed (protected) residential buildings and charitable buildings, additions which resulted in the issue of an enlarged VAT leaflet 708 in August 1997 defining standard- and zero-rated site restoration and landscaping services in section 11.3 and including Appendices listing examples of standard-rated loose furniture, electrical and gas appliances, fitted cupboards and equipment in schools, churches and other charitable buildings and the reconstruction of listed buildings.

HEALTH AND SAFETY AT WORK ACT 1974

The forerunner of the 1994 Construction (Design and Management) Regulations, brought about by the EEC Construction Sites Directive (92/57/EEC), the Health and Safety at Work Act 1974 applies to all employers and employees, who have a duty while in the course of their employment to take reasonable care for their own and the safety of others by providing training, supervision, safe plant machinery and work systems to minimize risk to health and safety, contravention of which would result in fines imposed by a magistrates' or Crown Court. Regulations affecting the construction industry had been previously imposed by a number of Statutory Instruments in 1961 originating from problems encountered in work underground in mining and tunnelling.

ANCIENT MONUMENTS AND ARCHAEOLOGICAL AREAS ACT 1979

Ancient monuments in the UK have been scheduled since 1882, the government policy for which is now covered by the 1990 PPG 16 – Archaeology and Planning. The 1979 Ancient Monuments and Archaeological Areas Act scheduled buildings, structures or work above or below ground, in caves or excavations, all of which required consent before undertaking any repairs, alterations, flooding or tipping work; the undertaking of any such work without such consent was considered to be a criminal offence. The Act made provisions for objections to such scheduling to be heard at a public inquiry similar to those for planning appeals. The Ancient Monuments and Archaeological Areas Act was amended by the 1983 National Heritage Act setting up a Commission with power to make grants and loans for the preservation and acquisition of Ancient Monuments and Historic Buildings.

Under Part II of the Ancient Monuments and Archaeological Areas Act, the Secretary of State keeps a schedule of monuments and areas where work cannot be carried out within the prior consent of the DETR. Monuments are considered to be buildings unoccupied except by a caretaker and include the remains of buildings and caves. Archaeological areas present particular difficulties since the occupier may be unaware of their existence, and landscape consultants should always take particular care to check with the local authority before commencing work on open land where such areas may possibly exist. Section 35 of the Act requires anyone intending to disturb the ground to give the district council six weeks' notice of an intention to commence 'operations', which include 'flooding and tipping'. The local authority then has to reply within four weeks if it intends to carry out any archaeological excavation itself, which must be completed within a further four and a half months. The restrictions contained in Section 35 have been interpreted as also including the planting of trees and shrubs on the site of a scheduled monument, when schedules of plant material may need to be submitted for approval.

HIGHWAYS ACT 1980

Defining a 'highway' as being one over which the public has a right of passage, and giving local authorities the right to adopt such thoroughfares if properly constructed, the Highways Act 1980 provided also for them to be stopped up or diverted subject to an order by the magistrates' court or extinguished by an order confirmed by the Secretary of State. Obstruction of a highway, which includes ploughing, scaffolding and even the placing of skips, is also a criminal offence, conviction for which results in a fine.

The ordinary citizen has a right to navigate and fish in tidal waters and freedom to travel on the public highway whether it is a motorway or just a footpath on public or private land. Part X of the Act therefore restricts the right of a farmer to plough up a public footpath. *Extinguishment* or diversion of public rights of way can be effected under either the 1980 Highways Act or the 1971 Town and Country Planning Act. In the case of the Highways Act an extinguishing order can only be made if it appears expedient on the grounds that pedestrian or vehicular access is not needed for public use. A *diversion order* can be made if it is expedient to do so either in the interests of the owner of the land, the lessee or occupier or the public, so long as it is not substantially less convenient to the public. Powers are, however, granted to local authorities under the Town and Country Planning Acts in respect of footpaths and bridleways to make orders to stop up or divert public rights of way affected by development for which planning permission has been granted. Footpaths or byways affected by a local planning authority development order require notification to and confirmation by the Secretary of State if they are opposed.

WILDLIFE AND COUNTRYSIDE ACT 1981 (SITES OF SPECIAL SCIENTIFIC INTEREST)

This Act excludes major development in AONBs and gives greater prominence to Sites of Special Scientific Interest (SSSIs) designated under the National Parks and Access to the Countryside Act 1949 by making English Nature responsible for identifying and notifying local authorities, the Secretary of State, and owners or occupiers of areas of land considered to be of special scientific interest by virtue of their flora, fauna or geological features. It requires the listing of any 'operations' which may damage the features and requires the occupier to give three months' notice of his or her intention to carry out any such operation. A planning consent overrides any restriction but the Secretary of State has power to forbid any operations threatening the survival of any animal or plant of national interest or covered by international obligations.

The Act also enables the Nature Conservancy Council to designate areas of foreshore or sea-bed as marine nature reserves to be managed by the Council for conservation or research.

Under Part III of the Act, county and borough councils are required to maintain definitive maps and descriptions of public rights of way, including bridleways and public footpaths over private land. The maps are conclusive evidence both of existing rights of way which may be extended and of new ones created by the public, and which the local authority must record. Section 59 of the Act makes it an offence to keep, on land crossed by a public right of way, bulls older than ten months unless they are a non-dairy breed left at large with cows or heifers.

An Amendment Act in 1985 provides for the Countryside Commission to direct the protection of AONBs and SSSIs.

NATIONAL HERITAGE ACT 1983

The National Heritage Act 1983 combined the Historic Buildings Council, Ancient Monuments Board and the DoE Department of Ancient Monuments and Historic Buildings into the Historic Buildings and Monuments Commission for England, now known as 'English Heritage'. It also provided for the preparation of a Historic Gardens Register to be completed on a county basis by the end of 1986. The criteria for inclusion on the register, which grades gardens dating before 1939 into Grade I – of exceptional interest, Grade II* – of great quality and Grade II – of special interest, are similar to those for listed buildings, but the gardens do not need to be the same grade as the building they surround and do not have to have the same planning restrictions. The purpose of the register is only to identify the gardens' merit to owners, local authorities and government departments to assist in conservation measures and to grant aid to which it might not otherwise be thought they were entitled.

BUILDING ACT 1984

Originating from the earlier Victorian laws and the Public Health Acts 1936 and 1961, the current Building Regulations are now covered by the enabling Building Act 1984 and implemented by the much shorter Building Regulations (SI 85/1065). These lay down only the principles necessary to achieve reasonable requirements for public health and safety, incorporating by reference 'approved documents' – for example British Standards and Codes of Practice – 'deemed to satisfy provisions' and certificates of compliance by 'approved persons' other than the local authority.

The regulations cover the erection of, and extensions and material alterations to, buildings, including alterations to services and fittings and repairs (that is, the replacement or making good of existing parts of buildings). Seven classes of exempt buildings are set out in Schedule 3 (similar to but not the same as permitted planning development). These exclude buildings controlled under other legislation, buildings not frequented by people (such as garages, greenhouses and agricultural buildings), temporary buildings and mobile homes, ancillary buildings, small detached buildings and extensions. Buildings by statutory undertakers, school buildings, buildings for mines and quarries and those for government departments were originally also exempt from the provisions but now have to comply with the regulations.

Notice of an intention to carry out work covered by the regulations must be given to the local authority under regulation 12 at least 48 hours in advance (except for shops and offices). Alternatively full plans may be deposited under regulation 13. Applicants do not have to wait until plans have been passed before starting work, and more plans may be asked for to assist in the inspection of the work on site. Plans must be passed in whole or rejected within five weeks of their submission (or if agreed within a further three weeks). Work that contravenes the regulations must be taken down or altered to comply with the regulations, unless it has been built in accordance with plans that have already been passed.

Irrespective of what is shown on the contract (as distinct from Building Regulations) drawings, the obligation to comply with the regulations is always with the contractor, but most standard forms of contract require the contractor to notify the consultant if he or she finds any divergence and for the cost of ensuring all alterations comply with the regulations to be recoverable from the client.

HOUSING AND PLANNING ACT 1986

The simplification of the Zones laid down in the 1971 Act is set out in Part 2 of the 1986 Act. Financial assistance of urban regeneration grants is covered in Part 3, and special provisions for conservation and other such amenity areas, with restrictions on or prohibition of advertisements, are set out in Part 4. Part 5 covers opencast mining and Part 6 listed buildings, conservation areas and revised controls of advertisements.

WATER ACT 1989

The consolidated 1989 Water Act paved the way for legislation for the complete restructuring of water and drainage management in England and Wales under the Water Industry, Land Drainage, Statutory Water Companies and Water Resources Acts, all enacted in 1991. The Water Industry Act, the Land Drainage Act and the Statutory Water Companies Act together dealt with the obligations of the internal drainage boards and local authorities; the Water Resources Act related to water resources and the responsibilities of the National Rivers Authority (NRA).

ENVIRONMENTAL PROTECTION ACT 1990

This Act served to clarify the obligations of the various authorities responsible for tackling or preventing environmental pollution. Its nine Parts and 16 Schedules deal with the integration of environmental control by means of the Inspectorate of Pollution, covering waste, clean air, litter and radioactive substances, and the setting up of three new Nature Conservancy bodies, all to be dealt with in future regulations requiring pollution to be controlled by the best available techniques commensurate with not entailing excessive cost, and with powers to impose fines of up to £20 000 by magistrates or unlimited amounts in the Crown Court and two years' imprisonment, these requirements applying to Crown land also. 'Environmental Assessment: A Guide to Procedures DoE 1989' transferred various functions to the NRA.

PLANNING AND LISTED BUILDING ACT 1990

This Act obliges the Secretary of State to compile (with the help of English Heritage) a list of buildings or groups of buildings of architectural or historic interest; it also provides powers to regulate the enforcement of measures for the protection and preservation of such buildings, such as the serving of Preservation Notices for repairs and Listed Building Consent being required for any proposed alterations, contravention of either being a criminal offence. There are currently nearly 500 000 entries on the list, including all buildings built before 1700, most of those built between 1700 and 1840, those of special quality or character by leading architects of the period built between 1840 and 1914, and buildings of special interest built between 1914 and 1939; of these, 10 000 are Grade I, 20 000 Grade II*, and the remaining 470 000 are Grade II.

ACCESS TO NEIGHBOURING LAND ACT 1992

An Act enabling an application for a court order for access to neighbouring land for the purposes of essential building work or landscape repairs, such as drainage, ditch clearance, or removing dangerous, damaged or diseased trees, shrubs or hedges. Compensation and conditions for such access may be involved.

ENVIRONMENT ACT 1995

This Act established the environment protection agencies in the UK and transferred to them the functions of the waste authorities and the functions and property from the National Rivers Authority.

DOGS (FOULING OF LAND) ACT 1996

This Act now allows local authorities to enforce dog owners to pick up dogs' mess when they defecate in a place in the open air to which the public has access, with a maximum penalty on the first conviction of £1000 and the ability to issue £25 fixed penalty notices if the £25 is paid within 14 days in lieu of the offence being prosecuted.

HOUSING GRANTS, CONSTRUCTION AND REGENERATION ACT 1996

An Act brought in to implement the DoE Latham Report for the construction industry and requiring (in Part II) all construction contracts, both in the construction operations themselves and in the design and advice on the building and laying out of landscape, to contain provisions for obligatory adjudication in accordance with a scheme (SI 98/649) laid down by the Secretary of State. Contracts, subcontracts and Conditions of Engagement are now also required to contain an entitlement to stage payments, the right to suspend performance for non-payment of fees and the prohibition of conditional payment (pay when paid) provisions.

STATUTORY INSTRUMENTS – REGULATIONS/ORDERS – —— DETR CIRCULARS

The procedures for the enforcement of the policies laid down in all Acts of Parliament are effected by Statutory Instruments – Regulations – and are explained in Ministry Circulars, which are issued when required to cover new legislation or to amend the procedures laid down earlier. In addition to the measures described in the following sections – which include those that relate to the control of pesticides, environmental assessment, and hedgerows – other examples of the most important of such instruments of policy are given in Appendix 7.

CONTROL OF PESTICIDES REGULATIONS 1986 (SI 86/1510)

These regulations came into effect in 1986 affecting all those who advertised, sold, supplied, stored or used pesticides (including aerial sprays), householders, and employers of those who used them. From 1 January 1987 advertising and certificates of competence for storage were controlled; from 1 July 1987 controls were applied to anti-fouling paints and surface coatings, and from 1 January 1988, those who sell or supply pesticides to require users to 'take all reasonable precautions to protect the health of human beings, creatures and plants, to safeguard the environment and in particular to avoid the pollution of water'.

ENVIRONMENTAL ASSESSMENT (SI 76/1419) AND GDO (SI 77/289)

In 1985 the Council of Environment Ministers of the European Communities adopted a directive 'on the assessment of the effects of certain public and private projects on the environment' generally known as the 'Environmental Assessment Directive' (85/337). Compliance by member states was required by 1988. The directive provides that for certain types of projects listed in an Annexe, developers must collect certain information about the environmental effects of a project which has then to be taken into consideration by the authority before giving consent to the development. The information to be provided, also set out in an Annexe, includes a description of those aspects of the environment likely to be significantly affected by the proposed project, for example:

1   Population, fauna, flora, soil and water.
2   Air, climatic factors and material assets.
3   The architectural and archaeological heritage.
4   Landscapes and interrelated spaces between them.

Also required is a description of the measures envisaged to prevent, reduce and where possible offset any significant adverse effects on the environment. Other bodies with environmental responsibilities are to be given the opportunity to comment before consent is given and the information is given to the public.

This information can already be demanded by the planning authority under General Development Order (SI 77/289). The options in terms of type of process and location of the proposed development must of course be prepared on an objective and factual basis, free of matters of opinion and with the advantages and disadvantages of each option set out.

TOWN AND COUNTRY PLANNING – ASSESSMENT OF ENVIRONMENTAL EFFECTS REGULATIONS (SI/88/1199)

This implemented the EC Directive 85/337 and required Environmental Assessments to be carried out for large-scale projects requiring planning consent that were likely to have a particular impact on the environment; the listing of compulsory assessments for large-scale engineering works, extractive industries and developments with a significant environmental impact if the planning authority thought it necessary, the information to be provided in the Environmental Assessment; and the Secretary of State to rule between the developer and the local authority in the event of any dispute. Decisions were required to be given within 16 weeks instead of eight.

This SI was amended by SIs 90/367, 92/1494 and 94/677, dealing with the obligations to require an Environmental Assessment before consent is given, procedures with appeals to the Secretary of State, the information required, and the publicity to be given to the statements submitted.

ENVIRONMENTAL ASSESSMENT: A GUIDE TO PROCEDURES DOE 1989

This describes the complex procedures for the preparation and submission of an Environmental Assessment, with extracts from the T&CP (Assessment of Environmental Effects) Regulations 1988, EC Directive 85/337 and DoE Circular 88/15, setting out criteria for Schedule II projects and a flow chart for procedures.

CONSTRUCTION (DESIGN AND MANAGEMENT) (CDM) REGULATIONS 1994

In an attempt to minimize the risk of accidents and injuries on site during construction projects and subsequently when the works are maintained, the government introduced the Construction (Design and Management) Regulations 1994, which came into force on 31 March 1995.

The 24 Regulations on Health and Safety in SI 94/3140 and the approved Code of Practice, L54 (any breach of which could involve criminal proceedings), applies to all construction projects except when the project is not notifiable to the Health and Safety Executive (HSE) because the construction period is unlikely to take longer than 30 working days (six weeks) or involve fewer than 500 person days of construction work. Where the project is not notifiable and fewer than five people are employed on site at any one time designers only have to notify the HSE in accordance with Regulation 13. Where the project is for a domestic client on property solely for his or her own occupation, only notification under Regulation 7 by the Health and Safety Planning Supervisor is involved.

Other aspects of the CDM Regulations include:

1. On all other projects the client must, before work starts on site, appoint a Health and Safety Planning Supervisor and a Principal Contractor (who the client is reasonably satisfied is competent in health and safety matters) to prepare a Health and Safety Plan assisted by the designer before work starts on site. Once work starts on site, the Principal Contractor must complete the Health

and Safety Plan, which is to be safely deposited and kept available at all times for inspection by any person who might subsequently need such information for any future work or maintenance of the project.

2. The Regulations require the client as soon as possible to appoint separately and to pay a Health and Safety Planning Supervisor to see that:

(i) the HSE has been notified;

(ii) the designers and other consultants have considered the health and safety aspects;

(iii) a Health and Safety Plan has been prepared;

(iv) the Health and Safety File is delivered to the client on completion of construction.

3. The Principal Contractor is required by the Regulations to:

(i) cooperate with the Health and Safety Planning Supervisor to develop the initial Health and Safety Plan before the start of any construction work;

(ii) advise the Planning Supervisor during construction of any amendments to the Plan;

(iii) obtain any information to be included in the plan;

(iv) ensure any employees and self-employed persons involved in the construction work are trained in health and safety and are fully informed of the Plan.

It is important to note that no work can start on site until the Principal Contractor has been given time to develop the Health and Safety Plan, and time must be allowed for this.

4. The designer appointed by the client must be competent and possess the resources to comply with the health and safety requirements, which impose on the designer the obligation to avoid foreseeable risks and to identify, eliminate and avoid whenever possible risk at source when designing. Designers must now therefore not only take into account costs, fitness for purpose, buildability and the impact on the environment in their design, but also considerations of the stability and temporary support of work under construction, site access, life expectancy of components and regular maintenance and cleaning. Full details of the designer's obligations are given in Regulation 13.

5. Health and Safety Planning Supervisors must always be separately appointed and remunerated. He or she will probably be the designer on a smaller project but may well be another person

on a larger project. In either case they must be fully conversant with the health and safety issues, procedures and quality management systems and be able to cooperate and coordinate the health and safety aspects of the work with the other consultants.

6.   The CDM Regulations require:

(i)   Notification of the project to be given to the HSE by the designer or Principal Contractor if the appointment of a Health and Safety Planning Supervisor is not required.

(ii)   An initial Health and Safety Plan to be prepared from all who have been involved in the design and the same Plan to be provided to all tenderers in the tender documents, warning of hazards particular to the project in addition to those which contractors would normally expect to encounter. This Plan has to be amplified to incorporate the contractor's and his or her subcontractors' health and safety policy and a method statement for informing, monitoring, reporting and collaborating with all involved on site, and it must be kept up to date with any variations or modifications arising during construction.

(iii)   The Health and Safety File, with record and 'as built' drawings, must be prepared and delivered to the client on completion of the project so that anyone working on the project in the future on structural repairs, alterations, mechanical and electrical installation, operating manuals, routine maintenance and cleaning is aware of any hazards that might arise. This File must be available for inspection by anyone who might need it and is to be passed on to whoever might need it in the future.

HEDGEROW REGULATIONS (SI 97/1160)

With effect from June 1997 it became against the law for a person to remove or destroy most hedgerows without the consent of the local planning authority, who have six weeks in which to prohibit their removal. Should the hedgerows be removed without permission, unlimited fines may result. Permission is required if a hedgerow is on or alongside agricultural land, common land and village greens, land used for forestry, horses, ponies or donkeys or is a SSSI, but not if it is shorter than 20m, is in or borders a garden. Moving an existing gate does not require consent if the original gap is filled. The hedge must be at least 30 years old and is considered to be 'important' if it complies with one or more of eight criteria specified in detail in the Regulations.

HOUSING GRANTS AND CONSTRUCTION REGULATIONS (SI 98/649)

Implementing the 1996 Housing Grants, Construction and Regeneration Act the 1998 Construction Regulations require all construction contracts, including those for professional services, to include the following:

1. Interim payments whenever work lasts 45 days or more.
2. Confirmation of when all payments are due.
3. Method of calculating the payment to be clearly stated.
4. The payer to notify the amount he or she will pay within five days.
5. The final date of each payment to be clearly stated.
6. Notification of any intention to withhold payment to be within a fixed period.
7. The right to refer disputes to adjudication for a decision within 28 days.

DETR CIRCULARS

Sometimes in an attempt to be more explicit or to describe procedures in more detail, often due to the efforts of uninformed parliamentary draftspersons, Acts, Statutory Instruments – Regulations/Orders – have become unintelligible, and therefore explanatory circulars are drafted and issued by civil servants in the Ministry concerned, their frequency directly related to the zeal of parliament in producing new legislation. A list of the more important Circulars relevant to landscape consultants is given in Appendix 7.

DETR PLANNING POLICY GUIDANCE NOTES (PPGs)

Until the late 1980s government advice on planning policies had been made known by White Papers and Circulars prior to the issue of legislation, procedures and planning policies. In 1988 these were superseded by Planning Policy Guidance Notes (PPGs) for the use of local authorities and developers over a wide range of subjects, and over the subsequent years these have been updated and supplemented as necessary and now provide authoritative guidance on all planning issues. Further guidance is now also available from Minerals Planning Guidance Notes (MPGs) and Regional Planning Guidance Notes (RPGs).

Drafts of proposed new and revised PPGs, like British Standards, are issued to professional institutions and representatives of organizations in the industries concerned for comment prior to publication.

Planning Policy Guidance Notes of particular importance to the landscape profession are listed in Appendix 7.

CHAPTER

4

PRACTICE MANAGEMENT

All landscape consultant offices irrespective of size require good personnel, an efficient financial and management structure and the ability to profit from past experience for current and future projects.

 ## FINANCIAL CONTROL

The basic essential for any office – and the cornerstone of any accounting system – is the cash book. In its simplest form it includes on the one side details of all income received, entered with the date, origin and amount, and identifying separately fees, expenses and VAT, and on the other side details of all expenditure, broken down into ten or more headings (see Figure 4.1). In landscape practices expenditure usually includes such categories as: salaries and consultancy fees, rent, heating, light and cleaning, office stationery, telephone and post, recoverable project expenses such as printing, travelling, photography, models, office furniture and equipment, insurance and sundries including items of single annual expenditure.

This one book with its supporting receipts, invoices and bank statements is often sufficient for the preparation of an annual statement of accounts and balance sheet at the end of each financial year for audit and tax purposes. Most mini and micro computer hardware now have an appropriate software system to enable this to be achieved automatically and, subject to the incorporation of audit trails and careful checking for errors, provide accurate and up-to-date information at short notice (see Figure 4.2).

It is, however, not sufficient to rely only on accurate records of past and even current income and expenditure without giving some thought to the future, and the preparation of an 'Annual Budget Forecast of Fee

INCOME

INV. NO.	DATE	JOB	JOB NO. (1)	TOTAL (2)	SUB-TOTAL	FEES (3)	EXP. (4)	SUNDRIES (5)	VAT (6)	(7)

EXPENDITURE

CHEQUE NO.	PAID TO:	DATE	TOTAL (1)	VAT (2)	SALS. (3)	ACCOM. (4)	CONSLTS FEES (5)	GENERAL (6)	PROJECT EXP. (7)	BOOKS PUBS. STAT. (8)	TRAVEL SUBS ENT. (9)	PETTY CASH (10)	FINANCE, BANK CHARGES (11)	PARTNERS DRWGS (12)	MISC. (13)

Figure 4.1   A page from a simple cash book

ON
CASH FLOW FORECAST
Financial year: 1998
Date: 10th August 1998

Year Month	1997	1998 :Jan	:Feb	:Mar	:Apr	:May	:Jun	:Jul	:Aug	:Sep	:Oct	:Nov	:Dec	:TOTAL
		ACTUAL	ACTUAL	ACTUAL	ACTUAL	ACTUAL	ACTUAL	ACTUAL						
RECEIPTS														
Fees/expenses received		81,342	149,237	36,015	70,676	100,455	29,682	24,501	59,000	29,000	21,300	28,100	48,000	677,308
Total		81,342	149,237	36,015	70,676	100,455	29,682	24,501	59,000	29,000	21,300	28,100	48,000	677,308
PAYMENTS														
Project expenses		8,631	14,512	7,796	5,826	14,424	8,269	8,232	11,000	11,000	11,000	11,000	11,000	122,690
Consultants fees		10,414	8,504	3,999	12,956	7,629	2,312	4,782	3,000	3,000	3,000	3,000	3,000	65,596
Salaries		23,866	26,990	21,780	21,522	20,972	22,472	25,129	18,000	18,000	18,000	18,000	22,000	256,731
Accommodation		10,262	2,809	4,709	1,292	6,263	7,972	3,361	2,500	3,000	3,000	3,000	3,000	51,168
office charges		5,459		5,459			3,875	250		4,000			4,000	17,584
VAT (net)		14,519	5,435	1,502	27,193	3,579	1,383	20,447	2,500	1,500	16,000	1,500	1,500	97,058
Partnership tax			16,785		16,785		16,033	16,785					16,000	32,033
Professional indemnity		4,896												50,355
Partners drawings			4,060	4,060	4,675	4,062	4,061	4,667	4,060	4,060	4,700	4,060	4,060	51,421
Pension		6,165												6,165
Total		78,753	79,095	49,305	90,249	56,929	66,377	83,653	41,060	44,560	55,700	40,560	64,560	750,801
Receipts less expenses		(2,589)	(70,142)	13,290	19,573	(43,526)	36,695	59,152	(17,940)	15,560	34,400	12,460	16,560	
Bank balance b/fwd		175,900	173,311	103,169	116,459	136,032	92,506	129,201	188,353	170,413	185,973	220,373	232,833	
Bank balance c/fwd		173,311	103,169	116,459	136,032	92,506	129,201	188,353	170,413	185,973	220,373	232,833	249,393	

Figure 4.2   A statement of forecast income and expenditure

ON
FEES FORECAST
FINANCIAL YEAR 1998
Date: 20th August 1998

| | | ACTUAL | ACTUAL | ACTUAL | ACTUAL | ACTUAL | ACTUAL | ACTUAL | ACTUAL | | | | | |
| | | 1998 | | | | | | | | | | | | 1999 |
JOB NO.	JOB NAME	1Jan	1Feb	1Mar	1Apr	1May	1Jun	1Jul	1Aug	1Sep	1Oct	1Nov	1Dec	1JFMA
941	Lectures			1,029	88	450		257			500			
1077	A Cope		1,027	1,995								4,500		
1086	Getwell Hospital													
1219	Iron Court										2,000			
1226	Shepherds Hill		247	745										
1245	Hazel Grove													
1251	Lime Close								12,420					
1253	Select Square				16,348									
1261	Ivy Green									3,000				
1285	Norborough	4,580												
1289	Treadwell	3,917												
1292	Daniels										500			
1305	The Bothy												3,600	
1309	Berry Farm						6,385				1,700			
1310	Faraway Borough		34,702											
1321	Contour Survey			815		59,961								
1323	The Studio										300	3,600		
1324	Primrose Cottage						2,070							
1329	Treadwell Green		2,747											
1390	Gnomes Homes	32,173												
1331	Gravel Court	8,425												
1334	Puddle Lane	7,545		10,623										
1342	Old Manor House										2,800		1,800	
1345	Cherry Avenue										3,200			
1346	Leafy Lane										100			
1347	Robins Row		91											
1349	Hollywell													
1350	Linden Crescent	1,437	1,506											
1355	Ridge & Cope										4,500			
1356	The Square, Nettleshire								9,044	15,000				
1357	Willow Close													
1361	The Cover													
1366	Templars		2,981								2,500			
1368	The Bungalow								12,219	15,000				
1369	Rainbow Build												600	
1372	Redhill Farm		47,245						16,695				17,000	

Figure 4.3 A fees forecast

Income' is essential even if it relies mainly on inspired guesswork in the calculation of the amount of the interim payments of fees and the dates when it is anticipated they will become due (see Figure 4.3).

A similar 'Monthly Summary of Income and Expenditure' can also be prepared to forecast monthly expenditure, with updated monthly sub-totals taken from the cash book and the monthly figures taken from the fee income forecast (see Figure 4.4).

A few hours spent at the beginning of each year and a few minutes each month to keep it up to date, substituting more accurate estimates when they are known and actual receipts and payments when they are made, will pay handsome dividends towards ensuring the future financial stability of the practice, and is absolutely essential when negotiating any necessary overdraft facilities with the bank.

 STAFF

It used to be said that one-third of the income of a practice was expended on technical and staff salaries and one-third on rent and overheads, leaving the final one-third for the remuneration of the working partner or partners, but today the proportion is nearer one-half, one-third and one-sixth respectively, with many partners earning little more than their most senior assistants. With the greatest single expenditure of an office being on staff, the careful husbanding and deployment of their resources must therefore be of primary importance.

It is often convenient to divide technical staff into four categories of responsibility and remunerate them accordingly:

1. *Technical (junior) assistants* – Unqualified and graduate (year out) assistants capable of performing simple jobs under strict supervision. Work at this level is not the job of a qualified consultant, but will normally be that of landscape technicians and students in training.

2. *Assistants* – Fully qualified assistant consultants capable of handling small jobs under supervision. They may also be members of a team working on a larger project. The work at this level should be seen as the task of staff in their early years after qualification.

3. *Senior assistants* – Assistants capable of taking responsibility for large jobs or of acting as team leaders in charge of a number of assistants engaged on either a large project or a series of smaller projects. This level should be regarded as the professional career

MONTHLY SUMMARY OF RECEIPTS AND PAYMENTS

Last Year		This year to date	Forecast to date
	INCOME		
....	Fees received	....	....
....	Expenses received	....	....
....	VAT received	....	....
....	Sundry receipts	....	....
....	Transfer from deposit	....	....
£ _____		£ _____	£ _____
	EXPENDITURE		
....	VAT inputs incl. HMC & Ex	....	....
....	Wages, salaries and staff pensions	....	....
....	Consultants fees	....	....
....	Rent, rates, ins., htng, ltng, clng	....	....
....	Books, stationery, materials, telephone, post	....	....
....	Non-recoverable pract. exp., i.e. photos & models	....	....
....	Recoverable pract. exp., i.e. printing, travel, xerox, maps etc.	....	....
....	Subs, indemnity ins., bank charges, sundry finance	....	....
....	Petty cash	....	....
....	Sundry items	....	....
£ _____		£ _____	£ _____
....	Repairs, furniture & fittings	....	....
....	Partners regular drawings, pensions	....	....
....	Partners irregular drawings, i.e. Tax Reserve Cert., capital drawings & tax	....	....
£ _____	**TOTAL**	£ _____	£ _____
	CASH		

Figure 4.4   Monthly summary of income and expenditure

grade and should normally be reached after some five years' or so experience and practical knowledge. Professional competence is misused if staff have not had the opportunity of undertaking work at this level of responsibility by their mid-thirties at the latest.

4. *Associates* – Assistants capable of directing the activities of a number of teams. Work at this level will be found mainly in the larger offices and is the level to which more able staff achieve promotion; they should expect to have influence in the framing of office policy in design and construction matters.

RESOURCE ALLOCATION AND JOB COSTING

Irrespective of the landscape consultant's office being reimbursed by the client on a percentage fee or time basis, accurate job costing from up-to-date time sheets prepared regularly by partners and staff is essential. When staff are used on projects where the practice is remunerated on a time basis weekly time sheets, recording the number of hours each day they have devoted to the job in question, are essential so that a detailed statement can be prepared to accompany the fee submission to the client. Although the hourly rate may be charged to the client on the basis of £0.18 per £100 gross annual salary, it is often advisable (if not essential) to work out the actual rate by adding to their gross salary actual overheads and dividing the total by the total annual actual hours worked full- or part-time (see Figure 4.5).

OFFICE ORGANIZATION

Without imposing unnecessary disciplines and bureaucratic procedures, and at the risk of damaging the creative spirit and vitality of the office, it is necessary at the outset to decide if the practice is to operate on a centralized specialist basis – that is to say, with one group of staff preparing all design drawings, which are then handed to another group to prepare working drawings, specification and tender documents, which are then handed in turn to a third group for post-contract administration and site inspections. This is certainly the most efficient method of organizing the office's workload, and one still adopted by some of the larger practices. Most practices today, however, choose to work on a dispersed or federal basis, each group being responsible for a project from conception to completion on site. The belief is that this

		hours	hours	hours	hours	hours	hours
compiled							
staff grade							
Part I: Time		hours	hours	hours	hours	hours	hours
Standard working hours	hrs/Yr						
Total hours this individual (if part-time employed)	hrs/Yr						

		£	p	£	p	£	p	£	p	£	p	£	p
Part 2: Costs		£	p	£	p	£	p	£	p	£	p	£	p
Basic annual salary	£/Yr												
Add: employer's contribution NI	£/Yr												
Add: employer's contribution graduated pension	£/Yr												
Add: employer's contribution supplementary pension	£/Yr												
Add: cost to employer of canteen facilities/ individual	£/Yr												
Add: other payments by employer (eg bonus)	£/Yr												
Add: ditto	£/Yr												
Sub-total items 4 to 9 employer's other costs	£/Yr												
Item 3 + Item 10 = total annual gross salary	£/Yr												
Estimated overheads for the year (transferred from Form A1, line 4)	£/Yr												

Part 3: Job costing

$\dfrac{\text{Item 11 + Item 12}}{\text{Item 2}}$ = Job costing rate (transferred to Form F2)   £/Hr

Part 4: Billing charges scale 5.11

$\dfrac{\text{Item 11}}{100}$ x 0.18 = rate for full time personnel   £/Hr

$\left[\dfrac{(\text{Item 3 x Item 1}) + \text{Item 10}}{\text{Item 2}} \right] \times \dfrac{1}{100} \times 0.18$
= rate for part-time personnel   £/Hr

Figure 4.5   Time sheet for job costing
(Reproduced with the permission of RIBA Publications Ltd.)

arrangement encourages a great spirit of creative design, personal involvement and more efficient management, while still enabling the composition of the groups within the office to change as and when necessary to suit peaks in workload, even if this means their employment on tasks of lesser responsibility than their greater experience would otherwise suggest. The organization of the office has a direct effect on the quality of its output. A good organization is essential if staff are to work congenially with their employer and other colleagues. No partner can usually manage more than 15–20 staff and the larger office will usually require, in addition to associates, senior and junior qualified and unqualified staff and an equivalent hierarchy of secretarial staff, a bookkeeper and librarian (see Figure 4.6). It is also important to remember that internal public relations are just as important as external, and the need for staff meetings to keep office staff informed of the work of the office other than their own, and possible new projects on which they might be employed, should not be overlooked. Social occasions, including those at Christmas and mid-summer, are equally important to engender a congenial spirit within the office.

Apart from the usual typing of letters, specifications, minutes and the other post-contract administrative services, there are many other supporting activities necessary for the efficient running of the office and it is often useful for the partners to delegate responsibility for certain items such as:

O   the acquisition of drawing office stationery and materials;
O   the office library of technical literature;
O   records and photographs of completed jobs for future publicity;
O   office furniture and equipment; and
O   office repairs and redecorations,

in whole or in part to other members of staff.

 PREMISES

The location of a landscape consultant's office accommodation in the centre of a city is no longer an essential requirement, if indeed it ever was, but most clients nevertheless feel the need for relatively simple close personal contact. Good communication by letter, drawing, telephone, fax, e-mail or in person are essential and the ability to achieve this is an important requirement in the choice of the location of an office, whether this be situated at the consultant's own home or in a block of offices in the city centre, the suburbs or in the country. The geographical location of existing major clients and of those who might have need of a consultant's services in the future, as well as the type of work in which the consultant is particularly successful, must also be considered. An office in London is of little use to a practice or consultant interested in forestry in the Highlands, while an office in Inverness will inevitably prove to be a handicap for consultants whose particular line of work revolves around the creation of atria offices for international conglomerates.

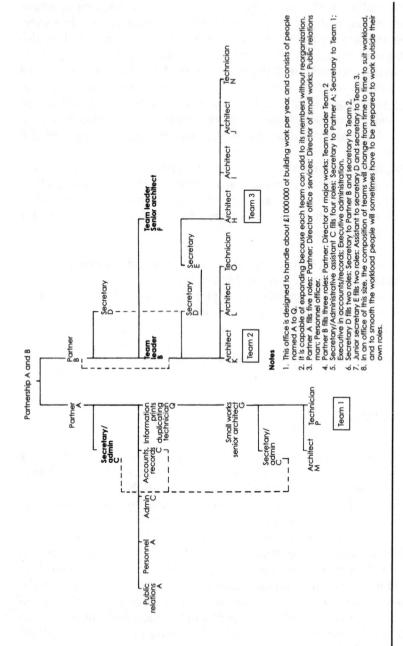

Notes

1. This office is designed to handle about £1 000 000 of building work per year, and consists of people named A to Q.
2. It is capable of expanding because each team can add to its members without reorganization.
3. Partner A fills five roles: Partner; Director office services; Director of small works; Public relations man; Personnel officer.
4. Partner B fills three roles: Partner; Director of major works; Team leader Team 2
5. Secretary/Administrative assistant C fills four roles: Secretary to Partner A; Secretary to Team 1; Executive in accounts/records: Executive administration.
6. Secretary D fills two roles: Secretary to Partner B and secretary to Team 2.
7. Junior secretary E fills two roles: Assistant to secretary D and secretary to Team 3.
8. In an office of this size, the composition of teams will change from time to time to suit workload, and to smooth the workload people will sometimes have to be prepared to work outside their own roles.

Figure 4.6 Staff organization
(Reproduced with the permission of RIBA Publications Ltd.)

Irrespective of the location of one's practice, the ability to adapt to changing circumstances is equally essential, particularly with regard to the need to expand or contract in response to a fluctuating workload, with the consequent increase or decrease in staff numbers and the effect on the amount of office space required. Facilities at home may only be a short-term expedient and the choice is often between sharing space with other practices on the one hand, or renting, leasing or purchasing the freehold of one's own premises on the other. Whatever the solution, temporary or long term, it is always better to have too much than too little space as this can subsequently be sublet if necessary (although not always at a higher rent than that due to the landlord). Remember also that one often expands into surplus space simply because it is available and then finds it hard to contract again when this becomes necessary. One should also not overlook the problems often encountered in assigning the end of short or long leases in unattractive areas or offices which are difficult to subdivide.

Not only should an office have enough space for technical staff but there must also be adequate accommodation for meetings, as well as sufficient secretarial staff, lavatories and tea-making facilities. Remember also the need to make the necessary arrangements for cleaning the office, the cost of rates, insurance against fire and theft, the statutory employers' liability insurance against personal accidents to visitors and staff and the need for the offices to comply with the Offices, Shops and Railway Premises Act 1963 and the Health and Safety at Work Act 1974.

 ## OFFICE ADMINISTRATION AND EQUIPMENT

The extent of administration involved in running even the smallest office can easily be underestimated. Not only are there salaries, PAYE, VAT and national insurance to be paid, but also bills have to be checked and paid, fee invoices issued, chased and receipted when paid, staff records kept up to date, vacancies advertised, interviews arranged, and correspondence with accountants, the bank manager, auditors and solicitors maintained.

OFFICE STATIONERY

Headed notepaper (usually A4) and envelopes must be clear and legible when photocopied and should not only attempt to reflect the 'style' of the office and incorporate the practice's name, address, telephone, fax numbers and e-mail address, together with the names and qualifications of all partners, associates and retired 'consultants', but must also leave space for the letter itself! Most offices also have printed continuation and copy letter sheets, memoranda of meetings, 'with compliments' slips and drawing enclosure sheets. They may also have printed or photocopied time sheets, and telephone message pads. Bulk purchases of notepads, ball pens, carbon paper, correcting fluid and other items of office stationery are usually ordered from travelling sales representatives.

OFFICE EQUIPMENT

Photocopiers

These are now indispensable in any office and should always be A3 with at least a reduction, if not enlargement, facility to enable them to be used by the drawing office also. The choice of hire, lease or outright purchase of copiers is a matter of individual preference and cash flow. When such specifications as larger sizes, coloured copying and the ability to produce large numbers of copies are required, the use of an agency is usually an option and saves office time, particularly when the cost is recoverable.

Telephones

These are now available by hire or purchase from sources other than BT. Again the facility for future expansion of not only extensions but also the number of outside lines is advisable. Nothing is more irritating to staff or clients than having to wait for an outside line or getting a continuously engaged tone when trying to call in. For the same reason a pleasant, polite and helpful telephonist/receptionist with a good telephone manner is essential to create the correct impression for any office, large or small. Landscape consultants are entitled to recover the cost of telephone calls; the installation of call logging equipment usually shows the costs, but few offices make more than a handful of calls costing more than 50p in any one day. Answerphones are, however, an essential facility if only for clients wishing to contact the office and leave messages before 9 am, during lunch time and after 6 pm, as are mobile telephones for partners and staff when away from the office and when they are urgently required to be contacted by clients and contractors (but not while in meetings, trains and restaurants!).

Fax machines

These have rapidly superseded telex machines and have become an essential adjunct for any office, due to their ability to provide the instant day or night transmission of both written and drawn information between client, consultant and contractor, but separate telephone lines are advisable.

COMPUTERS

Computers and word processors

The major item of office equipment is of course one or more computers or word processors, which have taken the place of typewriters on account of their being able to offer such facilities as a memory, ease of editing, justification, variable fonts and point size, ease of correction and accuracy. It is important always to obtain the best that one can afford. The choice of software is a matter for the individual practice.

Computer hardware

In the past decade, the use of computers for professional services has moved from simple tasks with one machine (used only for word processing letters, minutes, reports, specifications and spread sheets, previously carried out on a typewriter), through the now almost universal use of fax machines (delivering letters to the addressee and calling for an answer within minutes instead of the next one or two days), plant selection and ground modelling programmes, to the world of e-mail, voice mail, inter office, national and international networking. Both the Landscape Institute's secretariat and its library are now contactable by members via an e-mail link for those who have a modem or Internet link, via world wide web pages, and video conferencing is already within sight.

Personal computers (PCs) and laptops are now available with the most sophisticated facilities at lower and lower prices. Equipment with the current 'Windows' facility 266 Mhz MMX, with Pentium II chips, USB connectors for speed and longevity, 440 LX mother boards, On Now feature and at least 16Mb, if not 64Mb EDO RAM, 24 x CD ROM, 33.6 kbps internal modem and 6 Gb hard disk drive, 15-inch colour screen and a HP, Epson or Canon ink jet or laser printer would seem to be able to meet all the demands of the average practice today.

Software

Software for landscape administration is little different from that required by any office for word processing, accounting and audit, graphic desk top publishing, reports, specifications, plant schedules and maintenance and normal database, and if not 'built in' to the hardware are readily available from suppliers and retailers without the need for the knowledge to program one's own tailor-made system. All that is required is the ability to diagnose any fault arising in its operation and any necessary maintenance.

Computer aided design (CAD)

For landscape consultants this has obvious advantages for ground modelling, volume cut and fill calculations, but the necessary software and equipment can be very expensive if not time-consuming for 3-D and any but the simplest two-dimensional drawing systems and equipment. Although drawing systems are available to enable architects and civil engineers to produce accurate detailed drawings of components and assemblies, often pre-prepared and available on disk by manufacturers, such admittedly attractive facilities as layout drawings to coordinate the drawings of quantity surveyors, structural, mechanical and electrical engineers in (coloured) overlays at common scales, the sophistication and choice of line thickness, curves, graphic symbols, repetitive nesting, handing, rotation and text are not always justified on landscape projects even in the hands of the most experienced technician.

E-mail and Internet

The need for an electronic (e-mail) address via a service provider for transferring information, messages and correspondence direct to a VDU and printer by use of a modem, together with the use of the Internet and a web site, are also matters which require careful consideration by each practice, depending on its individual requirements.

OFFICE FURNITURE

In addition to drawing boards – normally melamine-faced with parallel motion stands, CAD terminals, padded seats with back and footrests – staff involved in practice and project administration can require desks with drawers and chairs both for themselves and visitors. Chests for the storage of photographic negatives and transparencies, either vertically or horizontally, and filing cabinets should always be fire resistant.

DESIGN OFFICE EQUIPMENT

Printing

Still the norm for any drawing larger than A3. Opinions are divided on the advantages of installing in-house equipment, but with the present three-hour collection and delivery service offered by most printing firms for all but the most unusual orders, the cost of in-house equipment can rarely be justified even when the cost of reproducing drawings can be recovered from the client.

Design office stationery

Printed cut sheets of tracing paper, especially A1 and A3, with the name and address of the firm, the name of the job, and the drawing scale, date, author and number are now the norm.

Most offices also provide pencils, pens, ink, Letraset, erasing machines or rubbers, colouring equipment, curves and templates for their staff; staff provide their own instruments, scales and set squares.

Levelling equipment

It is often better, quicker and more accurate and economical to arrange for site surveys to be prepared by specialist surveyors, but most offices have dumpy levels and staffs of their own to save hiring them in the case of emergencies or when a contractor's equipment is not available.

INSURANCE

Apart from the insurance of the office building itself, insurance of the furniture, fixtures and fittings against damage from fire, theft, and so on, including the cost of renting alternative accommodation, replacing lost or destroyed drawings and even loss of profit, must be taken out, as well as insurance against any accidental injury to staff and visitors while on the premises. Consideration should also be given to insuring against the possibility of accidents to staff while travelling to site visits, during their duties on site, or while returning to the office; long-term staff illness or disablement; any private medical insurance for partners and staff; and retirement pensions for long-serving staff.

TECHNICAL LIBRARY

Next to competent staff, a good technical reference library is probably the most important resource an office can have. It is not, however, a 'loan' library with essential technical literature subsequently hidden away or forgotten beneath the drawing board of one member of the staff and denied to the remainder. Where a particular item of technical information is required for one particular job and needs to be referred to frequently, duplicates or photocopies should be obtained. Even when this item has been removed from the library for only a short time, a note should be left behind of its whereabouts – often a tedious chore but really only good manners on the part of the borrower. Staff should, however, always be encouraged to seek information through the 'librarian' and only in his or her absence should they seek out the information for themselves.

Equally, landscape technical libraries must be more than a collection of unsolicited technical literature, passively received in the daily post and filed haphazardly irrespective of value or present or future relevance. Even valuable existing information must be kept up to date and ideally should be checked at regular intervals with the manufacturer concerned, to confirm that it is still current and has not been superseded. Literature filed when the library was first set up and never since updated is worse than no information at all; indeed, some offices make a point of asking for fresh, up-to-date and accurate trade information, if necessary, for each individual job, accepting the delays that this may sometimes cause. Technical libraries are, however, more than just shelves of technical literature; they are also for books and should at least contain the essential technical references featured in the Landscape Institute (LI) book list.

Other types of technical literature no landscape consultant's library should be without are copies of the essential fifteen or so British Standards and the National Building Specification Library of standard clauses for landscape works. As with trade literature, it is equally essential that these are kept up to date, either by constant vigilance or by subscription to or membership of such professional amenities as the Barbour Microfile or the Royal Institute of British Architects (RIBA) Product Data subscription services. Much information is available today on CD or microfiche and ideally not only a reader/printer but a photocopier should be installed in the library so that hard copy is readily available when required.

Libraries should also be the point of access to other sources of material, either directly or by telephone with or without fax. Not only technical libraries such as the Royal Horticultural Society, Wisley, the LI, the RIBA, the Building Research Establishment (BRE) and the

Building Centre, but also local public authority libraries are usually only too willing to help in tracing and acquiring historical and technical information.

Most offices subscribe to at least one or more technical journals or periodicals and their receipt, circulation and subsequent disposal is also one of the librarian's responsibilities. In all but the smallest office distribution to members of staff, from one to the other, can mean it may take weeks or months for literature to circulate around the whole office, and it is probably better for the librarian to identify and forward those items of interest to a particular member of staff, and to circulate only a monthly summary of acquisitions and items of general interest to all members of staff on a regular basis.

Not to be forgotten is other non-technical information such as professional directories of members' names and addresses, not only of the LI but also of the RIBA, Royal Institution of Chartered Surveyors (RICS) and the Institute of Chartered Engineers, not to mention train timetables and hotel guides. While strictly speaking such tasks are not within the librarian's duties, some offices make the librarian responsible for practice promotion literature (prepared either in-house or by a public relations consultant), and preparing and filing photographs and articles of recently completed jobs.

CONTINUOUS PROFESSIONAL DEVELOPMENT (CPD)

The Landscape Institute's Rules for the Continuous Professional Development (CPD) of a member require him or her to maintain their competence to practice by:

> The systematic maintenance, improvement and broadening of knowledge and skill and the development of personal qualities necessary for the execution of personal and technical duties throughout the practice member's working life.

It proposed that members should accept an obligation to undertake a minimum of 20 hours CPD per annum in an organized and recorded format.

Just as it is obvious that no one would entrust their health to a GP who had not made an effort to keep up to date with medical science since he or she had qualified ten or twenty years previously, so the medical, legal, surveying and architectural professions have now imposed a similar obligation on their members to maintain their knowledge and skills.

The Landscape Institute recognizes that this obligation should include not only knowledge of changing legislation and technical advances but should also apply to members' personal specialized interests such as urban and rural planning, planting techniques, conservation, ecology and historical research. The form of such study should be on a systematic basis in accordance with a carefully considered programme and not rely solely on attendance at randomly selected all-day, half-day or evening lectures, seminars, conferences and workshops, but should also include individual reading, research, visits and the preparation of articles and papers and service on BSI and Landscape Institute Committees.

It is obvious therefore that the requisite 20 hours can easily be achieved by attendance at one all-day seminar, two three-hour afternoon or evening meetings and four two-hour periods gathering research for a project within the office in any one year.

PROFESSIONAL INDEMNITY INSURANCE (PII)

To comply with the spirit of their Code of Professional Conduct, landscape consultants are expected to ensure they have sufficient financial resources to meet their professional obligations should it be found that the service they have provided a client falls short of that which could be expected from a suitably experienced consultant engaged for the service required, and the client has suffered damages as a consequence.

This can best be ensured by professional indemnity insurance (PII), taken out on an annual basis, to include the work of assistant staff and to cover any allegations of professional negligence (often arising as a result of litigation to recover unpaid fees) for any claims made during the year covered by the insurance, irrespective of when the negligence is alleged to have occurred. Such insurance is normally required to provide indemnity in any one year for each and every claim up to twice the total fee income of the individual or practice, subject to a minimum of £250 000 for each and every claim up to £1 million. Currently premiums for such cover range from £750 to £2 000 p.a. On retirement consultants or their practices should obtain 'run off' cover for any claims that might be attributable to the retiring consultant and that might arise during the first five years of his or her retirement.

DIRECTORY OF REGISTERED LANDSCAPE PRACTICES

The Landscape Institute maintains a Register of Landscape Practices. To be eligible for inclusion practices must have as their principal a professional member of the Institute who has full legal responsibility in the practice as a sole practitioner, partner or director and who holds professional indemnity insurance for a minimum of £250000 for each and every claim; such practices are then eligible to be included in any list of practices nominated through the Institute's nomination procedure, in response to an approach to the Institute for suitable names.

If the principals are not in full-time attendance at the practice but the office is staffed full-time by a professionally qualified Institute member, the office is designated as a branch office; an office which is not so staffed but where the principal is available for a minimum of two days per week is designated as a part-time office.

Although practices are listed in the Directory under geographic regions, most practices, wherever their office is located, are able to undertake work throughout the United Kingdom and abroad.

CHAPTER

TENDER AND CONTRACT DOCUMENTS

PRE-CONTRACT PROJECT AND TENDERING PROCEDURES

FREEZING THE DESIGN

Once the outline, sketch and detailed proposals have been completed and approved by the client, it is essential that the design is now considered to be 'frozen' – indeed, once such approval has been given by the client the landscape consultant has no authority to make any material changes to the design other than those specifically requested by the client. It is equally essential to point out to the client after the design has been frozen that, although changes can subsequently be made, when necessary, to suit changing circumstances or to incorporate better ideas, these changes frequently incur the payment of additional fees due to the landscape consultant having to incorporate the changes in the existing design, and possibly also due to the need to involve other consultants during the making of these changes.

PRODUCTION INFORMATION AND BILLS OF QUANTITIES

Once the design has been finalized, it is now necessary to put in hand the preparation of the necessary information – both drawn and written – in order to select a contractor to be entrusted with carrying out the work on site. The way in which the contractor is selected depends entirely on the client's priorities with regard to the date by which the landscape works must be completed, the cost control, the need for a finite or contractual authorized expenditure, the time available to ascertain the client's detailed requirements and the scope of the work required. Irrespective of these priorities it is almost certain that in the majority of cases drawings, specifications and details of the contract conditions (covering dates for commencement and completion, control of the works, payment and compliance with statutory obligations with regard to insurance against injury to persons and damage to property) will have to be prepared.

The work of a landscape consultant is achieved and created on site 'rather like painting a portrait by numbers with the contractor holding the brush and the consultant trying to tell him or her what colours to use and where to put them'. Unless this working arrangement and the degree of cooperation and mutual understanding it entails can be achieved effectively the project is doomed to failure from the start.

The translation of the design into instructions to the landscape contractor, so that the latter can implement the design and be remunerated accordingly, is covered contractually in four different documents:

1. *Illustrative:* Drawings illustrating the layout and assembly of the materials and components specified.
2. *Qualitative:* A detailed description of the standards of materials and workmanship required.
3. *Quantitative:* Schedules and bills itemizing the labour and materials required.
4. *Conditions of contract:* The legal document covering the conditions under which the work described in the other documents is to be executed and paid for.

All these aspects must of necessity be included in the contract documents prepared by the consultant and signed by the client and the contractor.

 ## LANDSCAPE DRAWINGS

The Foreword to BS 1192: Part 4: 1984 (*Landscape Drawing Practice*) states the intention of drawn information to be:

> to provide communication with accuracy, clarity, economy and consistency of presentation between all concerned with the construction industry ... Familiarity with commonly accepted forms of presentation is likely to result in greater efficiency with the preparation of landscape drawings and minimise the risk of confusion on site.

Figures 5.1 and 5.2 show examples of landscape drawings.

GRAPHIC SYMBOLS

The need for common and easily understood graphic symbols to convey the consultant's intentions cannot be overemphasized. BS 1192: Part 4: 1984 provides a comprehensive range of 50 conventions which should meet the majority of requirements and should convey the maximum information with the minimum time and effort. Figure 5.3 gives examples of BS-approved graphic landscape symbols.

COPYING OF DRAWINGS

Sometimes it is hard for us to remember that the benefits of photocopying and dyeline techniques have been with us for less than half a century and that the drawings of Nesfield and Olstead, let alone those of Bridgeman and Brown, all had to be laboriously copied by hand.

Nowadays contractors take it for granted that they are entitled to as many copies as they need and for this reason, if no other, colour, other than on single copies with a felt pen, rarely has a place in contract documentation. Colouring drawings is costly and time-consuming and the chances of errors being made are directly related to the number of copies required. The increased availability of copies which reduce and enlarge drawings suggests that the reintroduction of the use of drawn scales on drawings is overdue. Quite apart from the obvious requirements for clarity and legibility when letters and drawings are intended for transmission by fax, the thickness of lines, symbols, dimensions, figures and text of landscape drawings must always follow the recommendations of BS 1192 to ensure that they are capable of clear and legible reproduction.

SIZE OF DRAWINGS

Drawings produced for use by the contractor must always be of a size capable of being handled easily on site, irrespective of the size of the project. On any one project there should rarely be more than two or three different sizes of drawing at the most, if the possibility of their being mislaid or misfiled is to be minimized. For most projects, therefore, A1- and A2-size standard sheets are the most appropriate for location, site, setting-out and layout plans at scales down to 1:100, and A3 and A4 for component and assembly drawings from 1:50 to 1:5.

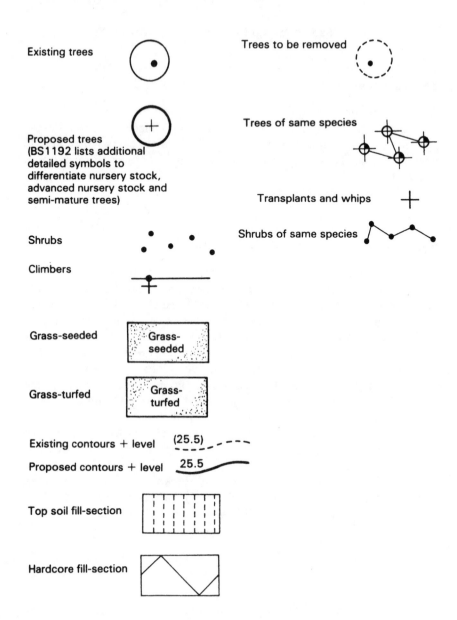

Figure 5.1   The basic British Standards landscape graphic symbols (Extracts from BS 1192: Part 4: 1984 are reproduced by permission of BSI. Complete copies can be obtained from them at Linford Wood, Milton Keynes, MK14 6LE.)

CONTENT

No rules exist at present regarding the minimum content of drawings required by a contractor for any one project, and it is difficult to see how such guidance could in fact be achieved. BS 1192 does, however, attempt to indicate how the information should be shown and includes a checklist of the information required on various types of drawing. It also lays down three categories of drawings: 1) layout, 2) component and 3) assembly. Landscape consultants will find it helpful if they conform to this discipline.

Drawings should rarely duplicate information to be found elsewhere or on other drawings, since this not only increases the risk of error but involves additional work when changes are made. In spite of being given written warnings about the advisability of always working to the largest-scale drawing, contractors often find it more convenient to work to the one containing the most information – that is, the ones drawn to the smaller scales.

LAYOUT DRAWINGS

Often produced on A1- and A2-size sheets, layout drawings must rigorously exclude design information and resist the temptation to show trees and shrubs fully grown and in leaf. The use of overlay draughting techniques whereby different elements of the work are shown on separate sheets (for example site clearance, setting out, foundations, drainage and site services) is particularly applicable to landscape projects, and involves creating one basic drawing from which overlays or copies are made before adding the other information – the addition of which may be essential, useful or just confusing depending on the circumstances. Sections always assist in the calculation of areas and the reduction of errors when cut and fill is involved. Indicating the location of additional component and assembly details for a particular area, with the drawing reference number enclosed within a circle, is especially useful.

Any restrictions on the location of the contractors' site huts and spoil heaps and any limitations on access should always be clearly indicated on layout drawings. Setting-out dimensions should always be related to an existing alignment, building, road or site boundary. Curves drawn from templates are rarely satisfactory and should always be capable of being accurately set out on site from clearly dimensioned centres and tangent points in the case of circular curves (which should be used wherever possible), even if this means the combination of a number of different radii. When irregular curves relying on dimensioned offsets

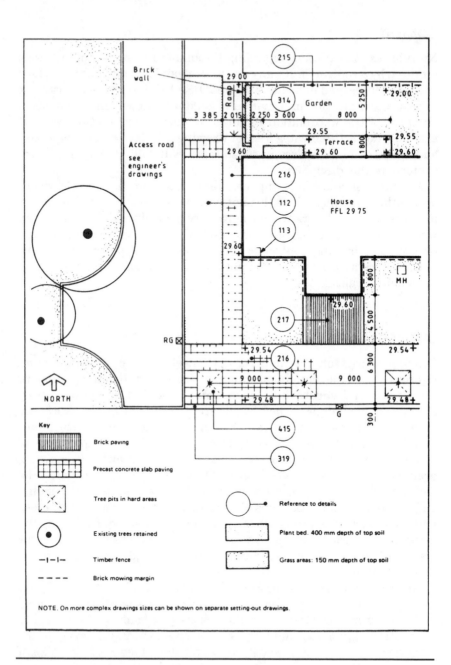

Figure 5.2   A hard-landscape layout drawing
(Extracts from BS 1192: Part 4: 1984 are reproduced by permission of BSI.
Complete copies can be obtained from them at Linford Wood, Milton Keynes,
MK14 6LE.)

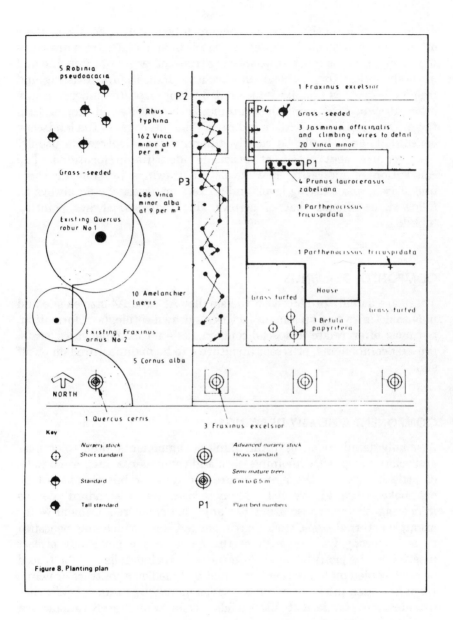

5 Robinia
pseudoacacia

P2

9 Rhus
typhina

162 Vinca
minor at 9
per m²

Grass-seeded

P3

486 Vinca
minor alba
at 9 per m²

Existing Quercus
robur No 1

10 Amelanchier
laevis

Existing Fraxinus
ornus No 2

5 Cornus alba

NORTH

1 Quercus cerris

3 Fraxinus excelsior

1 Fraxinus excelsior

P4   Grass-seeded

3 Jasminum officinalis
and climbing wires to detail

20 Vinca minor

P1

4 Prunus laurocerasus
zabeliana

1 Parthenocissus
tricuspidata

1 Parthenocissus tricuspidata

House

Grass turfed

Grass turfed

3 Betula
papyrifera

Key

⊕	Nursery stock Short standard	⊚	Advanced nursery stock Heavy standard
◉	Standard	⊚	Semi mature trees 6 m to 6.5 m
◉	Tall standard	P1	Plant bed numbers

Figure 8. Planting plan

Figure 5.3   A planting layout drawing
(Extracts from BS 1192: Part 4: 1984 are reproduced by permission of BSI.
Complete copies can be obtained from them at Linford Wood, Milton Keynes,
MK14 6LE.)

are unavoidable on the drawing, they must be closely spaced with their origins clearly indicated. Scaling curves, radii and offsets from drawings inevitably involves much time-wasting trial-and-error work on site and is rarely satisfactory. A clear and accurate indication of existing and proposed levels is equally important on landscape (as indeed in any other) drawings. Showing the contours, both existing and proposed, on the drawings is very useful in indicating the intention of the landscape consultant, and should be clearly differentiated. Contractors usually also require spot levels at precisely identifiable locations. The convention of indicating new levels on drawings by showing them unenclosed, and existing levels in brackets or boxes, should always be followed, as should that of arrows, like tadpoles, always pointing 'uphill'.

COMPONENT DRAWINGS

These are usually produced on the smaller A3- and A4-size sheets and may sometimes rely on a manufacturer's drawn catalogue information, but most often relate to special components – for example gates, seats, pre-cast components, or street furniture – to be manufactured on or off site.

COMPONENT ASSEMBLY DRAWINGS

Assembly details relating to the fixing of components, their tolerances and relationship with adjoining work and components often seem to be of little interest to the manufacturer or supplier but should not be overlooked (see Figure 5.4). Many offices have 'standard' details indicating their own solution for any particular requirement – for example external steps, curbs, paving or fencing – which may be issued as a photocopy with or without the name of the particular project inserted in the job title panel. Alternatively such details may be traced or photocopied on to a larger sheet and included as a contract drawing. Including such information on drawings merely by means of reference to a library of standard details is a false economy and rarely satisfactory, particularly when they are subsequently amended.

It is essential that as many drawings as possible are made available to the contractor and included in the contract documents at the time of tender. Any delay in their issue to the contractor during the contract period may well give rise to a delay in progress and a justifiable claim by the contractor for the reimbursement of the direct loss and expense he or she has incurred as a consequence and to which they are entitled.

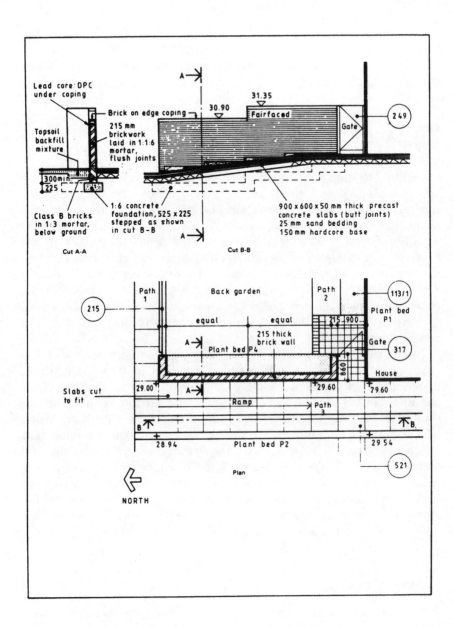

Figure 5.4   A landscape component assembly drawing
(Extracts from BS 1192: Part 4: 1984 are reproduced by permission of BSI.
Complete copies can be obtained from them at Linford Wood, Milton Keynes,
MK14 6LE.)

Such additions to the contract sum arising from delays caused by the landscape consultant are rarely appreciated by the client, nor do they encourage the consultant's involvement in any of the client's subsequent projects.

 ## LANDSCAPE SPECIFICATIONS

In addition to supplying drawn information on the layout and assembly of the materials and components to be provided by the landscape contractor, the landscape consultant also has to instruct the contractor about the quality of workmanship and materials required. This is usually referred to as a 'specification', or as 'trade preambles' in the bills of quantities. The detailed description of the construction, workmanship and materials to be provided by the contractor is clearly a matter for the landscape consultant and should be included in the contract between the client and the contractor, as one of the essential documents describing the work which the contractor has undertaken to provide for the contract sum.

In addition to being set out in a recognizable and orderly way the requirements of the specifier must be immediately recognized, understood and priced accordingly by the estimator so that the latter can allow in his or her tender no more and no less than he or she considers necessary to satisfy the requirements of the consultant. When bills of quantities are included in the contract documents it is important to ensure that all reference to the quality of workmanship and materials (for example the name of the manufacturer of the paving bricks) is excluded from the measured items and covered only in the trade preambles, otherwise the contractor may refer only to the measured items and ignore the specification in the day-to-day arrangements of the work on site.

STANDARD CLAUSES

For these reasons it is clear that, when drawing up specification documents, there are great advantages in the use of standard clauses which the estimator will immediately recognize. From past experience he or she will then know the cost involved without the need for a careful line-by-line consideration to ensure that there are no ambiguities (which the estimator can only allow for in his or her tender by including a hidden contingency sum within the rate so as to cover the risk involved).

While each office can select from these clauses only those options which they require for all their projects, even then they cannot select a 'standard' specification for all projects since they will rarely if ever be on the same site nor need the same materials, and will therefore never require exactly the same clauses. All offices require a regularly updated 'library' of standard specification clauses from which they can select for each project only those applicable in that instance. If specifications are only based on those of a previous project, the possibility of error – either from including an inappropriate clause from the previous project or from omitting those clauses that are necessary for the new project but which were not covered by the previous one – is almost inevitable.

Such a library of clauses requires constant vigilance to ensure that it is regularly updated to incorporate the latest good practice, regulations, British Standards and codes of practice.

ESSENTIAL PHRASEOLOGY

Specification clauses must be written clearly and concisely in a manner that communicates the consultant's intentions simply and unambiguously, by using the same words and phrases consistently throughout. Clauses should always start with a key word – 'TOPSOIL', 'WEEDS', 'HERBICIDES' and so on – followed by a verb in the imperative – for example 'to be', 'provide', 'lay', 'plant', and so on. Vague phrases such as 'in all respects', 'the best of their respective kinds', 'free from all faults' and the like should be avoided in case they are interpreted literally, beyond the limits of that which is practicable, or involve exorbitant costs to achieve standards far higher than the specifier intended. Equally, describing operations in great detail or requiring an accuracy or tolerance that is unnecessary or impossible to achieve should always be avoided. Clauses should not only be capable of being carried out in the actual work on site but also be capable of being checked for compliance by the specifier, either visually or by testing. Otherwise, unscrupulous contractors, secure in the knowledge that they cannot be checked up on, will leave the work undone, to the detriment of the conscientious contractor who has priced the work properly and included it in his or her tender, which is then not the lowest submitted.

National Building Specification Ltd (NBS) have prepared a library of standard specification clauses covering hard and soft landscape work, which can be obtained on disk as 'NBS Landscape' (available on subscription). This covers most if not all of the items likely to arise on landscape works, including those clauses specially written for site preparation, the planting of trees, plants and shrubs, and their subsequent upkeep. Examples of some NBS landscape specification clauses can be seen in Table 5.1.

Table 5.1   Examples of NBS landscape specification clauses

Excavating and filling   D20

860
The following minimum depths are recommended: Grass areas: 10 – 150 mm according to use. Planted areas: 450 mm. Tree pits: Dimensions depend on the size of tree(s) and may need to be scheduled on drawings.
   Greater depths may be appropriate where there are large quantities of stockpiled topsoil or poor quality subsoil.
   Omit this clause if using clause 865 for the entire project.

865
Use this clause when using low grade topsoil and 'neatness' of finish is less important than achieving some plant growth afterwards.
   Unless applying to the entire project, complete the heading appropriately, e.g. *IN ZONE B RECLAMATION AREA:*

870
Some sports (e.g. tennis, cricket squares) require higher standards and should be specified in accordance with the recommendations of the appropriate sporting organisation.

880
Insert, e.g.:
30 mm above adjoining paving or kerbs.
Not less than *150* mm below dpc of adjoining buildings
30 mm higher for shrub areas than for adjoining grass areas.
   If turf or a layer of mulch is specified, allow for it by increasing the figures given, and adding a sixth item, e.g.
• *The above requirements allow for the laying of turf/addition of mulch where appropriate.*
An acceptable estimate for the root spread of trees is approximately one metre beyond the branch spread of broad crowned trees or half the height of fastigiate trees. These may vary considerably depending on species and location, especially where the tree roots have been covered by hard surfaces. Soil level changes or other construction activities outside of the protected zone can still threaten trees by changes to water supply. If it is important to preserve particular trees, seek specialist arboricultural advice as remedial options may exist.

900 – 960
Complete as appropriate if using clause 625.

860^ SPREADING TOPSOIL:
• Remove temporary roads or surfacing before spreading topsoil.
• Spread over prepared subsoil in layers not exceeding 150 mm and gently firm each layer before spreading the next.
• Overall minimum depths after firming and settlement to be:
   ....
• Do not compact topsoil. Preserve a friable texture of separate visible crumbs wherever possible.

865 LOOSE TIPPING OF TOPSOIL ....
• Do not firm, consolidate or compact topsoil when laying. Tip and grade to approximate levels in one operation with the minimum of trafficking by plant.
• Overall minimum depths after settlement to be: ....

870 SPORTSFIELDS: Grade to even levels and within the following permitted deviations:
• From planned gradient or given levels: ±75 mm.
• From line between boning rods 30 m apart: ±25 mm.

880^ FINISHED LEVELS OF TOPSOIL after settlement, unless otherwise stated, to be:
• ...... mm above adjoining paving or kerbs,
• Unchanged within the root spread of existing trees,
• Not less than ...... mm below dpc of adjoining buildings, grass areas,
• ...... mm higher for shrub areas than for adjoining
• Married-in with adjoining soil areas.

HIGHWAYS AGENCY EARTHWORKS SPECIFICATION APPENDICES

900^ APPENDIX 6/1 – REQUIREMENTS FOR ACCEPTABILITY AND TESTING ETC. OF EARTHWORKS MATERIALS: ....

905^ APPENDIX 6/2 – REQUIREMENTS FOR DEALING WITH CLASS U2 UNACCEPTABLE MATERIAL: ....

910^ APPENDIX 6/3 – REQUIREMENTS FOR EXCAVATION, DEPOSITION, COMPACTION (OTHER THAN DYNAMIC COMPACTION): ....

915^ APPENDIX 6/4 – REQUIREMENTS FOR CLASS 3 MATERIAL: ....

920^ APPENDIX 6/5 – GEOTEXTILES USED TO SEPARATE EARTHWORKS MATERIALS: ....

Table 5.1 (concluded)

Planting

359
Typical materials are:
• Those listed in clause 355, but improved by processing or treatment, e.g. to remove contaminants or provide uniform consistency.
• Recycled domestic waste.
• Expanded minerals, e.g. vermiculite, perlite.
• Inert plastics, e.g. polystyrene granules.
• Water holding agripolymer gels.
• Wood fibres.

365
Use this clause for specialized growing media or soil mixes in, e.g. raised beds, planters, etc. or for particular types of plant growth. Complete the clause heading to show the relevant location(s).

375
See also section D20. Cultivation in poor soil conditions can be extremely damaging. Never allow the use of machinery such as rotary cultivators on heavy soils if they are wet.

In situ topsoils that have been well protected will probably have a good structure and may not need cultivation.

The CPSE 'Handling and establishing landscape plants' recommends that soil should be prepared over an area of a minimum of three times the width and one and a half times the depth of the roots of the plants to be planted.
Second Item: Insert, e.g. *150 mm.*
Third Item: Insert, e.g. *75 mm.*

385
See general guidance 7. Use this clause for materials laid before planting. Specify individual mulch mats (in similar materials, but pre-slit and positioned around the stem after planting) in clause 490 and loose materials in clause 485.

Materials available include polyethylene, jute or woollen fibres, bitumenized paper and composite mats of straw and coir bonded to polypropylene mesh or sheet. Many biodegradable products are available. Plants and shrubs are inserted through slits cut at the edges, or flaps cut in the middle of sheets.
Last Item: Some fabrics can be overlaid with further materials, e.g. gravel or bark. This may be desirable where appearance is important. Insert details and clause number (e.g. 485 or 590), or delete the last item, as required.

405
Size(s): Insert, e.g. *150 mm wider than roots when fully spread and 200 mm deep.*
Alternatively, provide a schedule of sizes in the clause, e.g.
Diameter Depth
Type(s) of shrub/plant ....
Otherwise, refer to a separate schedule by inserting *As scheduled.*

Insert any additional requirements, e.g.
Increase dimensions where necessary to ensure that pits are at least 75 mm deeper than root system and wide enough to accommodate roots when fully spread.
➜

359^ PROPRIETARY SOIL CONDITIONER/AMELIORANT:
• Manufacturer and reference: ....
• Apply evenly over .... at 1 m³ of material ......m² immediately before cultivation.

365 TECHNICAL/SPECIALIST IMPORTED GROWING MEDIUM FOR ....
Supplier and reference: ....

375^ CULTIVATION:
• Break up any compacted topsoil to full depth.
• Within a few days before planting, but in suitably dry weather and ground conditions, cultivate top .... mm of all planting beds, using suitable plant to loosen, aerate and break up the soil into particles of 2–8 mm.
• Leave surface regular and even, with levels as required in section D20 and within .... of levels specified on drawings.
• Remove weeds, perennial weed roots and undesirable material brought to the surface including stones and clods larger than 50 mm in any dimension, roots, tufts of grass and foreign matter.
• Do not dig or cultivate within the root spread of trees and shrubs to be retained.

385^ MULCH MATTING/GEOTEXTILE FABRIC:
• Manufacturer and reference: .... Type/size: ....
• Water soil thoroughly before laying. Lay before planting, taking care to ensure close contact with the soil surface. Lap or butt joints as recommended by manufacturer with no gaps.
• If required, cut neat slits or flaps for planting. Refit mat or fabric closely around plant stems.
• After planting, overlay with......... as clause ....

PLANTING SHRUBS/HERBACEOUS PLANTS/BULBS

405^ SHRUB PLANTING PITS:
• Excavate not more than .... days before planting and retain topsoil for re-use where specified.
Size(s): ....
• Break up bottoms of pits to a depth of ....
• Backfilling material: ....

THE COMMON ARRANGEMENT

A joint committee comprising representatives of all sides of the building industry was set up in 1979 at the request of the Department of the Environment to establish the need to coordinate the presentation of project information (Coordinating Committee for Project Information – CCPI). As a first step 200 work sections were established, grouped into 60 or so categories and brought together under the 10–15 broad headings similar to those used in the Standard Method of Measurement (SMM) for bills of quantities, but in this case applicable to drawings and specifications. The two headings most relevant to the landscape industry were Group D (Groundwork) (see Table 5.2) and Group Q (Site surfacing, planting and fencing, including Q30 seeding/turfing and Q31 planting) (see Table 5.3).

Specifications are usually written in two parts, the first being the 'preliminaries' section covering the responsibilities of the parties to the contract, the procedures to be followed, a description of the scope of the work, the site and any special restrictions with regard to access, sequence of work, hours or working rules. The second part of the specification describes the materials and workmanship required. The latter are now normally listed separately and include reference to the location, accuracy, tolerances and fit of the various elements in the scheme and emphasize any special requirements for appearance, performance testing on or off site, and the submission and retention of samples.

CLAUSE SELECTION

Selecting the right clauses requires skill and judgement on the part of the specifier, something often only achieved by experience. Nothing shows up lack of experience or competence more quickly than a specification which includes inapplicable clauses or those incapable of achievement. It is important also to achieve a balance in the specification, dealing only in great detail with those items which are important or which form a significant part of the work, with only a brief but nevertheless accurate reference to the less important items.

With the increased use of computers there is no longer any excuse for not producing an individual specification using a selection of the appropriate standard clauses for each project. Specifying by reference that 'The contractor is to allow for all workmanship and materials to be in accordance with the relevant clauses in the ... standard specification', or even just listing the reference numbers of the clauses required, is not good enough.

Table 5.2 Common Arrangement work sections – Group D (Groundwork)

D11
Soil stabilization

Stabilization or improvement of bearing capacity or slip resistance of existing ground by injecting or otherwise introducing stabilizing materials, by power vibrating or by ground anchors.

Included

Cement or chemical grouting

Electrochemical stabilization

Sand stowing

Forming regular pattern of holes, compacting surrounding soil, and filling with aggregates or hard fill, all by means of power vibrators

Ground anchors

Dynamic compaction

Freezing of ground water and sub-soil where specified

Stabilizing soil in situ by incorporating cement with a rotovator

Excluded

Stabilization by temporary lowering of water table
(Relevant section, D12 or D20)

Consolidating and compacting existing ground/formation levels
(Excavating and filling, D20)

Soil-cement sub-bases to roads and pavings
(Hardcore/Granular/Cement bound bases/sub-bases to roads/pavings, Q10)

Stabilization by permanent ground water drainage
(Drainage below ground, R12)

D12
Site dewatering

Temporarily lowering the ground water level over the whole or significantly large parts of the site to facilitate construction, the work being required to be executed by a specialist firm.

Included

Forming well points

Gravel or other filling

Installing and removing drain tubes and ring mains

Excavating sumps

Pumps and pumping

Off site disposal of water

Excluded

Removing ground, surface or storm water by pumping from open sumps in basements, trenches, pits or similar excavations, the work not being required to be executed by a specialist firm
(Excavating and filling, D20)

Land drainage, R13

D20
Excavating and filling

Forming bulk, pit, trench and surface area excavations other than for services supplies,
m and e services and drainage. Filling holes and excavations other than for ditto. Making up levels by bulk filling or in layers, including hardcore but excluding bases and sub-bases to roads and pavings.

Included

Information regarding site conditions and water levels

Applying herbicides to soil before excavating

Excavating topsoil, subsoil, made ground or rock

Breaking out existing substructures

Breaking out existing hard pavings

Removing existing underground storage tanks and services

Removing existing trees, shrubs, undergrowth and turf

Consolidating bottoms of excavations

Trimming excavations to accurate shape and dimensions

Keeping the excavations free of water (other than site dewatering)

Temporary diversion of waterways and drains

Benching sloping ground to receive filling

Making stockpiles of excavated material

Disposing of surplus excavated material

Earthwork support

Filling with and compacting:
   Excavated material (including selected)
   Imported material
   Rock
   Hardcore and granular material

Consolidating/compacting general areas

Blinding surface of filling with fine material

Preparing subsoil by ripping, grading, etc. before spreading topsoil

Transporting from stockpiles or importing and spreading topsoil

Filling external planters, beds, roof gardens with soil and drainage layers, including filter mats

Excluded

Excavating and filling for temporary roads and other temporary works
(Preliminaries)

Ground investigation, D10, but not information on the results

Soil stabilization, D11

Stabilizing soil in situ by incorporating cement with a rotovator
(Soil stabilization, D11)

Site dewatering required to be executed by a specialist firm
(Site dewatering, D12)

Excavating and backfilling for underpinning
(Underpinning, D50)

Filling internal plant containers
(Interior planting, N14)

Excavating and backfilling for engineering services and service supplies
(Trenches/Pipeways/Pits for buried engineering services, P30)

Hardcore/Granular/cement bound bases to roads/pavings, Q10

Gravel/Hoggin roads/pavings, Q22

Cultivating and final fine grading of soil for seeding, turfing or planting
(Relevant sections, Q30, Q31)

Spreading peat, compost, mulch, fertilizer, soil ameliorants, including working in
(Relevant sections, Q30, Q31)

Excavating and filling treepits
(Planting, Q31)

(Reproduced with permission of NBS Services Ltd.)

Table 5.3   Common Arrangement work sections – Group Q (Seeding, turfing and planting)

Q30
Seeding/Turfing

Preparing soil and seeding or turfing to form lawns and general grassed areas.

Included

Applying herbicides

Cultivating topsoil, including removing large stones and weeds

Fine grading topsoil

Providing, spreading and working in peat, manure, compost, mulch, fertilizer, soil ameliorants, sand, etc.

Edging strips for lawn areas

Mesh reinforcement for grass areas

Seeding and rolling

Turfing, including turf edges to seeded areas

Hydro-seeding

Grass cutting

Work to existing grassed areas, including scarifying, forking, fertilizing, applying selective weedkillers, local re-seeding or re-turfing, rolling, edging, etc.

Protecting new and existing grassed and planted areas with temporary fencing, etc.

Watering, including during Defects Liability Period

Work specified to be executed during the Defects Liability Period

Replacement seeding and turfing

Excluded

Earthworks and other preparation:
   Clearing existing vegetation
   Removing existing hard paving and obstructions
   Removing existing topsoil and stockpiling
   General site contouring and adjusting levels
   Transporting from stockpiles or importing and spreading topsoil
   Filling external planters, beds, roof gardens with soil and drainage layers
(Excavation and filling, D20)

Grass block paving:
   Sub-base
   (Granular/Cement bound bases/sub-bases to roads/pavings, Q20)
   Blocks and bedding
   (Slab/Brick/Block etc. pavings, Q25)

Special surfacings/pavings for sport, Q26

Land drainage, R13

Irrigation, S14

Maintenance (as distinct from making good defects) other than that specified to be carried out during the Defects Liability Period

Q31
Planting

Preparing soil and planting herbaceous and other plants, trees and shrubs.

Included

Applying herbicides

Cultivating topsoil, including removing large stones and weeds

Fine grading topsoil

Forming raised or sunken beds, borders, etc.

Providing and spreading peat, manure, compost, mulch, fertilizer, soil ameliorants and working in if required.

Planting herbaceous plants and bulbs

Planting shrubs and hedges

Planting nursery stock and semi-mature trees

Excavating and backfilling tree pits

Fence supports for hedges

Support wires, etc. for climbers

Tree stakes, tree guards, tree guys

Wrapping and other protection of trees, shrubs and plants

Labelling

Applying anti-desiccants

Tree surgery, thinning and pruning

Protecting new and existing grassed and planted areas with temporary fencing, etc.

Watering, including during Defects Liability Period

Work specified to be carried out during the Defects Liability Period

Replacement planting

Excluded

Earthworks and other preparation:
   Clearing existing vegetation
   Removing existing hard paving and obstructions
   Removing existing topsoil and stockpiling
   General site contouring and adjusting levels
   Transporting from stockpiles or importing and spreading topsoil
   Filling external planters, beds, roof gardens with soil and drainage layers
(Excavation and filling, D20)

Interior landscape, N14

Tree grilles
(Slab/Brick/Block/Sett/Cobble pavings, Q24)

Seeding/Turfing, Q30

Fencing, Q40

External prefabricated plant containers
(Site/Street furniture/equipment, Q50)

Land drainage, R13

Irrigation, S14

Maintenance (as distinct from making good defects) other than that specified to be carried out during the Defects Liability Period

(Reproduced with permission of NBS Services Ltd.)

SPECIFYING QUALITY OF MATERIALS

Materials can be specified in one of three ways:

1. *By type:* Provided the quality and minimum standard required can be clearly described, it is always in the employers' interest to allow a contractor the maximum freedom of choice in the selection of the sources of the materials required. In the case of plants an indication of which of the dimensions of height, stem girth and container size are to have priority is essential.

2. *By British Standards:* Even when these exist for the material in question it is important to remember that a range of options and sizes is almost invariably included within the one standard – for example, the stem circumference of extra-heavy advanced nursery stock to BS 5236 can range from 12 to 20cm and the height from 4.25 to 6.0m (see Table 5.4).

3. *By naming the supplier:* The precaution of listing three suppliers, or of restricting the contractor to one single supplier from whom the plants must be obtained, while never to be used unnecessarily, is often the only way of ensuring delivery of plants of an adequate size, condition and state of health. Although this restricts the element of competition of pricing by the contractor of the items concerned, it does at least ensure the minimum standard of the plants to be provided and the comparability of this part of the tender. When naming a single source it may be necessary to add the words 'or equal and approved' so as to ensure that what is supplied actually does comply with the client's or consultant's stated requirements, in which case it is essential to check, preferably by inspection, that what is being offered is indeed equal. It is also advisable to include in the specification the requirement that 'approval of the alternative source must be obtained in writing from the specifier at least seven days before the latest date for the submission of tenders', to prevent a contractor submitting a very low tender by incorporating prices obtained from an alternative substandard supplier.

SPECIFYING WORKMANSHIP

There are three ways in which standards of workmanship can be assured from contractors:

1. *By finished effect:* Describing to the contractor precisely how the finished work is to appear is by far the best method wherever

possible, since it tells the contractor what is wanted but leaves it to his or her expertise as to how this is to be achieved; it also has the advantage of ensuring the contractor is entirely responsible should things go wrong.

2. *By British Standard Codes of Practice:* BS 4428 (*Landscape Operations*) lays down in general terms the minimum standards of workmanship for earthworks, topsoil, preparation, seeding, laying turf, and planting trees, shrubs and herbaceous plants. Site conditions or the requirements of the project frequently require more than these minimum standards, however, and reliance solely on the requirement to comply with BS 4428 is rarely sufficient except for the simplest work.

3. *By method:* Describing *how* a job is to be accomplished is in some ways the easiest means of specifying workmanship and ensuring the contractor prices and provides exactly what is required. It does, however, relieve the contractor of any responsibility should the work subsequently be found to be inadequate. The requirement 'to supply and fix' a semi-mature tree without reference to the size and content of its tree pit is clearly insufficient, but specifying the sequence and time of its planting could certainly relieve the contractor of his or her responsibilities for its subsequent survival.

PLANT PROTECTION

Temporary fencing of trees and shrub borders until they become established must always be described in detail and its provision insisted on. Phrases such as 'Provide such temporary fencing as is necessary and remove on completion of the defects liability period' are quite inadequate and only indicate to the contractor that the specifier does not consider this to be very important and is unlikely to enforce its provision. The estimator will therefore only allow a nominal amount for this item in the hope that it will not be insisted on and thus enable him or her to submit the lowest tender. Since the protection may be required for longer than the length of the defects liability period, it is often advisable to specify that it is to remain in the ownership of the employer. The question of the enclosure of the site in order to ensure the safety of the public and protect the plants from vandalism during the progress of the works is, of course, quite a different matter and should be left entirely to the discretion of the contractor.

Table 5.4   Essential landscape British Standards

There are over 70 British Standards for gardening, horticulture and landscape work listed in the February 1983 Sectional List of British Standards, of which two thirds are available in summary form.

Twelve British Standards are considered essential references for all those concerned with landscape work.

1. NURSERY STOCK (FAC/1)
   BS 3936 parts 1–10 Specification for trees and shrubs, and so on.
   Part 1 (1992) Trees and shrubs
   Part 2 (1990) Roses
   Part 3 (1990) Fruit
   Part 4 (1984) Forest tree planting
   Part 5 (1985) Poplars and willows
   Part 6 – not used
   Part 7 (1989) Bedding plants
   Part 8 – not used
   Part 9 (1987) Bulbs, corms and tubers
   Part 10 (1989) Ground cover plants
   Part 11 (1984) Culinary herbs in containers
2. OPERATIONS (BDB/5)
   BS 3998: (1989) Recommendations for tree work.
   BS 4043: (1989) Recommendations for transplanting root ball trees.
   BS 4428: (1989) Recommendations for general landscape operations.
   BS 5837: (1991) Code of Practice for trees in relation to construction.
   BS 7370 parts 1–5 Ground Maintenance (EPC/2).
   Part 1 (1991) Ground Maintenance organizations
   Part 2 (1994) Hard areas
   Part 3 (1991) Turf (excl. sports)
   Part 4 (1993) Soft landscape
   Part 5 (1996) Water areas
3. MATERIALS (FAC/2)
   BS 3882: (1994) Recommendations and classification for topsoil.
   BS 3969: (1990) Recommendations for turfing grass areas.
   BS 4156: (1990) Peat.
4. TERMINOLOGY
   BS 1831 Part I: (1985) Recommended common names for pesticides.
   BS 2468: (1963) Glossary of terms relating to agricultural machinery.
   BS 1192: (1984) Part 4 Recommendations for landscape drawings.
   (1990) Part 5 Structuring computer graphics.

WATERING OF PLANTS

It is equally insufficient just to specify that the contractor is to water the plants 'as and when necessary during the defects liability period'. The specification must state not only the quantity of water to be provided, depending on the needs of the particular species and subsoil conditions, but also the number of visits to be allowed for. It can still be left to the contractor to suggest to the consultant when these visits are required, and should the total number not have been necessary by the end of the defects liability period the contract sum will be adjusted accordingly.

A clause should also be included in the specification requiring the contractor to inform the consultant if he or she is unable to carry out any necessary watering of the plants due to the water supply being restricted by emergency legislation as the result of drought conditions, and requiring the contractor to ascertain the availability and cost of second-class water from a sewage works or other approved source. The consultant can then issue such instructions to the contractor as he or she considers necessary. Detailed advice regarding the watering of plants is given in the Landscape Institute's technical bulletin *Watering Restrictions and Watering Specification* (1996).

 # LANDSCAPE QUANTITIES

The primary objectives of any set of tender and contract documents are to ensure that the contractor is provided with all the information necessary for him or her to include in his or her tender all that is required for the proper completion of the works, and to ensure also that the lowest-priced tender is, in terms of meeting specification and quality requirements, strictly comparable with the tenders of the competitors. It has to be accepted that if competitive tenders are being invited the lowest tenderer will usually be the one who has included no more than the minimum standards specified. The secondary objective is to provide comparable rates for the landscape consultant to use for the evaluation of variations and Interim and Final Certificates.

The Joint Council for Landscape Industries' (JCLI) contract and all other standard forms of contract therefore contain an obligation for the contractor, whether tendering on the basis of a specification and drawings, schedules, schedules of rates or bills of quantities to the contractor, to break down his or her tender. This breakdown will provide the necessary details of build-up, lump sum or otherwise, for the landscape consultant to be able to check that the tender contains no significant errors, and will assist in the valuation of variations and Interim Certificates.

TENDERS BASED ON SPECIFICATION AND DRAWINGS

Even when the tenderer has to take off his or her own quantities from a specification and drawings it is essential to ensure that, even if no quantities are given, the tender is at least broken down so that the landscape consultant is given details of the cost of the individual components of preliminaries, soil preparation, grassing, shrubs, trees and elements of hard landscape. A tenderer's individual circumstances may result in a wide range of different prices for the various elements of the work being presented by the respective tenderers competing for a contract (although the totals may not be dissimilar), but breaking down tenders in this way always indicates areas where, in the event of a large divergence, at least checks can be made. Wherever possible – even on small projects – it is always advisable in tender summaries to include an approximation of the total area involved for each element, so that all tenders are submitted on the same basis. One tender in which the estimator has measured 55m² of grass and 45m² of shrub border can never be comparable with one which has allowed for 45m² of grass and 55m² of shrub border.

SCHEDULES

BS 1192: Part 4 defines schedules as 'tabulated information on a range of similar items' and gives as examples those for tree work and planting shrubs and climbers, with various columns for the numbers involved – for instance name, type, size, position, unit rate and total cost.

Name	Type	Size	Location	Unit rate No	Total cost

SCHEDULE OF RATES

It should be noted that the JCLI contract provides the option of either schedules or schedules of rates to be included in the contract documents. This enables the contract to be used not only for lump sum contracts but also for those based on schedules of rates where the actual work required is not known at the outset and is remeasured and valued only when it has been completed. A comprehensive schedule of rates including all that is likely to be required may often be little less than a bill of quantities without the quantities. Under such circumstances, it is often useful to include 'notional' quantities based on an approximation of the area or volume envisaged, which – although it must be remeasured on completion – at least encourages the inclusion of a more accurate tender rate.

BILLS OF QUANTITIES

Clearly tenders will be more accurate if submitted on the basis of full bills of quantities prepared by the landscape consultant or quantity surveyor and paid for by the client direct. The cost of this can rarely be seen to be justified on landscape contracts or subcontracts of a lesser value than £20 000. On the larger contracts, however, bills of quantities are essential for proper cost control.

To provide a uniform basis for measuring building work, an independent committee (the Standing Joint Committee) of builders and quantity surveyors was set up in 1922 which has ensured that the minimum information necessary to define the nature and extent of the work are provided to estimators in a standard sequence and format. This enables them to submit accurately priced, comparable tenders. Any departures from the standard measurement conventions must be specifically drawn to the attention of the tenderer.

STANDARD METHOD OF MEASUREMENT OF BUILDING WORKS (SMM7)

Prior to 1988, in the earlier SMM6 guidance, landscape operations were covered by only 48 words in section D44 (Landscaping):

> Soiling, cultivating, seeds, treating top surface, fertilising and turfing to surfaces shall be given separately in square metres, stating the thickness of soil and the quantity per square metre of the seed or fertiliser. Any requirements for watering, weeding, cutting, settlement, reseeding and the like shall be stated.

SMM7, published in 1988, was based on the Common Arrangement (which as we have seen is also used for drawings and specifications) to produce a coordinated set of documents. In addition to the bills of quantities being used for tendering, evaluating Interim Certificates and variations, the new format enabled them to be used also for production planning, ordering materials, cost control and analyses.

JCLI PLANT LISTS

The Joint Council for Landscape Industries published in 1989 and revised in 1997 a list of about 1200 species and cultivars of trees, shrubs and climbing plants recommended as being suitable and generally available for landscape work throughout the UK, together with their size, soil and aspect preference; in 1994 a similar list for herbaceous perennials was also published. The specification of plants from these lists for use in those locations for which they are appropriate minimizes any future argument as to their availability and suitability. Figure 5.5 shows a JCLI list of trees and shrubs suitable for landscape planting.

HTA NATIONAL PLANT SPECIFICATION

Based on the JCLI lists, the 1997 HTA Plant Specification amplifies the requirements of British Standards by listing and describing the range and sizes of those plants which are most commonly grown and available. The specification incorporates the 1995 revised version of the Committee for Plant Supply and Establishment (CPSE) Code of Practice for the Handling and Establishment of Landscape Plants, as well as the CPSE Recommended Form of Tender for the Supply and Delivery of Plants. Supported by a HTA Nursery Certification Scheme, and integrating the NBS Landscape and HTA National Plant Specification, it ensures, by means of a regular inspection audit both in the nursery and subsequently on site, compliance with the standard and quality of the plants specified and tendered for.

CIVIL ENGINEERING CONTRACTS

Landscape contracts let in accordance with the provisions of the Institution of Civil Engineers (ICE) Form, in which the work is paid for on a remeasurement basis, have similar and simpler, but not identical, rules for the preparation of civil engineering and planting measurements, with more items grouped together.

 # TENDER PROCEDURES

When the drawings, specification and if necessary bills of quantities are approaching completion (provided that it has not been decided to negotiate a tender with a single contractor) it is necessary to give

TREES AND SHRUBS FOR LANDSCAPE PLANTING

SECTION 1   TREES

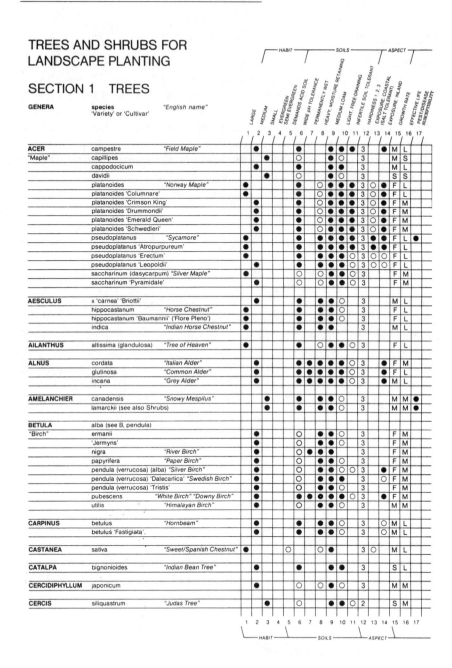

Figure 5.5   JCLI tree and shrub list

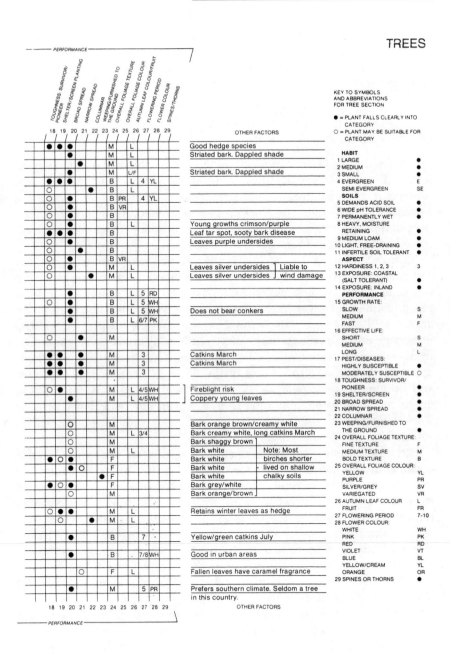

Figure 5.5   (concluded)
JCLI Plant List © The Landscape Institute

consideration to which firms are to be invited to tender in competition for the work, either by submission of rates or a lump sum. In either case it is necessary to ascertain, beforehand, if the tenderers are interested and willing to submit a tender in competition.

INVITING TENDERS

When the details of the work to be included in the contract have been finalized and fully set out in the documents on which the landscape contractor is to be invited to tender, it is then necessary to select a suitable firm to whom the work can be entrusted. This is achieved by negotiation or by inviting competitive tenders from those firms considered to be most appropriate.

'Open' tendering, in which tender documents are sent to any contractor replying in response to an advertisement in the local and technical press, is neither considered to be good practice nor is it recommended by government departments. Where a client's standing orders still require it, they can best be complied with – once the necessary advertisements have been made – by inviting tenders only from a limited number of the best-qualified contractors of those applying, taking care to include in the list only firms of the same size and standards of competence. It is unrealistic to expect Rolls-Royce to quote a cheap price for repairing a Ford, nor will Ford provide workmanship of the same standard as Rolls-Royce. Their quotes will be comparable neither in quality nor in price.

Strict adherence to the proper procedures in preparing tender documents and inviting tenders is essential if they are to be submitted expeditiously and accurately. Depending on the time available, scope of work and type of contract selected, a choice has to be made between remeasurement contracts based solely on schedules of rates, which only require the contractor to quote his or her percentage additions to the standard labour, materials and plant rates (which include overheads, travelling time, emoluments and holidays with pay, and so on) or lump sum tenders based on drawings and specifications alone or with full bills of quantities prepared and paid for by the client.

In either case the same tendering procedures will apply. Those for the building industry are set out in the National Joint Consultative Council (NJCC) for Building Codes of Procedure for Single, Two Stage and Design/Build-tendering and are equally applicable to the landscape industry.

Selective tender lists must always be prepared in consultation with the client, using only those firms known to the consultant to be of proven ability, whether this knowledge comes from personal experience, from references from other consultants, or because the firms in question have satisfactorily executed similar work for the client in the past.

In order to ensure a reasonable choice of applicants, six is normally the maximum number of contractors invited to submit tenders. This allows for the possibility of one or two contractors returning the tender documents uncompleted and declining to apply for the contract, documents due to changes in their circumstances, as well as tenders being submitted after the tender expiry date (or not returned at all). It is always advisable to ensure that at least three bona fide tenders are received and reported to the client. Any fewer tenders often leads to a completely new tender invitation, to include additional contractors, with the delay that this inevitably causes.

To minimize the risk of this happening the NJCC Code provides for all those whom it is intended to include in the tender list to be written to or telephoned beforehand, informing them of:

○   the location and scope of the work;
○   the consultants involved;
○   the composition of the tender documents (for instance, if quantities prepared on behalf of the client will be provided);
○   the form of contract to be used; and
○   the proposed dates for the invitation and submission of tenders,

asking that they confirm their willingness and ability to submit a tender by the date and time stated.

The tender documents must always state if the tender is to be on a fixed price or fluctuations basis and state the contract period during which the work must be completed. The Code provides for tenders to remain open for acceptance within 28 days, or in exceptional circumstances, if the approval of a funding authority or a government department is involved, 56 days. If these requirements are complied with, subject to an arithmetic check, the choice of contractor will be a relatively simple matter, almost invariably being automatically the lowest tender submitted. If any bona fide errors in the tender are discovered the Code provides for them to be corrected in one of two alternative ways, the choice of which is also confirmed in the Form of Tender.

Alternative 1 requires the contractor to stand by his or her lump sum tender and the error to be covered subsequently by a percentage correction to all the contractor's rates (this is the option normally adopted by local authorities). In the event of the error being such that the contractor is unable to unwilling to stand by his or her tender (often the wisest course from both the client's and contractor's point of view, if the error is substantial) the next lowest tender is accepted.

Alternative 2 is normally the option chosen on private sector projects, the amount of the error being added to or subtracted from the tender sum and the contract being let in the revised amount. This gets over the problem when the corrected tender is still less than that of the next lowest tender, although of course, if the corrected tender is then above that of the second lowest tender the contract will naturally be placed with the latter.

The other problem, which unfortunately is by no means uncommon, is when the tender is greater than anticipated and exceeds the client's authorized expenditure. The Code provides in this instance that reductions must always be negotiated only with the lowest tenderer, and only if negotiations break down should an attempt be made to negotiate a lower tender with the second lowest tenderer. If, however, the necessary reductions are so great as to have materially changed the scope of work, then the best course is to prepare a new set of tender documents and invite further tenders from the same or, if appropriate, another selected list of contractors.

Contractors must always be told that 'qualified' tenders, such as those offering an alternative contract period or being 'subject to the availability of labour and materials', will be automatically rejected, as should those including substitutes for those plant species or sizes specified, although the Code does provide for such tenders to be considered, if they are submitted as supplementary or additional tenders to that submitted in accordance with the tender documents.

In landscape contracts, it is also essential to state in the tender documents the anticipated contract commencement date (having allowed four weeks for acceptance and for the contractor to mobilize and allocate the necessary labour, plant and materials), since the cost of any upkeep required to be allowed for after practical completion will vary considerably depending on the time of year – six months' upkeep during the summer months costs the contractor considerably more than six months during the winter.

Figure 5.6 shows an example of a covering letter for enclosing tender documents to ensure all tenders are submitted on a comparable basis, while Figure 5.7 shows a Form of Tender.

REPORTING ON TENDERS

Tenders should only be opened after the date and time for their submission has passed – usually noon on Monday, to allow for contractors' estimators to work over the weekend and, due to the uncertainties of postal deliveries, for tenders to be delivered by hand. Those tenders which have been delivered too late are marked 'returned – received out of time' and returned unopened.

Dear Sirs,

Heading

Following your acceptance of the invitation to tender for the above, I/we now have pleasure in enclosing the following:

a two copies of the bill(s) of quantities/specifications/ schedules; [1]
b two copies of the general arrangement drawings indicating the general character and shape and disposition of the works, and two copies of all detail drawings referred to in the bills of quantities; [1]
c two copies of the form of tender;
d addressed envelopes for the return of the tender (*and priced bill(s)*†) and instructions relating thereto.

Will you please also note:

1 drawings and details may be inspected at …
2 the site may be inspected by arrangement with the employer/architect [1]
3 tendering procedure will be in accordance with the principles of the 'Code of Procedure for Single Stage Selective Tendering'
4 examination and adjustment of priced bill(s) (Section 6 of the Code), Alternative 1/Alternative 2 [1] will apply.

The completed form of tender is to be sealed in the endorsed envelope provided and delivered or sent by post to reach … not later than … hours on … the … day of … 19…

* *The completed form of tender and the priced bill(s) of quantities sealed in separate endorsed envelopes provided are to be lodged not later than … hours on … the … day of … 19… the envelope containing the tender should be endorsed with the job title: that containing the bill(s) of quantities should be endorsed with the job title and tenderer's name.*

Will you please acknowledge receipt of this letter and enclosures and confirm that you are able to submit a tender in accordance with these instructions.

Yours faithfully,
Architect/Quantity Surveyor [1]

References   [1] Delete as appropriate, before issuing.
         *   Applicable in Scotland only in which case the preceding sentence would not be used.
         † Applicable in Scotland only.

Figure 5.6   Example of covering letter enclosing tender documents

A full list of the names and tender sums received can then be prepared, including the names of those invited to tender but who had subsequently declined or did not submit (with the reasons, where known). At this stage the Code requires all but the lowest two or three to be notified that their tender is unlikely to be recommended for acceptance, but without giving any indication of the other tenders received nor their amounts.

A financial analysis and arithmetic check only on the lowest should then follow to confirm that the tender has been fairly, accurately and consistently priced and is free from major arithmetical errors; any such mistakes that are found are corrected by whichever alternative has been previously chosen.

Once this has been done it is then possible to prepare a report for the client containing:

1.   a list of the names and amounts of the tenders received and in whose presence they were opened, together with the names (and reasons if known) of those not submitted;
2.   any qualifications and confirmation that the latter had been withdrawn;
3.   any amendments to the tender documents made during the tender period;
4.   any corrections required as a result of arithmetical errors;
5.   confirmation that the tender has been fairly, accurately and consistently priced;
6.   any savings to be made to bring the tender within the authorized expenditure or any revised budget; and
7.   confirmation of the ability of the contractor to commence and complete the work within the time and to the standards required.

If the procedures laid down in the Code have been followed, only rarely will the recommendation for acceptance of a tender other than the lowest be justified.

When, and only when, approval for acceptance of a tender has been confirmed by the client should the other tenderers be formally notified of the results of all the tenders submitted, including their own and that accepted. This can be achieved by a standard letter which lists only the amounts of tenders received, in ascending order, so that the tenders themselves cannot be identified with a particular firm. Names of firms can also be included if required but they should be separately listed in alphabetical order, so as to preserve confidentiality.

LANDSCAPE PROFESSIONAL PRACTICE

Tender for .... Landscape Improvements, Forest Glades ....

To ..... I C Green, Landscape Architects Dept Ambershire District Council, ...
High St, Amberham

Sir(s)

I/We having read the conditions of contract specification and schedules of quantity delivered to me/us and having examined the drawings attached thereto do hereby offer to execute and complete in accordance with the conditions of contract the whole of the works described within the period specified from the date of possession for the sum of £..16 501....
(.sixteen thousand, five hundred and one. pounds).

I/We agree that should obvious pricing errors in arithmetic be discovered before acceptance of this offer in the priced schedules of quantity submitted by me/us these errors/~~will be dealt with and adjusted (Alternative 1)~~/ will not be adjusted and we will stand by our tender (Alternative 2) (1) in accordance with Section 6 of the current NJCC for Building Code of Procedure for Single Stage Selective Tendering.

This tender remains open for consideration for 28/~~56~~ days (2) from the date fixed for the submission for lodgement of tenders.

Dated this ..twenty-third...... .... day of ..November... ... 19 98...
Name . Doug Potterton & Sons ....
Address .Greenacre.......................................
. . . . . .Amberham.......................................
Signature . . . . . .Doug Potterton..........................

REFERENCES: 1 Delete as appropriate before issuing.
             2 The period specified should not normally exceed
                28 days and only in exceptional circumstances
                should be extended to 56 days.

SUMMARY OF TENDER

Preliminaries	2 000.00
Hard landscape	7 329.00
Topsoil	1 000.00
Grassed areas	1 120.00
Shrubs and herbaceous plants	2 647.00
Trees	2 405.00
	16 501.00

Figure 5.7   Example of a Form of Tender

CHAPTER

6

LANDSCAPE CONTRACTS AND CONTRACT CONDITIONS

 THE MEANING AND ESSENTIALS OF A VALID CONTRACT

Both the law of tort and the law of contract are derived from common law, but whereas tort involves a civil wrong or unreasonable behaviour and can be independent of any contract, the law of contract depends on a commercial bargain between two individuals or legal bodies. This is not to say, however, that the existence of a contract does not prevent one of the parties from suing the other in tort instead, in the event of a dispute. To bring a case of negligence under contract, however, the plaintiff has to prove that the defendant owed him or her a duty of care, that there was a breach of that duty and that he or she suffered damages as a result.

Simple contracts do not have to be in any special form: they can be made orally and do not need to be in writing unless they are, such as hire purchase (HP) agreements, contracts of employment or are under seal. Even if such contracts are not in writing, however, for them to be legal there has to be an offer and it has to be accepted. Only when accepted does the contract come into being, even though any formal contract documents may not yet have been signed.

To be legally binding there must also be benefit to both parties and a *consideration* (unless the contract is under seal). This usually takes the form of the payment of money although the consideration may equally involve the provision of goods or services in return. Whatever the amount of the consideration – whether only a penny, blatantly unjust as in the case of Shylock's bargain, or a contractor offering to carry out work for a price which must inevitably cost him or her more – it nevertheless makes the contract binding. If the contracting party does not carry out their duties for the agreed price they must pay damages to the other party to the contract. The price to be paid is irrelevant, once fixed and stated in the contract, and the courts cannot alter it. If the amount of the consideration is, however, not stated, the courts will fix a *quantum meruit* payment – £12 000 against the £64 000 claimed in *L. Obermeister* v. *London Rodwell Properties* (1967).

Contracts usually contain express terms or conditions for the execution of the work and the method and time of payment. Even when not explicitly or expressly stated there are other terms which can be implied – for example, in order for a contractor to be able to carry out the duties required of him or her under a contract for landscape works there is an implied obligation on the contractor to give the landscape consultant (but not the client!) access to the site and for the employer to give possession of the site within a reasonable period. It can also be implied that the contractor will exercise all reasonable skill and care in the execution of the works unless expressly stated to the contrary and subject always to the provisions of the Unfair Contract Terms Act. If, however, the contractor has built something strictly in accordance with the drawings and it subsequently fails, it cannot be argued that he or she has any responsibility or implied warranty as to its fitness for the purpose for which it was designed (*Lynch* v. *Thorne*, 1956).

Privity of contract arises when only those directly concerned in the contract receive the benefits, have any liability under it and are bound by it. Contracts can be held not to be binding on the parties under certain circumstances, the most common being those arising from a mistake by one or both of the parties, when the mistake is undisputed and fundamental to the contract – for example in the ownership of the land on which the contract is to be executed. Equally, especially if arising from an ambiguity, if one or both of the parties believe they have entered into a contract with fundamentally different intentions, it can be held there is no binding contract.

Misrepresentation is also grounds for determining or rendering a contract void, arising when a statement which is induced into, but which is not a term of, the contract is found to be untrue, whether made fraudulently or innocently; if the statement has been made fraudulently the other party will be entitled to damages in tort whether he or she opts to determine or not. Contracts which are against the law, where the work itself contravenes the law – for example planning or building regulations – or when one of the parties is legally precluded are also unenforceable.

The discharge of most contracts occurs when both parties have *performed* all their obligations under the contract, for example when the contractor has completed the work and made good all defects and the employer has paid the contractor all the monies due to him or her in full and final settlement. Equally, if one or other of the parties, usually the contractor, has been *frustrated*, not because what he or she has contracted to do is too expensive or proves to be impossible but because if (as rarely happens) the contractual obligation becomes radically different from what is in the contract, the parties may be discharged from their obligations also.

A *breach of contract*, on the other hand, when a contractor refuses to obey an instruction to remove defective work or some event occurs for a reason not provided for in the contract, entitles the employer to consequential damages.

Repudiation of a contract arises when one or other of the parties refuses to discharge his or her contractual obligations; if it is so serious as to go to the root of the contract it is considered to be a fundamental breach, entitling the other party, for example, to cease work and withdraw from the site or to refuse to pay for the work and claim damages for delay until the work is properly completed.

Most standard forms of contract envisage these situations and provide for them so that only the contractor's employment is determined and the parties remain bound by the contract conditions.

THE TYPES OF CONTRACT FOR LANDSCAPE WORKS

There are six different types of contract currently used to procure building and landscape work in this country today:

1. Management
2. Cost plus
3. Approximate quantities
4. Lump sum
5. Design and build
6. Package deal.

There are a variety of standard forms of contract for each such contract type, for use by government departments and in both the public and private sectors. The choice of which form to use depends on a variety of factors, the most important being determined by the client's priorities in respect of the time available for completion, the client's knowledge of the requirements of the project at the outset and the need for the cost of the work to be contained within the limits of the authorized expenditure.

MANAGEMENT

A management contract – in which a landscape contractor is appointed to manage the construction of a landscape contract for a new work – is usually the most suitable type of contract to use when the completion date is so important that the work on site must start before the client's requirements and the design are finalized and costs ascertained. The main contractor is employed only to manage the project in general, without employing the subcontractors him- or herself.

COST PLUS

Cost plus contracts are also equally often used when the scope of the project is unknown at the outset and the need for quality requires the client to choose some but not all of the specialist subcontractors. In this case the subcontractors are all actually engaged by the main contractor.

APPROXIMATE QUANTITIES

Approximate quantities contracts are possible when there is time to complete the design and most of the drawings before the work starts but not to measure them in detail. Quotations are then obtained based only on approximate quantities and specification and the contract is entered into on the basis of a tender sum before the work starts on site. The work is then remeasured as it is completed on site and the 'ascertained final sum' valued in accordance with the rates in the bills of quantities.

LUMP SUM

Lump sum contracts are used when there is time to complete the tender documents with full drawings, specification and with or without complete bills of quantities, so that a lump sum for the work to be finished by a certain date can be agreed at the outset. For local authority work and all other contracts where staying within the authorized expenditure is of prime importance, this is still the type of contract most often used for building and landscape work and it can be let on either a fixed price or fluctuations basis if the duration of the work is more than 12 months.

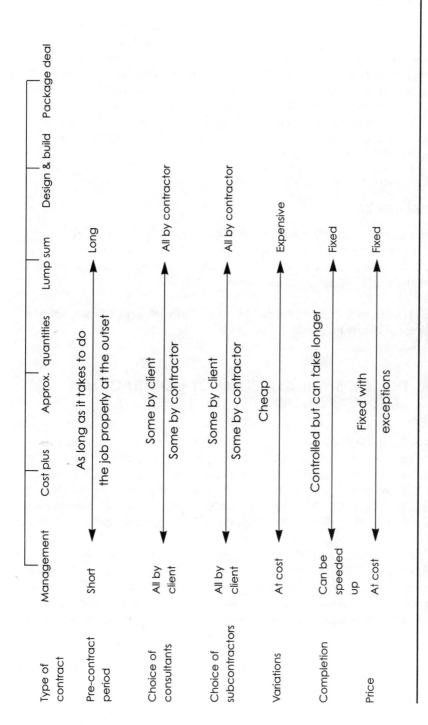

Figure 6.1   The advantages and disadvantages of different types of contract

DESIGN AND BUILD

Design and build contracts are applicable when the scope of the work is relatively simple and no more than an adequate quality of workmanship is required. Under these circumstances the client may not need to choose the consultants or any of the subcontractors him- or herself but may find it preferable for this to be left to the contractor, who then takes full responsibility for the satisfactory completion of the work, within the time stated and for the contract sum. In this instance variations are undesirable and expensive. If they arise many of the benefits of this type of contract are lost.

PACKAGE DEAL

Package deal contracts are really for a standard design of work which, if not already built, is at least similar in almost every respect to an existing example on another site that the employer or contractor can visit and build, using the same design and details.

The relative advantages and disadvantages of each type of contract are illustrated diagramatically in Figure 6.1.

THE JCLI STANDARD FORM OF CONTRACT FOR LANDSCAPE WORKS

The Landscape Institute first published a Standard Form of Agreement for Landscape Works for use without quantities in 1969. This closely followed the 1963 edition of the Standard Form of Building Contract, as did the Landscape edition for use with bills of quantities which was published in 1973. The two forms did not, however, incorporate subsequent Joint Contracts Tribunal (JCT) amendments, and five years later in April 1978 the Joint Council for Landscape Industries with the cooperation of the Landscape Institute published a much shorter form. This version, with additional clauses appropriate for the planting aspects, was almost identical to the then current JCT Form of Agreement for Minor Building Works which they had first published in 1968. This close and deliberate resemblance between the two forms of contract had been agreed with the JCT in the interest of conformity and ensured the acceptance of the JCLI Form by the local authority and county councils' associations who were represented as constituent members of the JCT.

Since the designation 'landscape architect' is not protected by legislation as is the architect, there was no need for the alternative designation of 'contract administrator' that is found, for instance, in the JCT contracts. Where the landscape work is under the direction of a local authority chief officer other than a landscape architect, or under a landscape manager or scientist, their title is entered accordingly in the 1st Recital and thereafter they are referred to as 'the landscape architect'. It is important to enter the office and not the name of the individual person, as this can cause difficulties should the named individual leave the practice or the authority before the contract is completed.

The JCLI Form was revised in April 1981 to conform with the section-headed format of JCT MW80 and was reprinted with minor corrections in 1982. It was again revised in April 1985 by the insertion of an additional Clause 1.3 enabling the form to be used with full bills of quantities prepared in accordance with SMM and the JCLI Rules for the Measurement of Landscape Works, provision for the naming of a quantity surveyor having always been provided for in a 4th Recital if required. An addition to the end of the 1st Recital also enabled the form to be used under either English or Scottish law as appropriate. (See Appendix 3.)

The JCLI Form was again revised in June 1996 and November 1998 to include the requirements for health and safety under the CDM Regulations, incorporate the recommendations of the Latham Report in respect of the prohibition of pay when paid 'clauses', and compulsory adjudication. It also adopted the substitution of 'Contract Administrator' instead of 'Landscape Architect', and 'aftercare' for 'maintenance' and a number of other amendments following similar revisions to the JCT Minor Building Works Contract. It is now therefore the recommended Form of Agreement for all local authority and private sector landscape contracts with or without quantities in the United Kingdom, up to a value of at least £75 000 at 1997 prices. For works executed as a subcontract under a building contract or of a higher value other conditions are appropriate, for example NSC4 for subcontracts under JCT 80 and IFC 84 for landscape contracts of up to £250 000, which are discussed later in this chapter.

An explanation of the Form of Agreement is given below (see also Appendix 3). Provision is made at the head of the Form of Agreement for it to be dated and the names and addresses of the employer and the contractor to be filled in.

THE RECITALS

There are five Recitals and five Articles in the Form.

1st Recital

Space is left for a short two-line description of the work, including any aftercare provided by the Contractor, to be carried out ('the works') for the sum stated in Article 2, and the name of the (practice of) the landscape consultant followed by the contract documents, namely the drawings, specification, schedules, schedules of rates, and/or bills of quantities – thereafter referred to as 'the contract documents' – with a footnote pointing out those not included to be deleted and concluding with the option of English or Scottish Law.

2nd Recital

This requires the contractor to price the contract documents.

3rd Recital

This requires the contract to be signed by both parties or their representatives.

4th Recital

This names the quantity surveyor (but with no mention in the subsequent conditions of what his or her duties are) with provision for the employer to nominate another, should the first die or cease to be the quantity surveyor for the contract.

5th Recital

The June 1996 revision primarily includes the additional alternative 5th Recital confirming that either (5A) the CDM Regulations do not apply, or (5B) in the event that they do apply whether or not all or only Regulations 7 and 13 apply. Should this be the case consequential additions to Clauses 1, 2, 3, 5 and 7 are included with corresponding additions to the footnotes.

THE FIVE ARTICLES

Article 1

This obliges the contractor to carry out and complete the works.

Article 2

The other part of the 'bargain' – the amount in words and figures the employer will pay the contractor to carry out and complete the works. It also states this to be exclusive of any value added tax, for which reason Interim Certificates are exclusive of VAT. This is the subject of a second invoice submitted separately by the contractor to the employer.

Article 3

Space again for the insertion of the name of the landscape consultant and, in the event of the latter's death or ceasing to be the consultant, for the employer to nominate another within 14 days who will not have the power to disregard or overrule any certificate or instruction given by his or her predecessor.

Article 4

In the event of any dispute at any time between the employer (or the landscape consultant on the former's behalf) and the contractor, other than those matters relating to VAT or the statutory deduction of tax, Article 4 provides for an arbitrator (who *does* have the power to disregard, or overrule, any certificate or instruction) to be agreed or to be appointed by the President or Vice President of the Landscape Institute.

Article 5

This additional clause provides for the appointment by the employer of the landscape consultant as Planning Supervisor and the contractor as Principal Contractor should the CDM Regulations so require to comply with the 5th Recital.

The JCLI Conditions of Contract appear on the following pages under nine headings as follows:

1 THE INTENTIONS OF THE PARTIES

1.1 The contractor's obligations

The first condition is the obligation of the contractor to carry out and complete the works with due diligence in accordance with the contract documents in a good and workmanlike manner, the only qualification being that where the quality of materials and standard of work are a matter for the opinion of the landscape consultant, this shall be to his or her reasonable satisfaction. The consequence of this is that, once the consultant has approved something, should it subsequently go wrong, the landscape contractor has quite rightly been relieved of further responsibility in the matter. Landscape consultants will therefore make use of this right only when it is otherwise impracticable to specify the work or material sufficiently accurately.

1.2   The landscape consultant's duties

Under the contract these are relatively few (the consultant's own duties to the client under the conditions of engagement to 'monitor' the work being an entirely separate matter), namely the issue of certificates, valuations, extensions and instructions.

1.3   The contract bills

These must be prepared in accordance with SMM, so that all the quantities are measured and prepared in a common form familiar to the estimators (particularly important in the age of computerized quantities). This is also so that estimators can ensure that everything necessary is itemized and included in their tender since, where bills of quantities are included in the contract documents, if something is not contained in the bill but is nevertheless essential for the successful completion of the project, and regardless of whether the missing item is shown on the drawings or not, the contractor is entitled to charge it as an extra. Departures from the rules are of course sometimes necessary due to special circumstances and these are of course permissible, subject to the estimators' attention being drawn to the problem affecting the item concerned.

1.4   CDM Regulations

Two new Clauses 7.4 and 1.5 provide for the appointment or reappointment of a Planning Supervisor *before* the work starts on site should the Regulations require it.

2   COMMENCEMENT AND COMPLETION

2.1   Dates

The date when the works may be commenced should be entered in the space provided on the form. It should be noted that this is the date when the employer intends to hand the site over to the contractor, after which its safety and security is the contractor's responsibility. There is no obligation on the part of the contractor, however, to start the work on site on this date (provided he or she still complies with the date for completion of the work), to be inserted on the following line. Contractors may wish to delay the actual start until they have received all the necessary plants and other material and arranged for the necessary labour and plants to be available when required, thereby reducing the amount of time the contractors themselves have to spend on site. A delayed actual start date is therefore a matter for mutual agreement. If, however, the delay in starting is caused by the employer then the contractor may be able to consider the whole contract frustrated and be entitled to renegotiate the contract sum. The clause also provides for aftercare to be carried out after Practical Completion.

2.2   Extensions

Extensions of the contract period are made by the landscape consultant when completion (but not the progress) of the work is delayed for reasons beyond the control of the contractor. Neither in the JCLI Form of Contract nor in the JCT Minor Works Contract is there any obligation on the part of the contractor to notify the consultant of any delays nor to list the reasons for the delay which are beyond the contractor's control. Equally there is no timetable within which the landscape consultant must make the necessary extension nor, when this has been done, to give the contractor the reasons or any breakdown of the period by which the consultant has extended the contract. Clearly, however, the more information the consultant can give the contractor, the less likely the contractor is to challenge the decision and refer the matter to arbitration. Reasons beyond the control of the contractor are usually considered to be equivalent to the 12 'relevant events' set out in Clause 25 of JCT 80 (see Table 6.1 on page 138).

Careful examination of bar charts showing the intended and actual commencement and completion dates of all types of work being carried out on a project are essential in order to establish the reasons and extent of any delays in completion, rather than simply accepting

Table 6.1 Events leading to extensions of the contract period and to reimbursement of direct loss and expense	
Relevant JCT 80 events justifying an extension to the contract period for the execution of the works delaying completion	Circumstances under which the contractor is entitled to reimbursement of direct loss and expense for delay of progress.
JCT 80 Clause 25 Relevant events beyond the control of the contractor	JCT 80 Clause 26 Direct loss and expense incurred by the contractor
25.4. 1. Force majeure	26.4.—
2. Exceptionally adverse weather	—
3. Loss or damage by fire etc.	—
4. Civil commotion, strikes etc.	—
5. Compliance with consultant's instructions on:	—
Discrepancies	26.4.3
Variations	.7
PC and Prov Sums	.7
Postponement	.5
Antiquities	34.3
Nominated s/c	—
Nominated suppliers	
Opening up satisfactory work	.2
6. Not having received instructions in due time	.1
7. Delays by nominated subcontractors or suppliers	—
8. Delays by artists and tradespersons	.4
9. Government restrictions	—
10. Unforeseeable shortages of labour and materials	—
11. Problems with statutory undertakers	—
12. Lack of ingress or egress to/from site	.6

the usual contractor's request for an extension until the actual date of Practical Completion has been certified by the Consultant.

2.3 Damages for non-completion

Damages for non-completion are provided to reimburse the employer for any damages he or she has suffered as a result of the landscape contractor not having completed the work within the contract period or any extended contract period. Forecasting the weekly sum that these damages are likely to amount to must be evaluated as accurately as possible, always bearing in mind that if the figure is too low the employer will not be adequately compensated and if it is too high not only will a court not enforce the damages, on the grounds that they were not a true estimate (liquidated and ascertained) and were intended to be punitive, but also that such an incidence of excessively high damages may cause contractors to inflate the costs of their tenders in future so as to offset losses suffered by them under such liabilities. Damages are normally considered to be covered under the following three headings:

1   the client's notional loss of interest on capital;
2   inconvenience or any actual consequential loss; or
3   additional professional fees.

The calculation of the loss of interest on capital is relatively easy, by the application of the formula:

$$\frac{\text{Contract sum} \times \text{bank rate}}{52 \text{ weeks}} = \pounds \ldots \text{ per week.}$$

This is explained more fully in the JCLI Practice Note 5 issued with the contract form (see Appendix 3) and compensates the employer for loss of use of the money that he or she has already paid under Interim Certificates to date, for which he or she has received no benefit and which could otherwise have been invested elsewhere and earning profit.

The second type of damage, involving inconvenience or any actual consequential loss, rarely arises in landscape contracts (it can be a considerable sum on certain commercial building projects).

The third type of damage, the entailment of additional professional fees, is often overlooked but the extra cost to the landscape consultant in visiting the site during the period of overrun, and which will not be reflected in any increase in the value of work certified, can often amount to several hundreds of pounds spread over a number of months.

There is no provision in the damages guidance for the involvement of the landscape consultant, the clause simply providing that if the work is not completed by the due date the contractor shall pay or allow the employer the liquidated damages at the rate stated.

2.4 Completion date

The completion date is to be certified by the landscape consultant 'when in his opinion the works have reached practical completion'. Every case must be decided on the merits of the particular situation prevailing in that instance, but it is generally considered that practical completion (signifying that the work has *actually* been completed – not 'practically' in the sense of '*almost* completed') has been achieved when the works can safely be used for the purpose for which they were designed. Clause 2.4 now provides for the issue of a schedule of this outstanding work at Practical Completion and a programme for its completion at an appropriate time of the year.

2.5 Defects liability

Defects liability covers the situation when after a period of use – usually six months in the case of building work and 12 months in the case of heating, electrical engineering services and landscape work – the work, material or plants, through no fault of the designer, are not performing as well as they could be expected to. The contract therefore provides for the work to be inspected at the end of the period specified, and the defects to be made good by the contractor at his or her own expense, after which the landscape consultant will issue a further certificate when these defects have been properly made good.

2.6 Partial possession

Partial possession by the employer was not included in the JCT Minor Works Contract, it being thought unlikely to arise. In landscape works, however, the previously unforeseen possibility of part of the works being finished in advance of another which might have been delayed, and the employer wanting to use it if the contractor would agree, was thought to be more likely. Circumstances could arise when all the work was finished in the autumn but it was too late to sow the grassed areas, or conversely in the spring when all the hard landscape was finished but it was too late to plant bare-root standard-size trees. This is therefore provided for in Clause 2.6 which allows, while the contractor remains responsible for the balance of the site, a certificate of partial completion to be issued for that part handed over, the relevant proportion of retention to be released and the contractor relieved of responsibility for the cost of any subsequent maintenance and for any liquidated and ascertained damages for the part handed over, for which he or she might otherwise be liable.

2.7 Plant failures

Failures of plants are not covered in the JCT Forms but are covered in the JCLI Form in Clause 2.7. All plants, other than those covered by Clause 6.5 (those stolen or subject to vandalism), found to be missing or defective at practical completion are to be replaced by the contractor entirely at his or her own expense. If this is during the dormant season the landscape consultant will delay his or her inspection until six weeks after the planting has come into leaf.

Two alternative sub-clauses, 2.7A and 2.7B, cover plants which subsequently die. The choice of clauses depends on whether subsequent aftercare of the planting after practical completion has been undertaken by the contractor or by the employer. Clause 2.7A covers the subsequent aftercare by the contractor and provides separate blank spaces on the form for various periods to be inserted, for making good grass, shrubs, plants, ordinary stock trees, advanced extra-large nursery stock and semi-mature trees. Any such that are found to be defective at the end of the periods inserted are to be replaced by the contractor entirely at his or her own expense unless the consultant instructs otherwise. When all necessary replacements have been provided the consultant issues a further certificate.

If, however, all aftercare subsequent to practical completion is undertaken by the employer then Clause 2.7B is appropriate. This relieves the contractor of all further responsibility, and any plants that subsequently die, whether due to inadequate work by the employer or for any other reason, are the employer's responsibility and it is the employer who is then responsible for the costs of any replacements.

If plant failures at practical completion are greater than 10 per cent, provision is made for their value to be deducted from the certificate issued at that stage before releasing half the retention monies under Clause 4.3.

3   CONTROL OF THE WORKS

3.1   Assignment

Assignment of the whole contract by either the employer or the contractor to another without written consent is precluded by Clause 3.1. This did not appear in the first edition of the JCLI Contract in 1978 but was added in 1981 to conform to the new JCT 80 Minor Works Contract when the revised version of the JCLI Form was published.

3.2   Subcontracting

This clause prohibits the landscape contractor from subcontracting any part of the works without the written consent of the landscape consultant. It should be noted that this consent is not to be unreasonably withheld and there is no obligation on the part of the landscape contractor to inform the consultant of the name of the firm to whom he or she intends to subcontract the work. Under such circumstances it is suggested that it would not be unreasonable for the consultant to withhold his or her consent until this information had been provided. As soon as the name of the proposed subcontractor is known, it is always essential for the consultant to take up references from other landscape consultants for whom the subcontractor has previously worked, if the subcontractor is not known to the consultant already. It should also be noted that there is no provision in this contract for the contractor to allow direct employees of the client (artists and tradespersons) to carry out other work at the same time as the main contract works, whether described in the tender documents or not. The consultant can of course 'nominate' such other firms to carry out work as a subcontract by the inclusion of a PC or provisional sum under Clause 3.7.

3.3   Contractor's representative

The contractor is to keep a competent person in charge on site when work is being carried out. Any instructions issued to that person are considered to have been issued to the landscape contractor in accordance with the terms of the contract.

This is important and no mere formality, since it safeguards the consultant from the possibility of mistakenly issuing an instruction to an employee of the contractor direct and assuming responsibility in the event of a subsequent accident. Such an accident occurred in the case of *Clayton* v. *Woodman* (1962), when a consultant instructed a bricklayer to cut a chase in brickwork and the bricklayer was injured when it subsequently collapsed due to lack of shoring.

3.4 Exclusion from the works

Exclusion from the site of certain employees of the contractor may be ordered by the consultant if he or she considers their behaviour to be offensive or detrimental to the works. The consultant cannot of course require their dismissal from employment by the contractor, since this might conflict with the employment protection Acts. This power should not be used lightly, and then only with tact. Contractors' (and landscape consultants') choice of employees most competent to carry out the work that has been entrusted to them is a matter entirely for their own discretion.

3.5 Landscape consultant's instructions

The power for the landscape consultant to issue instructions on the employer's behalf to the contractor is covered by Clause 3.5. All instructions are to be in writing (oral instructions to be confirmed within two days) and are to be complied with by the contractor 'forthwith' – that is, 'as soon as reasonably can be'.[1]

In addition to the normal duties of:

1. issuing certificates for interim payments and the final account;
2. attending at practical completion and when defects have been made good;
3. valuing variations;
4. extending the contract period for completion as may be reasonable; and
5. issuing such instructions as are necessary for the proper carrying out of the works,

the landscape consultant can, if the contractor does not comply with a written notice to do so within seven days, instruct others to carry out the works and deduct the cost from the money due to the contractor. (This power was added to the JCLI Contract in 1981 to follow JCT Minor Works.) The case of *Sutcliffe* v. *Thakrah* (1974)

---

[1] Osborne, P.G. (1964) *A Concise Law Dictionary* (5th edition), London: Sweet and Maxwell.

confirmed, however, that the consultant was not carrying out these duties as a 'quasi-arbitrator', since his or her decisions could always be challenged, however 'fairly and reasonably' the consultant was required to act. The consultant was only an agent of the employer, and the contractor could always refer a decision of the employer and/or the consultant on his or her behalf to the court. (See also Chapter 8 – Dispute Resolution.)

3.6 Variations

Instructions to vary the work from that stipulated in the contract documents, including the order in which it is to be carried out, may be issued on behalf of the employer by the landscape consultant under Clause 3.6. The employer must pay for such changes accordingly whether he or she wants them or not. They are to be valued by the landscape consultant (not the contractor) on a 'fair and reasonable basis', using where relevant the rates in the contract documents priced by the contractor as laid down in the 1st and 2nd Recitals. There is, however, a proviso in the clause for the consultant (not the employer) and contractor to agree the price between themselves before the work is put in hand.

3.7 PC and provisional sums

The ability for the landscape consultant to include prime cost (PC) and provisional sums in the contract and to issue the necessary instructions for their expenditure is covered by Clause 3.7. PC and provisional sums can be defined as follows:

> Provisional sums are provided for work or for costs which cannot be entirely foreseen, defined or detailed at the time the tender documents are issued.
> Prime cost (PC) sums are provided for work or services to be executed by a nominated subcontractor, a statutory authority, or a public undertaking, or for materials or goods to be obtained from a nominated supplier. Such sum shall be deemed to be exclusive of any profit required by the general contractor, and which provision shall be made for the addition thereof.

It should be noted that there is no requirement for any cash discount for prompt payment to be allowed to the landscape contractor, nor is there any reference to any obligatory procedures or documentation to be used when PC sums are used to enable the consultant to instruct the contractor to obtain the work from a single nominated subcontractor, or supplier.

However, in 1986 JCLI produced a Standard Form of Tender and Subcontract, the use of which ensures that the subcontract conditions match those of the main contract. This form is suitable for both those subcontractors chosen by the main contractor and those chosen by the landscape consultant (see Appendix 4).

Contingency sum: PC and provisional sums are not to be confused with 'contingency' sums, which are separate amounts included in tender documents 'to be expended or deducted from the contract sum in whole or in part as instructed by the landscape architect'.

Depending on the complexity of the project it is inevitable that certain additional work of a larger or smaller amount may be required. This will range from a relatively small amount on a simple new project to a higher value on a large and complex alteration scheme (between $2^{1}/_{2}$ and $7^{1}/_{2}$ per cent of the estimated contract sum is normal). These are covered both by the inclusion of a lump sum and also by a notional amount of time and materials to be provided on a 'dayworks' basis, which the contractor then has to price, thereby introducing a competitive element for variations to be valued in this way.

3.8 Objections to nomination

The acknowledgement of the fact that PC sums may be used for nomination is covered by Clause 3.8, which gives the landscape contractor the right to refuse to accept the nomination of any person or firm to carry out part of the works against whom the contractor may make a reasonable objection or who requires subcontract conditions at variance with those in the standard main or subcontract forms.

To reduce the likelihood of this occurring it is always advisable to include in the tender documents, when known, the name of the firm to whom the work is to be subcontracted or by whom the materials are to be supplied; the scope of the work; and, wherever possible, the period the subcontractor requires to execute the work or deliver the materials if this is known at the date of tender. It is always advisable to include in the tender documents the requirement that, should any tenderer wish to raise any objection against any of the firms named, he or she must do so no later than ten days before the latest date set for the submission of tenders.

When it is not considered necessary to select a single firm but nevertheless for quality reasons it is necessary to restrict the main contractor's choice, and the work is capable of being accurately described and specified, it is always possible to restrict the contractor's choice of subcontractors to three or more firms, to any one of whom the landscape contractor may subcontract the work.

3.9 Disturbance of regular progress

All standard building contracts, except the JCT Minor Works Form, provide for the main contractor to be reimbursed for any direct loss and expense he or she has incurred due to any disturbance of the regular progress of the work (even if completion is not delayed) caused by the employer, the employer's agents or servants (which includes the landscape consultant) and any other delays arising from lack of instructions (see Table 6.1 on page 138). JCLI Clause 3.9 requires in such an event that the landscape consultant should ascertain the amount of such loss and expense, and include it in any progress payments. While there is no obligation on the contractor to provide any details of such loss, it is clearly in his or her interest to do so, particularly as there are over 50 different headings under which some contractors may claim reimbursement.

4   PAYMENT

4.1 Correction of inconsistencies

The possibility of the existence of inconsistencies within or between the contract documents being discovered after the contract has been signed is acknowledged in Clause 4.1, which simply states that they will be corrected and that, if this involves a variation, instructions should be issued and it should be valued as such. This leaves every case to be treated on its merits. The clause goes on to say that the contract conditions take precedence over the other contract documents. It is generally accepted that drawings take precedence in respect of matters affecting location, assembly and fixing, the specification takes precedence in respect of quality and the bills or schedules have precedence for quantities – for example, if the drawings show five trees and the bills or schedules list only three the contractor is deemed only to have included for the three scheduled, although he or she will have to provide the five shown on the drawings and be paid for them accordingly.

4.2 Progress payments

The contractor is allowed, at intervals of not less than four weeks or at the stages specified in tender documents, to request the landscape consultant to certify progress payments, on receipt of which request the consultant must issue a certificate for the value of work properly executed to date, less that which has been previously certified. The inclusion of the word 'properly' is considered to mean 'in accordance with the *terms* of the contract and not to imply that it is in accordance with the contract documents', since this is the contractor's responsibility under Clause 1.1. Should the consultant find at this stage that any work is unsatisfactory he or she must of course exclude it from the value of the work certified.

Progress payments are to include the value of variations and work executed under PC and provisional sums and also of any materials brought on site but as yet unfixed, if this is reasonable and proper and they are adequately stored and protected. Since legally such materials may not become the property of the employer until they have been fixed, even if included in a certificate and paid for, it is usual to include in the tender documents a requirement for the contractor to provide evidence that he or she has in fact paid for them him- or herself and that they have therefore become the contractor's own property. There is no provision in the contract for the inclusion in a certificate for materials stored *off* site, for instance in a landscape contractor's nursery or yard, and it is unwise for a landscape consultant to do so, without at least ensuring that they are properly labelled as the property of the employer, with everything properly insured against any subsequent damage while in the care of the contractor.

The clause also provides for 5 per cent (or other such sum as had been included in the tender documents and inserted in the clause) to be deducted from each certificate to cover any defects which may subsequently arise and which have to be made good under Clauses 2.5 and 2.7. The employer has to honour the certificate within 14 days of the date of the issue. Lack of compliance with this obligation entitles the contractor to terminate the contract under Clause 7.3. There is no express provision in the clause for the consultant to condemn work and/or order its removal from site and replacement, nor for the consultant to instruct the contractor to execute any remedial work to bring it up to specification. To issue instructions for the latter could make the consultant responsible for its adequacy, which would be unwise.

4.3 The Penultimate Certificate

Within 14 days of issuing the Certificate of Practical Completion, the consultant has to certify a further progress payment on the basis of $97\frac{1}{2}$ per cent (or such other percentage stated in the tender documents) of the contract sum adjusted for the cost of variations, PC and provisional sums and any fluctuations to which the contractor is entitled. The clause also provides that where the landscape contractor is being paid under the contract for the subsequent maintenance during the defects liability period, the cost of this is to be excluded from the certificates also. Like progress payments, the Penultimate Certificate must also be honoured within 14 days of issue.

It is important that the valuation of this certificate is as accurate as possible since the contract does not provide for the issue of any other before the Final Certificate.

4.4   The Final Certificate

The landscape contractor now has three months (or such other period of time as has been inserted) in which to forward to the landscape consultant all the necessary details to enable the consultant to prepare the Final Account and Certificate (see Figure 7.1 on page 000). The landscape consultant then has 28 days in which to do this and issues his or her certificates as soon as the defects liability period has expired, any defects have been made good in accordance with Clause 2.7 (if applicable) and the consultant has certified accordingly that such remedial work has in fact been carried out. The employer must then honour the certificate within 14 days of issue.

It must be remembered that certificates are always issued for the full value of work properly executed, without the deduction of any liquidated and ascertained damages which the employer may be entitled to deduct.

Of the three cases to reach the High Court concerning the JCT/JCLI Contract two concerned arbitration (the first being *Pincot* v. *Fur Textile Care Ltd*, 1986) on the relationship between a main contractor and subcontractors. In *Oram Builders* v. *M. and C. Pemberton* (1985) the court decided that where an arbitration clause such as that in Article 4 (see page 000) covered the appointment of an arbitrator who (even though the clause did not so state) could open up and review certificates, that right did not apply to the courts or the Official Referee unless they were specifically appointed as an arbitrator. In *Crestar* v. *Carr* (TLR 6/5/87) a firm of contractors, Crestar Ltd, entered into a contract to alter a house in Essex and by the date of practical completion had issued Interim Certificates to the value of £77 698, at which time the contract envisaged that a retention of only a further 5 per cent would become due. The Final Certificate was, however, issued three months later for an additional £39 975, and when the building's owners, Mr and Mrs Carr, attempted to refer the matter to arbitration they were told by the builder that this was not possible since, not having settled the certificate within 14 days, they were now in breach of contract. The Court of Appeal, however, held that such a relatively large sum outstanding on the Final Certificate was not envisaged under the contract and the matter could therefore be referred to an arbitrator.

While in no way allowing oneself to be influenced by the client it is of course always good practice to inform him or her of the imminence of a Final Certificate, just as it is equally good practice to discuss the matter with the contractor and obtain his or her agreement wherever possible before its issue.

The clause now includes for interim payments at intervals to be specified for aftercare.

4.5 Contribution, levy and tax changes

The sudden imposition of tax changes, contributions and levies could impose a considerable burden on landscape contractors under a fixed price contract. Should this arise therefore, Clause 4.5 provides for its recovery by the contractor from the employer using the JCLI Contract's Supplementary Memorandum incorporated by reference. Since this covers only the cost of 'workpeople' and excludes site and head office supervisory staff, provision is made for an additional percentage to be added to cover the latter, 20 per cent being considered appropriate for contracts in excess of 12 months and 10 per cent for contracts for a shorter period. The whole clause can be deleted if the period is of such a limited duration as to be inappropriate.

4.6A Fixed price

When the duration of a landscape contract is 12 months or less, most contractors can reasonably accurately forecast any increases in the cost of labour and materials and therefore make such allowances in their tenders as they consider necessary or prudent. In such cases Clause 4.6A will apply which states that the contractor will not be entitled to any payment in respect of any increase or decrease in the cost to him or her of labour, materials, plant or other resources.

4.6B Fluctuations

It is, however, not unknown for some landscape contract work to extend over a period of more than 12 months and to cover two planting seasons, when future increased costs of labour or materials are more difficult to forecast. To reduce the risk to contractors and therefore in the tenders submitted, it is often in the employer's interest to arrange for the landscape contractor to be reimbursed by payment of a sum more closely related to the actual increased costs that may have been incurred. Clause 4.6B therefore makes provision for the calculation of increased costs by reference to the current retail price index or part D of the Supplementary Memorandum setting out the use of the Formula Rules published by the RIBA, RICS and Building Employers Confederation (BEC), prepared in accordance with DoE Circular 158/73 (313/73 in Wales and 2/74 in Scotland). These include a set of indices, which in the case of Category 48 (soft planning) are based on information supplied monthly by the horticulture trade and published by HMSO. The amount of the increase is calculated as follows:

$$\frac{\text{Valuation month index} - \text{base month index} \times \text{value of work done in the month}}{\text{Base month index}}$$

(Costs are based on June 1976 = 100)

Provision is also made for the recovery of increased costs during any aftercare period.

5   STATUTORY OBLIGATIONS

5.1   Statutory obligations, notices, fees and charges

Compliance with all statutory obligations, giving the necessary notices and paying all fees and charges is always the responsibility of the landscape contractor. Should the latter, during the progress of the work, consider that anything that he or she has contracted to do conflicts with any statute, Statutory Instrument, rule, order, regulation or bye-law, he or she must notify the landscape consultant and ask for instructions in writing. Provided, however, that the contractor has followed the contract documents and instructions, he or she cannot be held responsible for any such divergence. If, therefore, work has to be carried out subsequently to ensure compliance with the statutory requirements, the contractor is entitled to be reimbursed accordingly.

5.2 Value added tax

The liability for the payment by the employer of value added tax is set out in Part B of the Supplementary Memorandum which describes the arrangement for its collection by the contractor direct from the employer, independently of any certificate, and also the procedures the contractor must follow if the employer wishes to challenge any taxes which he or she considers have been incorrectly charged. Most landscape work is liable to tax at the standard rate and on the smaller contract many contractors delay its collection until the Final Account.

5.3 Statutory tax deduction scheme

The Income and Corporation Taxes Act 1988 requires that contractors and subcontractors, particularly self-employed individuals who do not have a certificate of exemption from the Inland Revenue, must have tax deducted before payment is made to them and the tax forwarded by the employer to the Collector of Taxes direct. Should this not be done and the necessary tax due is not paid, the employer is still liable for payment to the Inland Revenue, even though he or she has in fact paid the contractor or subcontractor in full. The necessary details are set out in Part C of the Supplementary Memorandum and it is clearly essential for all employers or landscape consultants to have sight of the relevant exemption certificates to ensure that they are current before any payments are made.

5.4 Fair wages resolution

The original 1946 Fair Wages Resolution of the House of Commons requiring contractors and subcontractors to pay no less than the current union rate was rescinded as being an anachronism in 1982. Although it may still remain in the standing orders of certain local authorities and councils it has now been deleted from the contract conditions.

5.5 Prevention of corruption

Clause 5.5 entitles the employer to cancel the contract and to recover any resulting loss from the contractor if the latter offers, gives or agrees to give any gift or consideration which constitutes an offence under the 1889–1916 Prevention of Corruption Acts or, if the employer is a local authority, under the 1972 Local Government Act.

5.6   CDM Regulations

Clauses 5.6 to 5.9 cover the obligations of the employer and duties of the contractor to comply with the Regulations.

6   INJURY, DAMAGE AND INSURANCE

6.1   Injury to or death of persons

The contractor is solely responsible under Clause 6.1 for the injury or death of any person which arises from the carrying out of work unless this is due to an act or neglect of the employer. The contractor must indemnify the employer against any claim which may arise and, to ensure that he or she has the financial resources to meet these obligations, the contractor is therefore required to take out the necessary insurance.

6.2   Damage to property

While the contractor is equally solely responsible in this instance, such responsibility extends only to that damage arising from his or her own negligence and for which he or she must take out the necessary insurance also. There is no provision for any minimum amount of insurance for damage to property, so that should employers doubt that the contractor has sufficient insurance cover, they should require him or her to submit the necessary evidence of this.

If the employer requires insurance for damage to adjoining property for which he or she could be held liable, this is best covered by a provisional sum in the tender documents.

The MW80 Insurance clauses were amended in November 1986 to bring them into line both with the revisions made to JCT 80 at the same time and with current practice in the insurance market. Although it was thought unlikely that 'all risks' insurance would be applicable on the type of work for which the JCLI Form was intended, it was, however, necessary to amend Clauses 6.1, 6.2 and 6.3A/6.3B to cover the correction to the specified perils under 6.3A. In Clause 6.3A, for the insurance of new work against fire, the proviso was added that *if* the contractor had an all risks policy, that policy would recognize the employer as being 'jointly' insured.

6.3A Insurance of the works

Damage to the landscape works from the normal perils of fire, flooding and so on on contracts for new work is normally to be the responsibility of the contractor under Clause 6.3A. The policy should be endorsed to indicate the employer's interest for the full value of the works, together with the landscape consultant's fees (for which space is left for the percentage to be inserted), loss of unfixed materials, the removal of debris, extra costs of reinstatement and any increased costs. Consequential loss to the employer and any damage to the contractor's temporary plant and buildings are normally excluded.

The clause also includes provision for the contractor to proceed with the works and to make good any damage as certified by the landscape consultant from monies received from the insurers.

6.3B Insurance of the works and any existing structures

When the works are within an existing site or are to be added to existing work, it is clear that any damage might not be confined to the new work and therefore insurance based solely on the value of the new work would be insufficient. Under these circumstances the alternative Clause 6.3B enables the employer, who no doubt already has the existing property insured, to add the new work to his present policy and cover the old and the new work together in the employer's and the contractor's joint names.

The relationship between Clauses 6.2 and 6.3 was clarified by Lord Justice Auld in the Court of Appeal in March 1997 when he held that recoverable damage under Clause 6.2 should not be reduced by the amount that would have been recoverable under Clause 6.3B insurance conditions if the latter had been effected; and it was not the intention of 6.3B insurance to benefit the contractor as well as the employer by providing a fund for reinstatement recoverable irrespective of fault.

6.4 Evidence of insurance

To ensure that the necessary contractor's policies are taken out and in force the employer is entitled to require evidence from the contractor, which is usually provided by a formal 'Certificate of Insurance'. The contractor has similar rights when the employer includes the new work in his or her insurance under Clause 6.3B.

6.5A Malicious damage

Landscape work is particularly susceptible to malicious damage and so the JCLI has provided a clause specifically to cover this eventuality. Malicious damage to the landscape works after practical completion is clearly the responsibility of the employer; damage of this nature which takes place prior to practical completion is the responsibility of the landscape contractor, who is responsible for the overall security and protection of the site. Clause 6.5A holds the contractor responsible for making good such damage entirely at his or her own expense.

6.5B High-risk areas

Where this risk of malicious damage occurring prior to practical completion is considered to be abnormally high the option of a provisional sum to cover such damage is provided in Clause 6.5B. While the contractor still has to take all such steps as are reasonably necessary to protect the works, in the event of such damage occurring the employer has the funds available from the provisional sum to pay for no more and no less than the actual cost of the remedial work required.

7.1 DETERMINATION

The employment of the contractor (but not the contract, which is an entirely different matter) can be terminated (that is, determined) by either the employer or the contractor, but for only a few specific reasons. Although determination is apparently quite straightforward, legal advice is always essential before taking such a step, to ensure that the termination is not to be considered to be invalid on account of some purely technical formality, such as the incorrect service of notices under Clause 7.1.

7.2 Determination by the employer

This can be effected for only one of three reasons: first, if the contractor, without reasonable cause, fails to proceed diligently with the works or wholly suspends the carrying out of the works before completion. While 'lack of diligence', although a matter of opinion, is relatively simple to establish, 'wholly suspends', as distinct from 'partially suspends' or 'postpones', is much more difficult to prove and it is for just such reasons that legal advice is always desirable.

The second reason is if the contractor becomes bankrupt, winds up his or her business or has a receiver appointed. This is of course a matter of fact, but it is not always easy to know when it has occurred, far less when it is imminent. When it does arise immediate action is essential to secure the site, to safeguard the works and to prevent the unauthorized removal of unfixed materials, plant and equipment, and so on from the site.

The third reason for determination by the employer is the contractor's failing to comply with the CDM Regulations.

In any of these cases, while the determination must not be made unreasonably, the employer is under no obligation to give the contractor any warning and, provided the notice is served by registered post, the contractor's employment is determined forthwith. The contractor must then immediately give up possession of the site and the employer need make no payment until the work has been completed by others.

7.3 Determination by the contractor

In this instance there are five grounds for determination:

1. if the employer is more than 14 days late in making progress payments or in paying any VAT that is due;
2. if the employer interferes with, or obstructs, the works or fails to make the site available by the date of commencement;
3. if the employer suspends the execution of the work for over a month or more;
4. if the employer does not comply with the CDM Regulations; and
5. if the employer becomes insolvent.

However, the contractor must give the employer seven days in which to rectify matters before the notice of determination takes effect and must be paid for all work completed up to the date of determination and the cost of removing his or her temporary buildings, plant and equipment.

8 SUPPLEMENTARY MEMORANDUM

This sets out the detailed provisions as follows: in Part A for changes in tax, levies and contributions, in Part B for the recovery from the employer of any value added tax due, in Part C for the statutory tax deductions under the 1988 Income and Corporation Taxes Act and in Part D for the recovery of fluctuations under the Formula Rules.

9   SETTLEMENT OF DISPUTES

The 1998 Revision amplifies the procedures for the settlement of disputes in Clause 9.0 by 9.1 Adjudication in accordance with Part D of the Supplementary Memorandum and 9.2 Arbitration in accordance with Supplementary Memorandum Part E.

JCLI PRACTICE NOTE NO. 5

The fifth practice note consolidates and supersedes the earlier notes and explains the various points covered elsewhere in the preceding chapters. It has special reference to the new 5th Recital and Article 5 in respect of the CDM Regulations, in addition to the other 16 guidance notes regarding the inclusion of schedules, bills of quantities, liquidated and ascertained damages, practical completion, defects liability, plant failures, the correction of errors, malicious damage and temporary protection and so on.

Various other minor amendments to correct typographical errors or to conform with the JCT Minor Works Conditions were also made.

The practice note was revised in November 1998 with ten amendments, five of which were additional clauses relating to aftercare, consequential loss, defects and outstanding work at Practical Completion, frost damage and plant specification clauses and five alterations to existing clauses. Defects Liability periods starting from the Certificate of Practical Completion, retention by exclusion from the cost of Aftercare, consequential loss to be included in Liquidated and Ascertained Damages are also covered. Guidance on specification for watering and procedures in the event of the imposition of watering restrictions is now to be found in the May 1996 Landscape Institute Technical Bulletin, *Watering Restrictions and Watering Specification*. Clause 18 suggests that in certain circumstances the employer may choose to share the cost of losses entirely due to severe winter weather after planting. Clause 19 recommends the use of plants to comply with the NBS National Plant Specification and to be supplied by a nursery in the HTA Nursery Certification Scheme.

THE USE OF THE JCLI FORM IN SCOTLAND

By inclusion of reference (in the 1st Recital) to the proper law under which the contract is carried out, the JCLI Form is suitable for use throughout the United Kingdom and even in some circumstances abroad, although it is also necessary to confirm the place where the works are to be executed, so that the contractor can make him- or herself familiar with any differences in statutory regulations and allow for them accordingly. This also applies to the arbitrations carried out under Article 4, although conformity to Scottish procedures if required causes no difficulty.

Notwithstanding its origins in Roman as distinct from Saxon and Norman law, the reliance on Sheriffs for administrative and judicial duties, and the lack of distinction between equity and common law (apart from a difference in nomenclature – for example pursuer and defender instead of plaintiff and defendant, and tort known as delict), Scottish practice and procedures differ from those in the rest of the UK in only three significant respects:

1. In Scottish law there is no need for a consideration to ensure a binding contract. Tender documents under such law must therefore refer to the execution of a formal contract in addition to that implied by the letter of acceptance. Nor is there any provision for contracts to be entered into under seal. Although *Jus quaesitum tertio* provisions in their own favour enforced by a third party are contrary to English partnerships, those in Scotland have a legal existence of their own, enabling parties to sue for debts in their own name (although the personal liability of the individual partners remains unaltered).

2. Delict (the righting of civil (not criminal) wrongs) is similar to but very different from the English law of tort; it usually arises from negligence and requires careful study to identify the differences of detail.

3. Scottish property law, however, differs in many respects from English law, primarily on account of the feudal rights remaining from the Norman Conquest and power vested in the Sheriffs. These were rationalized and simplified by the Conveyancing and Feudal Reform (Scotland) Act 1970, the Land Tenure Reform (Scotland) Act 1974 and the Land Registration (Scotland) Act 1979.

 THE JCT INTERMEDIATE FORM IFC 84

Conditions in the JCT Minor Works Form made no provisions for plant failures and malicious damage, nor did the Form cover partial possession, the valuation of variations using tender rates, PC sums, the ability to object to nominations, the payment of direct loss and expense due to disturbance of regular progress, or fluctuations – all of which were incorporated into the JCLI Contract.

However, in 1984 the JCT published an Intermediate Form suitable for use on larger contracts of a value of up to £250 000 at 1981 prices. While still not covering plant failures or malicious damage, this form did provide for the other circumstances previously omitted.

The JCLI has therefore prepared a single-page supplement to IFC 84 with an accompanying Practice Note 4, incorporating the two outstanding items covering plant failures and malicious damage, so that this form of contract can now also be used for the larger landscape contracts (see Appendix 6).

 ## THE INSTITUTE OF CIVIL ENGINEERS (ICE) FORM

This form is applicable for the larger engineering contract involving large quantities of groundworks, movement of earth, and the construction of roads and footpaths. It is not a fixed price, lump sum contract but has quantities prepared in accordance with a simplified method of measurement and is a remeasurement contract, all work being remeasured as the work proceeds and being paid for accordingly. The conditions are broadly similar but not identical to those under the JCLI Form, but the engineer has far wider powers with regard to the programme and sequence of work on site.

 ## THE ICE NEW ENGINEERING AND CONSTRUCTION CONTRACT (NEC)

First published in 1993 as the ICE New Engineering Contract, this contract was reissued in 1995 as a second edition retitled the New Engineering and Construction Contract, both to emphasize that it was as equally applicable to building projects as to engineering projects and to incorporate additional clauses so as to comply with the criteria for the most effective form of contract for modern conditions as set out in paragraph 5.18 of the Latham Report ('Constructing the Team', HMSO, 1994).

The NEC Contract attempts to minimize the adversarial nature of other forms of contract; it comprises nine core clauses, six main and 15 secondary option clauses, and aims by the use of simple language to provide as wide a range of options as possible to meet every different type of procurement required. The six main options cover different strategies for fixed or fluctuation price based contracts, with either 'activity schedules' or bills of quantity, target contracts with activity schedules or bills of quantity, cost-reimbursable and management contracts, applicable to both local authority and private sector projects. The Contract also includes provision for resolution of disputes, adjudication within four weeks and – while site supervision costs will be higher than usual under this form of contract – attempts to make use of the role of the project manager by recommending management-driven procedures involving the use of programme and method statements instead of the stick-and-carrot approach. The form has only to date been used by devotees on the larger engineering type of project and time alone will tell if it is appropriate for landscape work.

 SUMMARY

The main forms of contract and subcontract on which landscape consultants may be involved can thus be summarized as follows:

1. *ICE Form:* Designed for large civil engineering contracts (that is, bridges, motorways, slagheaps, sewage works and so on). A very simple form for few trades with wide powers (for instance, the engineer can dictate the sequence of execution of a project), and involving simple quantities (for example, supply and fix 1 number manhole). All work remeasured as it proceeds.
2. *ICE NEC Contract:* Applicable to both building and engineering projects and attempts to meet the Latham Report's recommendations for improving contract forms, through the use of easily understood language and a wide range of options intended to meet all types of procurement.
3. *JCT SFBC (JCT 80):* Incorrectly known as RIBA Form. By now a very complex document available in a variety of forms – for example, with or without quantities, private or local authorities (virtually the same), approximate quantities, phased completion, variants.
4. *JCT 80 (Clause 35) Form of Subcontract for Nominated Subcontractors:* Applicable to the major building contracts, with the soft planting around buildings being carried out by a specially selected specialist, enjoying special privileges with regard to direct interim payment if the main contractor defaults, and so on.
5. *IFC 84:* JCT Form published in 1984 for both medium-sized private sector and public sector building projects, with or without quantities, with provision for naming a single subcontractor. A 1991 JCLI one-page supplement to the IFC 84 conditions is available, with additional appropriate clauses applicable for the larger landscape project.
6. *JCT Minor Works:* The smaller version designed for 12-months' or less contracts up to £75 000 value, for use on private, local

authority, new and alteration *fixed price* contracts. Very useful for a wide variety of minor projects. No standard form of subcontract.

7.   *JCLI Form of Landscape Works:* The JCLI variant of the above, replacing the Institute of Landscape Architects form (as it was then known).

8.   *JCLI Form of Tender and Conditions of Subcontract:* For use with the JCLI Agreement for Landscape Works.

SUBCONTRACTS

It is a regrettable fact that today much of the work of a contract is subcontracted to firms or individuals who are not on the payroll of the main contractor. Not only does the JCLI Contract preclude both the contractor and the employer from assigning the contract to another, without the written consent of the other (Clause 3.1), but the contractor may not subcontract the work or any part of it without the written consent of the landscape consultant (Clause 3.2). This consent, however, shall not be unreasonably withheld, and while the contract does not require the identity of the subcontractor requested to be disclosed in order for the consultant to be able to decide whether to consent or not, it is clearly incumbent on the consultant to know whom the contractor intends to use, in order to decide whether the work can be entrusted to another of the contractor's choosing. Under these circumstances it is helpful for the contractor not only to inform the consultant of the identity of the subcontractor concerned but also to provide the names of at least three other consultants for whom the subcontractor has previously worked, as references. It is then possible for the consultant to send a questionnaire such as that in Figure 6.2 to the people or firms named in the references and obtain confirmation of the subcontractor's competence and suitability for the work.

CONSECUTIVE DIRECT CONTRACTS

It is sometimes possible and preferable to leave the completion of the landscape works until the building contractor has finished. It is clearly the simplest solution on projects such as those connected with industrial civil engineering or hospital work to delay the start of the planting, if the seasons permit, until the main contractor has finished and cleared up, before the landscape contractor starts. On other projects such as housing and schools, it is clearly essential to have all planting completed and well established before the buildings and their surroundings are occupied, to minimize possible future vandalism.

CONFIDENTIAL:

FIRM:

WORKS CARRIED OUT:

Please enter details or tick box as appropriate:

1. How long have you known this firm? YEARS ☐

2. What do you consider the maximum value of any one contract this firm is capable of excuting?

   AMOUNT

   ☐ £ _____

How would you assess the following:

	POOR	REASONABLE	GOOD	EXCELLENT	COMMENTS
3. Their office organization and management capabilities.	☐	☐	☐	☐	
4. Their ability to formulate practical programmes.	☐	☐	☐	☐	
5. Their ability to maintain programme.	☐	☐	☐	☐	
6. Their standard of workmanship.	☐	☐	☐	☐	
7. Their site organization.	☐	☐	☐	☐	
8. Their conduct of labour relations.	☐	☐	☐	☐	
9. Their relationship with subcontractors and statutory authorities.	☐	☐	☐	☐	
10. Their attention to site welfare and safety.	☐	☐	☐	☐	
11. Their degree of cooperation.	☐	☐	☐	☐	

	YES	NO
12. If the firm was the main contractor, did they rely extensively on subcontractors?	☐	☐
13. If the firm was the main contractor, were there any problems with payments to subcontractors and suppliers?	☐	☐
14. Were defects remedied promptly?	☐	☐
15. Were final accounts settled satisfactorily?	☐	☐
16. Would you use this firm again?	☐	☐

Figure 6.2   Standard letter for a reference on a subcontractor

CONCURRENT DIRECT CONTRACTS

When it is not possible or desirable to carry out the landscape works after the main contractor has finished, it is sometimes possible for the work to be carried out at the same time as the building work. JCT 80 (Clause 29) permits the employer to engage others of his or her own choosing to enter the site and undertake the landscape works while the main contractor is still on site, provided that this is made clear in the tender documents. Great care, however, is necessary to ensure that each does not blame the other for any errors or delays. Primarily intended to enable the employer to arrange for his or her own artists or tradespeople to work on site alongside the main contractor, this type of subcontract is equally appropriate when used for landscape contractors.

DOMESTIC SUBCONTRACTS

When the work is fully described in the tender documents and consent is given to the main contractor to subcontract the works to specialists entirely of his or her own choosing, these are known as 'domestic subcontracts'. Under these circumstances the main contractor remains entirely responsible for the quality of the subcontractors' work and any delays that the subcontractors may cause him or her. There are therefore many advantages in this arrangement but it does require the landscape works to be fully designed, detailed and carefully specified to ensure the correct quality is provided. The main contractor can use a landscape contractor with whom he or she has developed a good working relationship in the past or with whom special financial arrangements have been made. The employer still has a reasonable right to object to the subcontractor proposed and the main contractor accepts full responsibility for any delays or substandard workmanship of the landscape subcontractor. The main contractor can also arrange for the work to be carried out at a time convenient to him- or herself.

The BEC has published, in conjunction with the Federation of Associations of Specialist Subcontractors (FASS) and the Committee of Associations of Specialist Engineering Contractors (CASEC), a standard form of subcontract (DOMI) for use, with the JCT 80 form of building contract, under these circumstances; it effectively transfers the obligations of the main contractor to the subcontractor, and is appropriate for engineering services and landscape subcontracts alike. The subcontract contains four Recitals and three Articles in the usual way, with an arbitrator appointed by the President of the RICS, and 37 contract conditions running to 44 pages. An additional Clause 21.4.5 was published in August 1984 dealing with the transfer of ownership to the employer of unfixed materials on site.

LISTED SUBCONTRACTORS

To ensure an adequate quality of workmanship it is sometimes preferable, instead of allowing the main contractor a completely free hand in choosing the landscape subcontractor, to require that he or she subcontracts the work to one of a list of three subcontractors named in the tender documents, the choice of which being entirely a matter for the contractor's discretion without further reference to the landscape consultant. It sometimes happens that the contractor wishes to add to the list a subcontractor of his or her own choosing, which under Clause 19 of JCT 80 he or she is entitled to do, but the consultant should require the contractor to give notice of such an intention at least ten days before the date when tenders are due. It is essential to take up references on the landscape subcontractor proposed when this happens, using a standard letter such as that shown in Figure 6.2. The main contractor remains entirely responsible for the performance of a subcontractor selected in this way (who then becomes his or her 'domestic' subcontractor) and cannot claim an extension to the contract period for any delays the subcontractor may cause.

NAMED SUBCONTRACTORS

The JCT Intermediate Form IFC 84 is unique in that it provides for the naming in the tender documents of a single subcontractor whom the main contractor must use without any option. For this to be made use of, however, the landscape work must be fully described in sufficient detail for it to be priced, and subcontract tenders must be previously obtained by the consultant on a special form, NAM/T, which includes space for the insertion of details such as any special attendance which the main contractor may be required to provide, subcontract commencement and completion dates, and so on.

NOMINATED SUBCONTRACTORS

Prior to the publication of JCT 80 nomination was the almost universal method of arranging for the execution of subcontract works, in cases when it was considered that the work was of too specialized a nature to be entrusted to the main contractor and where the contractor could not be left to select a subcontractor of his or her own choosing. The Banwell Report stated that nomination – namely when the employer retains the selection to a single subcontractor of his or her own choosing – was only justified to meet one of the following three requirements:

1.   when special techniques are required,
2.   when early ordering is necessary, or
3.   when a particular quality of work is essential,

and this still holds true today.

In these instances it is often necessary to issue a letter of intent to the subcontractor concerned on the lines of that shown in Figure 6.3.

JCT 80

Under these circumstances, when the work is required to be carried out by a subcontractor under the JCT 80 form of building contract, a prime cost sum must be included in the tender documents accordingly and the subcontractor is then nominated under Clause 35. These procedures, which are set out in great detail, must be followed irrespective of whether the subcontract works are in connection with landscape, structural steel or pre-cast concrete, fixing metal windows, cladding, mechanical or electrical engineering works (even though the provision of shop drawings are unlikely to be required for landscape work).

```
Dear Sirs

We are pleased to confirm that your quotation dated
.............. in the sum of ............. for ............. works at the
above is acceptable and the main contractor will be
instructed to enter into a subcontract with you after
the main contract has been entered into.

Would you therefore please proceed with the preparation
of the necessary shop and fabrication drawings/arrange
for the necessary labour and materials.

We enclose therefore a copy of an Employer/
Subcontractor Agreement for your signature and return
for endorsement by our client confirming our
acceptance of any expense reasonably and properly
incurred by yourselves as a result and your agreement
to our client's subsequent use of them without
further obligation should the subcontract not be
proceeded with.

Yours faithfully
```

Figure 6.3   Letter of intent to nominated subcontractor

Clause 35

When a subcontractor nominated under Clause 35 delays the completion of the work, the main contractor is automatically entitled to an extension of the contract period and the employer loses his or her liquidated and ascertained damages as a consequence. If the main contractor defaults in handing over money stated in Interim Certificates as being due to a landscape subcontractor, the subcontractor is entitled to payment from the employer direct. In view of the complexity of the 1980 procedures, in March 1991 the JCT combined the two alternative methods of nomination into an obligatory procedure using the standard forms NSC/W, NSC/T and NSC/C.

NSC/W

The use of this separate obligatory agreement (warranty) signed by both employer and subcontractor overcomes the problem of the loss of liquidated and ascertained damages by the employer as the result of an extension of time having been granted to the contractor due to a delay having been caused by the nominated subcontractor. NSC/W achieves this through the inclusion of sub-clause 3.4, which states that:

> the subcontractor shall so perform the Subcontract that the Contractor will not be entitled to an extension of time for completion of the Main Contract by reason of the relevant event in clause 24.4.7 of the Main Contract conditions.

The employer is thus able to recover direct from the subcontractor the liquidated and ascertained damages he or she has lost by having to grant an extension of time to the main contractor, the amount of which is to be stated in the obligatory Form of Nominated Subcontract Tender (NSC/T). NSC/W also requires the nominated subcontractor to warrant that he or she has and will exercise all reasonable skill and care in his or her design and selection of the necessary goods or materials.

NSC/T

In addition to NSC/W this nine-page Standard Form of Nominated Subcontract Tender, the use of which is also obligatory, ensures that all the information required by the main contractor and subcontractor are known to each of them before they enter into the subcontract. The Form comes in three parts: the invitation to tender, the subcontractor's tender, and the particular conditions to be agreed between the contractor and subcontractor before they sign the seven-page Articles of Agreement (NSC/A) to undertake the work in accordance with the

Standard Conditions of Subcontract (NSC/C) incorporated into the Agreement 'by reference'. The key sections of NSC/T are on pages 2, 3 and 4 (see Appendix 5), completed in turn by the landscape consultant, the nominated landscape subcontractor and the main contractor before signing the Articles of Agreement to undertake the work (see Figure 6.4).

NSC/C

The standard nominated subcontract conditions, with 34 main clauses, run to 42 pages and have been drafted to reflect in every respect the provisions and obligations of the main contractor, particularly those dealing with insurance, disturbance to progress and tax certificates. NSC/C includes the same provisions as were included in the 1963 JCT contract, for direct payment, early release of retention, responsibility for attendance, making good defects, extensions to the contract period, adjudication, arbitration and determination. Clauses 23 and 24 set out the provisions for the right of 'set off' by the main contractor, either by agreement or by an award of the court or arbitrator, including 'costs', and determination by the architect in the event of default or insolvency. Determination by the subcontractor is also provided for in Clause 29, which states that any extra costs of a new nomination, if valid, have to be borne by the main contractor.

THE JCT 80 NOMINATION PROCEDURES

These are now carried out in successive consecutive stages as follows:

1. The landscape consultant invites tenders on NSC/T Part 1, sending Part 2 and NSC/W for completion and return by the subcontractor.

2. On receipt the landscape consultant gets the employer to countersign the completed NSC/W and NSC/T forms of the selected subcontractor and sends them all with NSC/N (the Form of Nomination) to the main contractor with copies to the subcontractor.

3. The main contractor and subcontractor have ten days from receipt of NSC/N to agree the programme, sequence and any outstanding details, completing and signing NSC/T Part 3 and the subcontract Agreement NSC/A accordingly, leaving the subcontract conditions NSC/C, incorporated in NSC/A by reference, 'on the shelf'.

NSC/T Part 3

Part 3 – Particular Conditions

Items to be completed by the Contractor and the Sub-Contractor

Notes on completion of these Particular Conditions

[a] Insert the same details as in NSC/T Part 1, pages 2 and 3. In NSC/T Part 3 the expression 'Contract Administrator' is applicable where the Nomination Instruction on Nomination NSC/N will be issued under a Local Authorities version of the Standard Form of Building Contract and by a person who is not entitled to the use of the name 'Architect' under and in accordance with the Architects (Registration) Acts 1931 to 1969. If so, the expression 'Architect' shall be deemed to have been deleted throughout Tender NSC/T. Where the person who will issue the aforesaid Nomination Instruction is entitled to the use of the name 'Architect' the expression 'Contract Administrator' shall be deemed to have been deleted throughout NSC/T.

[b] The Sub-Contractor's entries in NSC/T Part 2, items 1 to 4 should be considered when agreeing the entries in NSC/T Part 3.

[c] Conditions NSC/C state in clause 2·1: 'The Sub-Contractor shall carry out and complete the Sub-Contract Works in accordance with the agreed programme details in NSC/T Part 3, item 1, and reasonably in accordance with the progress of the Works but subject to receipt of the notice to commence work on site as detailed in NSC/T Part 3, item 1, and to the operation of clauses 2·2 to 2·7.' *(extension of Sub-Contract time).*

[d] The period of notice must take account of any period stated for the execution of the Sub-Contract Works off-site prior to commencement on site.

© 1991 RIBA Publications Ltd

---

[a]   Main Contract Works and location:

[a]   Sub-Contract Works:

---

[b]

1   (1)   Period required by the Architect/the Contract Administrator to approve drawings after receipt will be that set out in NSC/T Part 1, item 14.

[c]   (2)   The earliest starting date and the latest starting date for the Sub-Contract Works to be carried out on site:

are   (earliest)

and   (latest)

(3)   Periods required for:

(i)   submission for approval of all necessary Sub-Contractor's drawings etc. *(co-ordination, installation, shop or builders' work or other as appropriate)*   weeks

(ii)   the execution of the Sub-Contract Works

off-site (if any)
prior to commencement on site   weeks

on site   weeks
from expiry of **period required for notice to commence**
[d]   **work on site** which is   weeks

(4)   Further details:

Figure 6.4   Unworked example of Tender NSC/T Part 3, pages 2–4 (reproduced with permission of RIBA Publications Ltd.)

Notes on completion

Part 3 – Particular Conditions

Items to be completed by the Contractor and the Sub-Contractor *continued*

1   *continued*

[e] If the Sub-Contractor and the Contractor are able to agree a programme for the Sub-Contract Works this should be set out here or on an attached sheet.

[e] (5) Other arrangements:
state whether they are additional to those in items (3) and (4) or whether they supersede the details at items (3) and (4).

57

[f] Clause 5B can only be used where the Contractor under the Value Added Tax (General) Regulations 1985, Regulations 12(3) and 26 or any amendment or re-making thereof has been allowed to prepare the tax documents in substitution for an authenticated receipt issued by the Sub-Contractor under Regulation 12(4) of the above Regulations; and the Sub-Contractor has consented to the use of this method.

2   Conditions NSC/C clause 6·5·2

Insurance cover for any one occurrence or series of occurrences arising out of one event   £

3   Conditions NSC/C clause 4·30·1·2   The Adjudicator is:

Conditions NSC/C clause 4·32·1·2   The Trustee-Stakeholder is:

[g] Clause 5A·5 or clause 5B·5 can only apply where the Sub-Contractor is satisfied at the date the Sub-Contract is entered into that his output tax on all supplies to the Contractor under the Sub-Contract will be at either a positive or a zero rate of tax. Some supplies by the Contractor to the Employer are zero rated by a certificate in statutory form. Only the person holding the certificate, usually the Contractor, may zero rate his supply. Sub-Contract supplies for a main contract zero rate by certificate are standard rated: see the VAT leaflet 708 revised 1989.

4   Conditions NSC/C clause 5A/5B

[f]   Value Added Tax – alternative VAT   clause* 5A / 5B to apply
[g]   provisions   clause 5A·5* to apply / not to apply
                                               clause 5B·5* to apply / not to apply

[h] The entries in item 5 must have regard to the entry in item 4 of NSC/T Part 2 and are to include any other matters in relation to safety or site security as agreed between the Contractor and the Sub-Contractor.

5   [h] Any other matters to be set out here or on an attached sheet.

© 1991 RIBA Publications Ltd   *delete as applicable   **Page 3**

Figure 6.4   (continued)

Part 3 – Particular Conditions

Items to be completed by the Contractor and the Sub-Contractor *continued*

[i] If these changes or additions cause the Sub-Contractor to reconsider his Tender on NSC/T Part 2 so that agreement with the Contractor on, and the signing of, NSC/T Part 3 is delayed see SF 80 clause 35·8·2 and clause 35·9·2.

58

6 [i]   Any changes or additions to the information given in NSC/T Part 1:
item 7: obligations or restrictions imposed by the Employer;
item 8: order of Works:.Employer's requirements;
item 9: type and location of access;
as confirmed in the Nomination Instruction (Nomination NSC/N) issued by the Architect/
the Contract Administrator

7   Conditions NSC/C
Section 9

Settlement of disputes – Arbitration

Appointor (if no appointor is selected the appointor shall be the President or a Vice-President, Royal Institution of Chartered Surveyors)

President or a Vice-President of:
*Royal Institute of British Architects
*Royal Institution of Chartered Surveyors
*Chartered Institute of Arbitrators

Signed by or on behalf
of the Contractor

Date   19

Signed by or on behalf
of the Sub-Contractor

Date   19

*delete as applicable   Page 4

Figure 6.4   (concluded)

If the contractor and subcontractor refuse the nomination or withdraw their tender when the identity of the other is made known to them, or are unable to resolve any differences and comply with the instruction and complete Part 3 within the ten days laid down, the landscape consultant must either extend the period in order to allow the matters to be resolved or, unless the consultant decides the matters in dispute are sufficiently fundamental not to justify his or her insistence that the nomination instruction be complied with, the consultant must revise his or her instructions, omit the work or make another nomination.

Full details of the JCT 80 revised nominated subcontract procedures are given in the JCT Guidance Notes issued in March 1991 as Amendment 10, which should always be referred to for detailed guidance.

SUBCONTRACTS UNDER THE ICE FORM

The standard form of subcontract prepared by the ICE for use with their main form is relatively simple, covering only 19 short clauses on seven pages followed by five schedules:

1. main contract particulars;
2. subcontract documents and the scope of the works;
3. price, retention and period for completion;
4. facilities provided by the contractor; and
5. insurance.

JCLI STANDARD FORM OF TENDER AND CONDITIONS OF SUBCONTRACT FOR LANDSCAPE WORKS

This is for use on domestic, named and nominated subcontracts alike under the JCLI Form and was published in January 1986 (see Appendix 4). Section-headed like the JCLI and JCT Minor Works Forms, it also provides all the main contract information needed by tenderers. The tender form includes daywork charges, tender and subcontract period and, in addition to the normal seven sections for the intentions of the parties, commencement and completion and so on. It includes also a final Section 8 (Temporary Works and Services, Attendance and Related Works) covering temporary site accommodation, welfare facilities, temporary services, use of scaffolding, delivery and storage of materials, removal of rubbish, cutting away and subsurfaces – all of particular interest to a subcontractor intent on submitting a keen price.

CHAPTER

7

LANDSCAPE CONTRACT ADMINISTRATION

EMPLOYER'S AGENT

The landscape consultant's authority to act on behalf of his or her client is laid down in the Landscape Consultant's Appointment, in which the approval of the employer is required before proceeding from one work stage to the next, and which authority can be revoked at any time.

Although the landscape consultant's authority under the JCLI Contract is laid down, he or she is not a party to it. Although the contractor has to comply with all the consultant's instructions, if the contractor considers the consultant is exceeding his or her powers the contractor can also challenge any instruction and submit the matter to adjudication arbitration. The contractor must, however, comply with all valid instructions, and if the consultant has exceeded the client's authority the client is entitled to compensation by the consultant.

It is important also, when the landscape works are being executed as a subcontract of a main construction contract, that all instructions of the landscape consultant are not given to the landscape subcontractor direct but are channelled through the architect or engineer to the main contractor and then from the main contractor to the landscape subcontractor, since only the architect or engineer can give contractual instructions to the main contractor or his subcontractors.

MOBILIZING RESOURCES

In addition to the obligations to the client to monitor the progress, cost and quality of the work, the contract conditions require the landscape consultant to undertake, as agent of the employer, the administration of the contract. This calls for the highest standards of management, technical competence and administrative ability if the client is not to be put to unnecessary expense.

When the landscape consultant's recommendation to accept a tender has been confirmed by the client the tenderer should be informed immediately and arrangements made to put the work on site in hand. It is important to remember that the contractor must be allowed sufficient time to arrange for the appropriate site staff to be made available and to ensure that all labour and materials will be ready when required. Equally, any delay in the start on site and consequently the completion of the work may well involve the client in additional costs, particularly when the contract is on a 'fluctuation' basis.

 PRE-CONTRACT MEETINGS

When the client has confirmed their agreement of the landscape consultant's recommendation on which of the submitted tenders to accept, a pre-contract meeting with the contractor and all other consultants concerned should be arranged, at which the following should be established:

1. *Names, addresses and telephone numbers:* It is always of assistance to all concerned if the names, addresses and telephone numbers of those others involved – architect, quantity surveyor, engineering consultants, clerks of works and contractors' staff – are identified by name and details distributed, either with the agenda or the memorandum of the pre-contract meeting.

2. *Site:* The details of the site, any restrictions as to access, arrangements for operatives' car parking and contractors' working area should be confirmed at the outset.

3. *Contract documents:* The contract sum, dates for commencement and completion, documents to be attached to the Form of Contract, evidence and details of the Contract Bond, insurance and contractors' tax exemption certificates should all be confirmed at this stage.

4. *Specifications and bills of quantities:* The numbers of copies of drawings, specification and/or bills of quantities to be signed by the parties and by whom they are to be retained, together with requests for additional and blank copies and to whom they should be sent, should be ascertained.

5. *Commissioning and maintenance:* Any requirements for commissioning and maintenance manuals and the operation of any mechanical services or equipment, either prior to or after practical completion, should be confirmed.

6. *Statutory obligations:* The need to comply with statutory requirements with regard to noise, building regulations, notices, confirmation of planning consent, tree preservation orders and any local restrictions should noted.

7. *Contract administration:* The requirement for the contractor to supervise the works, to submit a progress chart, and the frequency and responsibility for chairing subcontractors' coordination meetings and carrying out site inspections, should be agreed. The consultant's arrangements for the promulgation and confirmation of oral instructions, the formal issue of written instructions, correspondence, valuations, dayworks and the recording of inclement weather should also be confirmed.

8. *Temporary works:* The contractor's proposals for the location of spoil heaps, site hut, offices and sanitary accommodation, temporary services, and the style, size and location of any site notice-boards both for the client and the contractor must be agreed.

9. *Quality control:* Requirements for samples both of materials and workmanship – for example bricks and pointing, concrete test cubes and grass seed mixes – and arrangements for attendance during the spreading of herbicides, mulches and fertilizers should be confirmed.

10. *Engineering services:* Any arrangements for the coordination of inspections, instructions, further information and approvals of any other consultants and statutory authorities should be clarified.

11. *Subcontractors and suppliers:* The acceptance of responsibility by the landscape contractor for the performance of all subcontractors and suppliers, whether domestic, named or nominated, must be emphasized (see also pp. 159–70).

12. *Frequency and dates of meetings:* The frequency, dates and times of visits by the consultants – whether daily, weekly or monthly – progress meetings and valuations will depend entirely on the adequacy of the contract documents, the complexity of the work and the stage reached. Some degree of formality is, however, essential and it is normal to fix at the outset of each project the dates for at least the regular site visits and progress meetings.

Landscape consultants have then four specific contractual administrative duties which they are required to undertake: those relating to certification, instructions, subcontracts and extending the period for the completion of the works.

 ## CERTIFICATION

PROGRESS PAYMENTS

The contract conditions require a landscape consultant to certify progress payments at intervals of not less than four weeks (or at certain specified stages of the work) in respect of the value of work properly executed to date; these have to be honoured by the employer within 14 days. Should this not happen the contractor is entitled to determine his or her employment having given seven days' prior notice of his or her intention to do so.

The use of the words 'properly executed' should be noted. This allows a landscape consultant to deduct from an Interim Certificate the value of any work improperly executed. It must be emphasized that this does not imply that by including its value in an Interim Certificate the landscape consultant is certifying that the work in question *has* been properly executed.

All contracts envisage that the value of work certified may include 'latent' defects, the existence of which could not have been foreseen at the time of certification and which may only become apparent during the defects liability period or even after the issuing of the Final Certificate. The larger forms of building contract include the phrase 'save as aforesaid [that is, except for items the consultant has reserved for his approval] no certificate shall of itself be conclusive evidence that any works, materials or goods to which it relates are in accordance with the Contract'. The apparent contradiction between these two clauses is explained by interpreting 'properly' as meaning properly executed in accordance with the contract *conditions* and not as a reference to the quality of workmanship or materials.

PRACTICAL COMPLETION

The landscape consultant must also certify the date when in his or her opinion the works have reached 'practical completion'. This is a phrase that has never been defined by the courts but which – as we saw earlier – is considered to signify the stage when the work is sufficiently complete to be safely used for the purpose for which it was designed. Although this is entirely a matter for the opinion of the landscape consultant, and although he or she is under no obligation to give any reasons for having made the decision that such completion has been satisfactorily reached, it is clearly in the interests of the client to have the use of the work for which he or she has already paid as soon as is practicable, without waiting for every last shrub to be planted, or litter bin fixed. There is no obligation, however, for the landscape consultant to prepare a 'snagging' list of defective items but a schedule and programme of work oustanding at Practical Completion is now required by the 1988 revision to JCLI Clause 2.4.

MAKING GOOD DEFECTS

Landscape contractors also have to make good any defects in the hard landscape or any plant failures arising during a specified period after practical completion, a percentage of the contract sum having been withheld to cover such eventualities. The landscape consultant has also a duty to certify when the contractor has made such defects good.

THE FINAL CERTIFICATE

Having received from the contractor all the necessary documentation within three months (or such other period as has been specified in the contract documents) from the date of practical completion, when all defects have been made good the landscape consultant has to issue, within a further 28 days, the Final Certificate covering the balance due to the contractor; this too has to be honoured within a further 14 days.

While landscape consultants can certify that these stages have been achieved by means of a letter to the client, the Landscape Institute has prepared forms (see Figures 7.1, 7.2, 7.3, 7.4 and 7.5) to enable them to discharge this duty accurately and expeditiously.

 ## LANDSCAPE CONSULTANT'S INSTRUCTIONS

Landscape contracts require the consultant, apart from issuing certificates, also to issue any further information necessary for the proper carrying out of the works and to confirm all instructions in writing (Clause 3.5). These are to be carried out by the contractor 'forthwith' (that is, as soon as possible); in the event of the contractor's failing to do so, the landscape consultant can, after seven days' written

Landscape Valuation/Financial Statement

No.

Employer:
address:
Contractor:
address:

Landscape
Architects

Valuation

Contract

Office reference

AUTHORISED EXPENDITURE

ESTIMATED FINAL COST

To amount of Contract   £ _____

To amount of Contract   £ _ _ _ _ _ _ _

Additional authorised expenditure   £ _ _ _ _ _ _ _ _

Less contingencies   £ _ _ _ _ _ _ _ _

£ _ _ _ _ _ _ _ _

Estimated value of Variations to date   +£ _ _ _ _ _ _ _ _

£ _ _ _ _ _ _ _ _

Estimated value of Variations yet to be issued   +£ _ _ _ _ _ _ _ _

£ _ _ _ _ _ _ _ _

Estimated increased costs (if allowable) £ _ _ _ _ _ _ _ _

Estimated increased costs (if allowable) +£ _ _ _ _ _ _ _ _

TOTAL AUTHORISED EXPENDITURE £ _____

ESTIMATED TOTAL COST   £ _____

Signed _____ Landscape Architect. Date _____

Distribution: Client ☐   Quantity surveyor ☐   File ☐   ☐   ☐

Landscape Interim/Final Certificate

No.

Landscape
Architect:
address:

Landscape
Architects
Interim/Final

Certificate

Employer:
address:

Certificate No.   _____

Date of Valuation   _____

Contractor:
address:

Date of Certificate   _____

Valuation of work
executed £ _ _ _ _ _ _ _ _

Value of materials
on site £ _ _ _ _ _ _ _ _

Contract:

£ _ _ _ _ _ _ _ _

Reference:

Less retention £ _ _ _ _ _ _ _ _

I/We hereby certify that under the terms of the Contract

Total to date £ _ _ _ _ _ _ _ _

dated: _____

Less amount previously
certified £ _ _ _ _ _ _ _ _

the sum of (words) _____

TOTAL   £ _____

(Exclusive of any Value Added Tax)

is due from the Employer to the Contractor

Signed _____ Landscape Architect: Date _____

Distribution: Client ☐   Contractor ☐   Quantity surveyor ☐   File ☐   ☐

Figure 7.1   Landscape Interim/Final Certificate. (Reproduced with permission of the Landscape Institute.)

Landscape
Architect's name
and address

Works

situate at

To contractor

Instruction

for Landscape Works

Instruction no.

Under the terms of the Contract

Date

I/We issue the following instructions. Where applicable the contract sum
will be adjusted in accordance with the terms of the relevant Condition.

Instructions	£ omit	£ add

Office
reference

Signed _____ —

Notes

Amount of contract sum £
± Approximate value of previous instructions £ _____
£
± Approximate value of this instruction £ _____
Approximate adjusted total £

Distribution: Client ☐   Contractor ☐   Quantity surveyor ☐   Clerk of works ☐   File ☐

© 1988 The Landscape Institute

Figure 7.2   Landscape Instruction Form. (Reproduced with permission of the Landscape Institute.)

Landscape Architect
address

Employer
address

Works
situated at

Contractor
address

Contract dated

Certificate of

**Non-
completion**

of Landscape Works

Job reference

Serial no.

Issue date

Under the terms of the above mentioned Contract,

I/We certify that the Contractor has failed to complete the Works by the
Date for Completion or within any extended time fixed under the contract
provisions.

To be signed by or for
the issuer named
above.

Signed _____

Date _____

Distribution: Client ☐   Contractor ☐   Quantity surveyor ☐   Clerk of works ☐   File ☐

© 1987 The Landscape Institute

*Figure 7.3   Landscape Certificate of Non-Completion. (Reproduced with
permission of the Landscape Institute.)*

Landscape Architect
address

Employer
address

Works
situated at

Contractor
address

Contract dated

Certificate of

**Practical
Completion**

of Landscape Works

Job reference

Serial No.

Issue date

Under the terms of the above mentioned Contract,

I/We certify that Practical Completion was achieved and the works taken into possession on

_____ 19 _____

the Defects Liability period
for faults other than plant failures will expire on

_____ 19 _____

for shrubs, ordinary nursery stock trees and other plants will expire on

_____ 19 _____

for semi mature and advanced nursery stock trees will expire on

_____ 19 _____

The Employer should note that as from date of issue of this Certificate of Practical Completion of the Works the Employer becomes solely responsible for insurance of the Works.

To be signed by or for
the issuer named
above.

Signed _____

Date _____

Distribution: Client ☐   Contractor ☐   Quantity surveyor ☐   Clerk of works ☐   File ☐

© 1987 The Landscape Institute

Figure 7.4   Landscape Certificate of Practical Completion. (Reproduced with permission of the Landscape Institute.)

Landscape Architect
address

Employer
address

Works
situated at

Contractor
address

Contract dated

Certificate of
Completion of

**Making good
defects**

of Landscape Works

Job reference

Serial No.

Issue date

Under the terms of the above mentioned Contract,

I/We hereby certify that the defects, shrinkages and other faults specified
in the schedule of defects delivered to the Contractor as an instruction have
in my/our opinion been made good.

This Certificate refers to:

The Works described in the Certificate of Practical Completion
Serial No. _____   dated _____

Signed _____

Date _____

Distribution: Client ☐   Contractor ☐   Quantity surveyor ☐   Clerk of works ☐   File ☐

© 1987 The Landscape Institute

Figure 7.5   *Landscape Certificate of Making Good Defects. (Reproduced with permission of the Landscape Institute.)*

notice and if the contractor has still not complied, instruct others to complete the work and deduct the cost from the balance of any money due to the contractor.

Any instructions to the contractor that have been given by the landscape consultant orally must be confirmed in writing within two days. To cover such eventualities consultants will either keep a duplicate pad on site, on which to confirm site instructions, or include written confirmation in memoranda of site visits and progress meetings. Instructions given by telephone can be confirmed by letter or by directions from the clerk of works if one has been appointed. It is normally convenient to cover instructions which do not have any monetary significance in this way. Where instructions are made which do have a monetary significance, these should be written down on the Landscape Institute's printed Instruction Form (see Figure 7.2). When such an arrangement is adopted it is useful to ask the contractor to notify the consultant of any instructions not yet covered by such a form, if the contractor considers them to have a monetary value, so that an instruction can be issued accordingly.

Instructions must always be orderly, precise and unambiguous, so as to indicate clearly both what action is required and by whom it should be performed. While telephones can be used for simple instructions and resolving question and answer problems, which are subsequently to be confirmed in writing, they are never suitable for complicated, difficult or delicate matters, for which personal meetings may be the only answer. Sufficient time can then be allocated for the problem to be investigated in depth.

Telephone messages left with the telephonist, even without specific requests to return the call, should always be recorded in writing and given to the individual concerned on their return to the office. Telephones should always be answered immediately and conversations kept brief and to the point. Telephones should not be used for lengthy or difficult discussions. Any call likely to last more than 10 minutes is always better covered by a letter or memorandum. Remember also that telephone calls nearly always interrupt the recipient, who is usually engaged on other equally important tasks, and it may well be better to put any problems or recommendations in writing and wait for a considered reply.

VARIATIONS

Landscape consultants must issue instructions for the expenditure of any PC or provisional sums and any addition, omission, or change in the works or the order or period in which they are to be carried out. These usually arise from a change in the employer's requirements (or lack of appreciation of what had been included in the contract) or from the realization by the landscape consultant either that a particular problem could be resolved in a better way or that a certain problem had been overlooked or forgotten. In any event the ability for the consultant to instruct changes is an essential requirement in any project. It is very rare for a designer to invent a perfect prototype without the need for further instructions.

It is very important, however, to ensure that this ability for the landscape consultant to issue instructions to the contractor to vary the contract is not abused, either by the consultant falling prey to second thoughts at too late a state ('wouldn't it be better if') or by their holding up the progress of the works through a delay in responding to a request for further information or instructions after the date on which the contractor had reasonably requested them.

The valuation of variations in accordance with the rates in the contract documents will rarely give a landscape contractor the proper recompense for the disruption and cost involved, the responsibility for their valuation on 'a fair and reasonable basis' being solely that of the consultant, using where relevant the prices in the priced specification, schedules, bills of quantities or schedule of rates. Although the contract provides for valuations to be agreed between the contractor and consultant prior to the work being carried out, this is all too rarely achieved. In practice a contractor will often price variations him- or herself and submit them to the consultant who will, if they appear to be reasonable, accept them without question. Contractually, however, it is the consultant's responsibility to value the variations, normally in accordance with the following building contract conventions:

1. the same work under similar conditions at the contract rates or prices;
2. similar work under different conditions based on contract rates;
3. different work for which no rates exist at fair and reasonable rates; and
4. work that cannot be measured at daywork rates.

If the variation involves a significant change in the scope or quantity of work, the contract provides for the effect of this on the contract rate or price to be taken into account.

CORRESPONDENCE

All letters and drawings whether delivered to the office by post or hand should be formally stamped with the date of receipt and distributed to the partner or staff concerned in an orderly, regular and not haphazard way. Whenever possible letters, e-mail and voice mail messages should be replied to on the date on which they are received and, when acted upon, filed daily in chronological order by the individual or secretarial staff concerned.

MEETINGS

It is important to remember that the meetings in which landscape consultants are involved are rarely 'committee' meetings wherein a number of people meet to reach a decision based on the majority vote of its members and from which the minority cannot disassociate themselves on a major point of issue without resigning, with the chairperson having a casting vote but the whole committee being collectively responsible for the decisions reached.

In contrast to such a way of reaching decisions, most consultants' meetings, both 'design team' and site progress meetings, are different in that subordinates and other consultants advise the lead consultant within their own individual sphere of responsibility so that the latter can come to a decision within the wider implications of the whole project.

Progress meetings are also 'information' meetings at which information about activities and operations can be exchanged and recorded, subsequently to be stated in a memorandum of the meeting confirming the decisions reached, what further action or information is required and from whom. Such memoranda are not minutes of a meeting attempting to precis and record the discussion. They should be confined solely to recording, in a clear and factual way, the matters discussed and the decisions taken.

DAYWORKS

The valuation of work that cannot be measured and which can only be valued on a 'daywork' basis – that is, on the actual cost of labour and materials used – must always be authorized beforehand (after reference to a quantity surveyor if necessary), and it is important to check not only that the rates and prices are correct but that the quantity of labour and materials are also reasonable, the contractor still being required to carry out the work as expeditiously, efficiently and economically as possible.

The valuation of work on a daywork basis consists of the actual (prime) cost to the contractor of labour, materials and plant, to which are added his or her incidental costs, overheads and profit evaluated and expressed as a percentage addition. The definitions of each are defined in their respective sections and published jointly by the RICS and BEC for the Building Industry *Definition of Prime Cost of Daywork carried out under a Building Contract* for building work and by the Federation of Civil Engineering Contractors for civil engineering works.

Variations valued on this basis must clearly be to a contractor's advantage since they entail the reimbursement of the contractor's actual costs together with the profit to which the contractor is entitled, irrespective of any fees for other work performed for the employer which the contractor has included in his or her tender and which may, due to unforeseen circumstances, now be less than the actual cost to the contractor. It is rare for contractors to suggest that variations be valued on a dayworks basis when the reverse is the case!

However, there are obviously situations – for example locating existing underground services, or site clearance to remove debris and large obstructions arising during subsoiling and tree surgery – where there is no other equitable way of fairly and reasonably measuring the work.

The same principles apply to the evaluation and correction of any errors or inconsistencies within or between the contract documents which may come to light after the contract has commenced and which may or may not constitute a variation to the contract sum.

Most contracts provide for the appointment of a 'competent person in charge' to be on site at all reasonable times as the contractor's representative, with authority to accept such instructions. This must be strictly adhered to if the problems of *Woodman* v. *Clayton* (1956), where the consultant was held to be liable having given instructions to a bricklayer direct and not through the contractor's site agent, are to be avoided.

Similar provisions are enacted entitling the landscape consultant to issue instructions for the exclusion of any person from the works, although this power must never be exercised lightly and only used in the most extreme circumstances.

PRIME COST (PC) AND PROVISIONAL SUMS

Circumstances also arise when the scope of some part of the work cannot be foreseen in the necessary detail at the outset – for example tree surgery – in which case contractors are instructed to include in their tender a provisional sum for the work inclusive of the contractor's profit and any attendance required. When at some later stage the full extent of the work is known, the consultant can then omit the provisional sum and instruct the contractor as to the full extent of the work required.

An appropriate prime cost (PC) sum can be included in the tender documents by a clause such as:

> Include the PC sum of £ ...... for .... work to be executed by a specialist subcontractor and allow .... weeks for its execution at an appropriate stage in the contract. Add for profit and attendance.

 ## SUBCONTRACT ADMINISTRATION

When the identity of the subcontractor is known at the time of preparation of the tender documents it is advisable for the name of the firm selected to be stated also in these documents. Should this not be possible, then the contract provides for the right of reasonable objection to be exercised by the main contractor when either the identity of the subcontractor concerned is made known to him or her or if the subcontractor requires the incorporation of any conditions in the subcontract which may impose on the main contractor any conditions which are contrary to those incorporated into his or her own contract with the employer (Clause 3.6). To minimize the chances of this occurring the JCLI has produced a four-page Standard Form of Tender and Conditions of Subcontract (see Appendix 4), the conditions of which mirror exactly those of the JCLI Main Form.

When the contract is let, a formal Instruction is issued to the main contractor to omit the PC sum and accept the tender of the subcontractor selected.

Some contracts for landscape works are often part of a building contract and have to be carried out concurrently and as a subcontract under the building contractor. In that case the appropriate subcontract standard forms of tender and subcontract conditions must be followed and used. Applying to all building subcontracts, the procedures for domestic, listed, named and nominated subcontracts are more detailed than those of JCLI and are described more fully on pp. 159–70.

EXTENSIONS TO THE CONTRACT PERIOD AND DISTURBANCE OF REGULAR PROGRESS

Landscape contracts provide for the contractor to notify the consultant 'if it becomes apparent the works will not be *completed* by the Contract Completion date for reasons beyond the control of the contractor'.

In building contracts there are 12 such relevant events beyond the control of the contractor (see Table 6.1 on page 138), the most important of which are:

1. *force majeure* (caused by Acts of God?);
2. loss or damage to the works by fire, storm, flood and so on;
3. civil commotion or strikes;
4. compliance with the landscape consultant's instructions;
5. delays in the receipt of such instructions; and
6. delays by nominated subcontractors.

These constitute a sound basis for evaluating 'reasons beyond the control of the contractor'. Should any of these arise then the contractor must notify the consultant who then makes in writing such extension of the period for completion as may be reasonable (Clause 2.2). In addition, should the contractor notify the consultant of any direct loss and expense incurred by reason of the *progress* of the work having been delayed for reasons that were within the control of the employer, then the consultant must ascertain the amount of such loss and expense involved and include it in any progress payments due.

The exercise of the judgement in respect of the extent of any extension granted calls for considerable skill and experience on the part of the landscape consultant, bearing in mind that:

○ extensions involve only delays to completion not progress;
○ many delays are concurrent and not consecutive;
○ some delays are on the critical path and some are not; and
○ some delays are within and some outside the control of the contractor.

It must also be remembered that while the consultant should notify the contractor of the extension granted and advise the latter of the events the consultant has taken into account as soon as possible, the consultant is under no obligation to give any reasons nor the individual amounts of the delays he or she has taken into account.

The advantages of coming to a decision while the events are still fresh in everyone's mind are obvious, but it is equally essential to give a decision before the contract date for completion, so that the contractor knows where he or she stands and can arrange accordingly, and also to prevent damages from becoming 'at large' and thereby obliging the employer to prove the loss or damage he or she has suffered instead of being able to rely on the 'pre-estimate' fixed beforehand and included in the contract.

However, should the consultant be of the opinion that completion of the works was not delayed for reasons beyond the control of the contractor, or progress was not delayed on account of any action of the employer, then the employer is entitled to deduct such liquidated damages as were stated in the contract conditions as being due for each week or part of a week that the works remain uncompleted beyond the contract completion date.

Should the consultant reject an application for an extension or for the reimbursement of direct loss and expense, it should be remembered that the latest conditions of appointment provide for the reimbursement by the client of the consultant's time involved. It is also the responsibility of the consultant to ensure that the amount of liquidated and ascertained damages per week provides not only for the reimbursement to the client of the financial costs incurred in payments already made, without the client's having the use of the works, but also for the reimbursement of the landscape consultant's costs incurred in additional site visits until practical completion is achieved by the contractor.

DETERMINATION

The financial consequences of either the employer or the contractor determining the contract are great, and termination of a contract should therefore never be embarked on without competent and experienced legal advice (see pp. 154–5).

The only grounds for the employer to terminate a contract are the lack of diligence of the contractor, if the contractor *wholly* suspends the carrying out of the works, or if the contractor becomes bankrupt.

There are similar grounds for the contractor to terminate a contract, namely: 1) the employer's failure to make progress payments by the due date, 2) if the employer interferes with or obstructs the carrying out of the works or fails to make the site available, 3) if the employer suspends the work or becomes bankrupt, or 4) if the employer fails to comply with the CDM Regulations.

In any such case the decision is not a matter for the consultants (although their opinion will no doubt be sought) but for the employer or contractor on the advice of their lawyers, and there must be strict adherence to the proper procedures laid down with regard to matters such as notification.

PROFESSIONAL OBLIGATIONS TO THE CLIENT

In addition to their administrative duties under the contract, landscape consultants also have responsibilities under the terms of their appointment with their client to advise the latter:

1. if the contract period is likely to be exceeded;
2. if the contract sum is likely to be increased; and
3. that the quality of workmanship and materials is generally in accordance with the contract.

IF THE CONTRACT PERIOD IS LIKELY TO BE EXCEEDED

The speed of construction and arrangements for the supply of the necessary labour and materials are solely matters under the control of the landscape contractor, regardless of whether or not delays are caused by the employer and therefore justify an extension of the contract period for completion of the works. The provision of a master programme, on which is indicated the critical path of several concurrent activities which must be completed before the next can be commenced, affords an essential tool to any contract, both for the contractor in properly managing the project and for the landscape consultant in monitoring its progress. Regular site visits to compare the progress actually achieved with that which was intended also make it relatively simple for the landscape consultant to advise his or her client if in the consultant's opinion the date for completion of the works is unlikely to be met. It is therefore useful to require the contractor to submit, a few days before each regular progress meeting, a report such as that indicated in Figure 7.6, which the landscape consultant can then discuss and check with the contractor on site.

IF THE CONTRACT SUM IS LIKELY TO BE INCREASED

The only person who can alter or control the cost of a landscape project is the consultant, since only the consultant can instruct the contractor to vary the work and it is the consultant who is responsible for the valuation of such variations in accordance with the rules laid down.

If landscape consultants complete and forward to the client the upper part of the financial statement attached to each Form of Interim Certificate (see Figure 7.1) for progress payments, few problems should arise since the client will be continuously appraised of the estimated

Document Ref.

K/CONPRO/Prelim.

Page No. ....

CONTRACTORS MONTHLY PROGRESS REPORT   for month of   ....

Report No. ....

Contractor ....

Contract   ....   Contract Ref. No. ....

---

1. <u>CONTRACT</u>

Contract commencement date   ... Contract completion date ...

Contract duration   ... Target completion date   ...

Weeks elapsed   ... Weeks remaining   ...

Contract sum   ... Value certified to date   ...

Inclement weather: rain/frost this month ...... total to date ......
Extension claimed ...... days. Extension agreed ...... days.

2. <u>PROGRESS</u>

REF:	ITEM:	% work programmed	% work achieved	weeks ahead/ behind	reason for change/ delay action taken

---

Overall percentage work programmed to date ....%

work completed to date ....%

Figure 7.6   Monthly report on contractor's progress

3. Shortages of labour, plant and materials   Action
taken

4. Subcontract difficulties and delays   Action taken

5. <u>Monthly Schedule of Outstanding Information Required</u>

REF: ITEM: Date required   Date received

Date: Prepared by:

Figure 7.6   (concluded)

final cost of the project and be able to take such action as is necessary if it appears the authorized expenditure might be exceeded.

MAKING SITE VISITS TO ENSURE THE QUALITY OF WORKMANSHIP AND MATERIALS

While the provision of the necessary labour and materials in accordance with the contract documents is a matter entirely within the responsibility of the landscape contractor, in practice, if the contractor is to submit the lowest tender in competition, he or she will include only for the lowest standard of workmanship and materials necessary to meet the specification, no more and no less.

It is the duty of the consultant, therefore, while not expected to be on site permanently, to visit the site at intervals, not to supervise but at least to monitor, inspect and check the work on the client's behalf, so as to ensure that the contractor and his or her workforce have interpreted the contract documents correctly and that the work has been carried out generally in accordance with the contract.

While there is no specific provision for a clerk of works in the JCLI Contract, there is no reason why one should not be appointed, if it is considered that constant supervision of the work of the contractor is required. It must be remembered, however, that such a person is there solely as an inspector on behalf of the employer, and has no responsibility to the contractor for quality control nor any powers to give any instructions to the contractor. When a clerk of works is considered necessary, it is normally better for him or her to be employed by the client direct although working under the direction of the landscape consultant; this avoids the possibility of the landscape consultant having to take responsibility for any errors the clerk of works might make. The consultant is, however, still responsible for setting the minimum standards which the contractor should meet.

Inspections carried out by landscape consultants at regular intervals are not sufficient to ensure compliance with the contract requirements and flexibility is essential to ensure the consultant's attendance on site at the crucial stages of a project, particularly for those items which are to be covered up subsequently. Such inspections should be made on a predictive basis, the critical stages being listed in the contract documents together with the requirement that the contractor should not be allowed to put the next stage of the work in hand without giving the landscape consultant at least 48 hours' prior notice that the previous stage has been completed and is ready for inspection. In this way the contractor will not be held up. Suggested stages for landscape projects are the following:

1. setting out;
2. excavation to remove topsoil and formation levels;
3. collection and spreading of materials already on site;
4. testing and spreading topsoil and applying herbicides;
5. ground preparation and the application of any fertilizer;
6. grass seeding;
7. hardcore beds for paving;
8. laying concrete and paving;
9. excavation of tree pits;
10. delivery and temporary storage of plants and other materials on site;
11. watering; and
12. maintenance visits.

Other items – for example tree surgery, plants, brickwork and pointing – which are difficult to describe or specify accurately can only be achieved by limiting their execution to certain subcontractors or suppliers of the consultant's own choosing or by giving the consultant the task of approving the particular item of the work. Since this then relieves the contractor of any further responsibility for its adequacy, such items should be kept to the absolute minimum necessary.

The stage at which these approvals are given will depend on the individual circumstances. Some can and should be given at the moment of their construction or delivery to site, others only after a sufficient period of time to establish their survival, efficacy or performance in use, or at the end of the defects liability or maintenance period.

Such approvals must, however, be given as soon as it is possible to do so if the contractor is not to be unfairly penalized by condemning, at a later stage, some item which could have been rejected much earlier before it was incorporated in the works, covered up or planted. It is equally important that an approval once given should not be reversed without a subsequent very good and valid reason.

Some specified landscape items – particularly herbicides, fertilizers, polymers and chemicals – are difficult to identify after they have been applied, without subsequent expensive analysis and tests. Since it is neither fair to other tenderers nor right for the employer to pay for an inferior substitute or something which they have not received at all, particular care should be taken to inspect the work at the same time as such items are being applied.

Specification clauses for such items should therefore require proof of their purchase to be provided and prior notice of their delivery to site and subsequent application. Advice of delivery and delivery notes should be verified at the time of delivery, copies of purchase notes alone being inadequate. Delivery notes must always include the name of the contractor, the type, quality and quantity of the materials supplied, and the name of the particular contract for which they are intended, if double presentation of the same proof of purchase for different contracts is to be avoided.

CHAPTER

8

DISPUTE RESOLUTION

 THE CODE OF CONDUCT

Members of the Chartered Landscape Institute are required to comply with the Institute's Code of Professional Conduct (see Appendix 1), which includes the obligation to 'promote the highest standard of professional services in the application of the arts and sciences of landscape architecture and management' and to 'interpret the conditions of contract with fairness as between their client or employer and the contractor'.

Should any client, employer, contractor or even member of the public consider a chartered member (and only a chartered member since the profession has no protection of title, anyone being able to call themselves a landscape architect, manager or scientist) has breached this Code they can inform the Institute who will then investigate the complaint; if the complaint is proven the Institute may reprimand, admonish, suspend or expel the member.

The Institute, however, has no powers to fine, compensate or make an award for any damages the complainant has suffered, even if the member has been convicted of a criminal offence, especially one resulting in a suspended or custodial sentence.

The Institute cannot become involved in disputes between a landscape consultant and his or her client or employer, such as an alleged breach of Conditions of Appointment in respect of fees due or inspection of the work in progress, unless they form part of a pattern of a number of similar complaints; nor can the Institute investigate complaints by contractors that the consultant has undervalued variations or has not granted an application for an extension to the contract period. These are matters for conciliation, adjudication, arbitration or litigation.

In certain circumstances it can, however, if requested by one of the parties concerned, recommend the appointment of a senior member of the Institute as a conciliator or mediator who will attempt to effect a reconciliation between the parties, although his or her recommendation may not be accepted by either or both of the parties.

 ## ALTERNATIVE DISPUTE RESOLUTION (ADR)

Notwithstanding the lack of a proper definition of the difference between mediation and conciliation, the advantages of attempting to resolve disputes by methods other than the now long-drawn-out procedures of arbitration and litigation have much to commend them, despite the fact that unless previously agreed to be so the result is non-binding on the parties involved.

These Alternative Dispute Resolution (ADR) provisions were brought into force by SI 96/2352 (C61) on 11 September 1996.

If the contract does not comply with these requirements the provisions of the 'Adjudication Scheme for Construction Contracts' published by the Department of the Environment, Transport and the Regions will apply. This Scheme was brought into effect under SI/649 as an alternative to the more detailed complaint procedures published by the JCT or the Official Referees Solicitors Association (ORSA), which many will prefer to use.

 ## ARBITRATION

In 1988 the JCLI Conditions of Contract introduced, in revision 5 to the Arbitration Article 4, a new section 9 (Settlement of Disputes – Arbitration), with five separate arbitration clauses setting out the powers and procedures for the appointment of an arbitrator to settle disputes arising under the contract. It must be remembered that since the landscape consultant is only the client's agent and not one of the parties to the contract, it is the client and not the consultant who becomes the claimant or respondent in the arbitration (unless of course the dispute is between the client and the consultant in respect of an alleged breach of the consultant's Conditions of Appointment).

The advantages of arbitration over litigation are often challenged by solicitors and lawyers, and each case must be considered individually on its merits before deciding on the best course of action; however, it is generally accepted that the advantages arbitration affords are that:

1. The hearing is in private with only the parties to the dispute, their experts and witnesses present.
2. The time and place of the hearing can be arranged at relatively short notice to suit the convenience of all concerned and not just the court.
3. If the parties want a fair, just and binding decision, this can be arrived at more quickly than in the courts.
4. The person chosen or nominated as arbitrator will usually be conversant with the technical aspects of the problem.
5. The award of the arbitrator is confidential and not made known to anyone other than the parties unless they so wish or appeal to the court.
6. The award is final and binding and can only be appealed against on legal grounds or errors on the part of the arbitrator.

 ## MEDIATION

Whereas in the past the long-standing legal principle that any evidence by one party should always be disclosed to or given in the presence of the other was observed, mediation permits the mediator, after a preliminary meeting with both parties, to discuss with each party separately and in confidence the strengths and weaknesses of each of their viewpoints and the consequences of their failure to agree, in an attempt by 'shuttle diplomacy' or 'caucasing' to achieve a compromise acceptable to both parties; however, the mediator makes no recommendation as to the solution to the problem.

 ## CONCILIATION

In this instance, while again hearing both sides' allegations separately from a 'without prejudice' standpoint, the conciliator makes a recommendation which in his or her opinion is the most equitable solution to the dispute. However, neither party is under an obligation to be bound by the conciliator's decision unless an agreement has previously been reached by the two parties that the decision shall be binding on both of them.

 ## ADJUDICATION

Originating in JCT contracts with nominated subcontractors (to provide them with a temporary resolution of a dispute involving 'set off'

or the withholding of monies due) and in the ICE Form of Contract (where it is called conciliation), adjudication was put forward as a solution in the Latham Report ('Constructing the Team', HMSO, 1994) to overcome the time taken by arbitration and litigation procedures to resolve disputes between employer and contractor, the Report ignoring the existence of JCT Arbitration Rules 5 and 7 laying down alternative procedures with written or oral evidence only and requiring an award to be made within four to six weeks from the adjudicator having notified the parties of having accepted his or her appointment.

As a consequence of the Latham Report the 1996 Housing Grants, Construction and Regeneration Act, Part II, Section 108(1) states:

> A party to a construction contract has the right to refer a dispute arising under the contract for adjudication under a procedure complying with this section.

The earlier Section 104 (before going on to define 'construction operations' in Section 105 as including site clearance, earth moving and landscaping) confirms 'construction operations' as including an agreement to provide advice 'on the laying out of landscape'.

Section 108(2) goes on to require the dispute to be referred to the adjudicator within seven days of one of the parties giving notice of the dispute to the adjudicator and the adjudicator to reach a decision within 28 days of the referral, or such longer period as is agreed by the parties after the dispute was referred, or within a further 14 days, if required by the adjudicator and consented to by the party by whom the dispute was referred (see Figure 8.1).

The decision of the adjudicator is binding until the dispute is finally determined by legal proceedings (or by arbitration if the contract provides for it), or if the parties reach an agreement, or if the parties accept the decision of the adjudicator as finally determining the dispute.

 ## THE JCLI ARBITRATION CLAUSES

Because an arbitration clause exists in the JCLI Contract Conditions signed and accepted by both parties, any attempt to have the dispute resolved in a small claims court, the Crown Court or the Official Referees High Court will be 'stayed' by the judge for the dispute to be resolved by arbitration, and only brought back to him or her if the arbitrator (or one of the parties appealing after the publication of the award) considers a point of law has arisen which requires resolution by the court. As stated by Lord Carswell in the 1997 appeal in *Beaufort*

PART II

Adjudication

108.—(1) A party to a construction contract has the right to refer a dispute arising under the contract for adjudication under a procedure complying with this section.

Right to refer disputes to adjudication.

For this purpose "dispute" includes any difference.

(2) The contract shall—

    (a) enable a party to give notice at any time of his intention to refer a dispute to adjudication;

    (b) provide a timetable with the object of securing the appointment of the adjudicator and referral of the dispute to him within 7 days of such notice;

    (c) require the adjudicator to reach a decision within 28 days of referral or such longer period as is agreed by the parties after the dispute has been referred;

    (d) allow the adjudicator to extend the period of 28 days by up to 14 days, with the consent of the party by whom the dispute was referred;

    (e) impose a duty on the adjudicator to act impartially; and

    (f) enable the adjudicator to take the initiative in ascertaining the facts and the law.

(3) The contract shall provide that the decision of the adjudicator is binding until the dispute is finally determined by legal proceedings, by arbitration (if the contract provides for arbitration or the parties otherwise agree to arbitration) or by agreement.

The parties may agree to accept the decision of the adjudicator as finally determining the dispute.

(4) The contract shall also provide that the adjudicator is not liable for anything done or omitted in the discharge or purported discharge of his functions as adjudicator unless the act or omission is in bad faith, and that any employee or agent of the adjudicator is similarly protected from liability.

(5) If the contract does not comply with the requirements of subsections (1) to (4), the adjudication provisions of the Scheme for Construction Contracts apply.

(6) For England and Wales, the Scheme may apply the provisions of the Arbitration Act 1996 with such adaptations and modifications as appear to the Minister making the scheme to be appropriate.

1996 c. 23.

For Scotland, the Scheme may include provision conferring powers on courts in relation to adjudication and provision relating to the enforcement of the adjudicator's decision.

Figure 8.1   Housing Grants, Construction and Regeneration Act 1996, Section 108 – Adjudication

Development Ltd. v. *Gilbert Ash*, 'the arbitrator can only substitute his opinion as to the parties' rights having applied the provisions of the contract to the facts'.

The Arbitration Act 1996 in 110 Sections, four Schedules comprising 59 pages repeals and consolidates the earlier Acts with the stated aim of obtaining a fair resolution of disputes by an impartial tribunal without unnecessary delay or expense, the parties to be free to agree how the disputes are resolved. Under the terms of the Act, the court will not intervene unless the interests of the public are involved.

Article 4 and Clause 9.1 provide for the settlement of any dispute arising during the progress of the work, after completion, or after determination (other than disputes relating to value added tax or the Statutory Tax Deduction Scheme). Such disputes shall be referred to arbitration under Clause 9 and if the parties cannot agree on an arbitrator (which they rarely can, each side thinking the person proposed by the other is likely to be favourably disposed towards the proposer), then an arbitrator is to be nominated by the President or a Vice President of the Landscape Institute.

Clause 9.2 gives the arbitrator power to open up, review and revise any certificates, opinions, requirements, notices or instructions of the landscape consultant. This power is not given to judges unless they are appointed to settle the dispute as an 'arbitrator'.

Clause 9.3 makes the award final and binding unless a dissatisfied party can obtain leave to appeal under sections 67, 68 or 69 of the 1996 Arbitration Act; such an appeal must be made solely on the grounds of a question of law which substantially affects the rights of one or more of the parties, and follows a House of Lords judgment that leave should only be given when the point at issue is applicable to standard contracts and not to one-off situations.

Clause 9.4 deals with the eventuality of the death of the arbitrator (or of that person otherwise ceasing to be an arbitrator) before making his or her final award; in such an eventuality a successor must be appointed who must abide by all the previous arbitrator's directions and awards unless required to do otherwise by agreement of the parties or the operation of the law.

Clause 9.5 requires the arbitration to be conducted in accordance with the JCT Arbitration Rules current at the date of the contract, or in accordance with any subsequent amendments if the parties so request.

Before arbitration procedures can be commenced, proper notification must be given by the claimant to the respondent. A letter on the following lines should suffice:

Dear Sirs,

Whereas disputes and differences have arisen between you and ourselves within the meaning of Article 4 of the Contract dated .... between .... and .... I here give you notice of our intention to have such differences settled by arbitration in accordance with the provisions of the Article.

Yours faithfully,

THE JCT AND CIMAR ARBITRATION RULES

Both these sets of procedural rules provide the options of:

1. A documents-only procedure requiring the statements of claim, defence and counter-claim (if any) to be exchanged within four/six weeks of the arbitrator's directions and the award to be published within a further four weeks, the costs of the arbitration being borne by the losing party.
    or
2. A short procedure with a hearing to be held within three weeks of the arbitrator's directions, any documents in support of the oral submissions to be served seven days prior to the hearing and the award to be published orally at the hearing and/or in writing within seven days of the hearing, both sides bearing their own costs.
    or
3. A full procedure with the service of statements of case and reply by claimant and respondent, together with counter-claim, witness statements and experts' reports consecutively at four-weekly intervals, followed by a hearing at which the parties give their evidence and are cross-examined over a period which takes several days at least and on conclusion of which the arbitrator has a further four weeks before publishing his or her award in writing, including directions for the losing party to pay the arbitrator's, their own and the costs of the successful party. When large amounts of money are involved, arbitrations under the full procedure are now as lengthy, costly and little different from disputes taken to the High Court.

Figure 8.2 shows JCT Arbitration Rules 5, 6 and 7 regarding differentiation.

 ## LITIGATION

If, for whatever reason, it is decided to resolve a dispute by litigation, this will be achieved through a default summons being issued by a county court, a writ by the High Court, or the Official Referees Court which deals only with disputes related to construction.

Should the dispute, for example, arise from a landscape consultant suing for fees outstanding, this will inevitably result in a counter-claim for professional negligence of one sort or another, however fanciful or unjustified.

In the case of county courts, defended claims for less than £5 000 are automatically referred to arbitration unless one party requests or the court decides otherwise. Claims in excess of £5 000 can also go to arbitration if both parties agree or the court orders it. Arbitration by the court involves an informal hearing taking place in private instead of a formal trial held in public.

Proceedings in court differ little from arbitrations under the Arbitration Act; the relevant procedural rules give standard directions for the exchange of particulars, evidence and witness statements in support of the plaintiff and the defence, and for setting a date for the trial at the next date available by the court, taking into account the estimated duration of the trial.

Most proceedings involve the appointment by each side of an expert witness to explain the technical issues in the case and to give an opinion based on his or her own experience as to the standards expected and the respective responsibilities of the parties.

Rules to be adopted if the parties agree

	Choice of Rules	Discovery	Documents	Oral evidence	Timetable extensions	Security and award of costs
RULE 5	Applies unless parties want Rules 6 or 7	If required	Full but no discovery	Nil	Extensions by arbitrator limited	Awarded (and taxed) by arbitrator
RULE 6	Applies if the arbitrator decides or the parties so request	If required	Full with experts and full discovery	Full	Arbitrator shall dismiss or extend. Timetable in Rules – (not by arbitrator) 12–26 weeks = 6 months + hearing	Awarded (and taxed) by arbitrator
RULE 7	Only if requested by claimant and agreed to by respondent	Unlikely to be necessary	Few and additional written evidence discouraged	Full	4–6 weeks	Low. Not awarded (borne by parties)

(1) Arbitrator has power to dismiss through lack of prosecution by claimant.
(2) Joinder provisions available.
(3) Note this is only a summary. The JCT Arbitration Rules should be referred to for full details.

Figure 8.2 JCT Arbitration Rules 5, 6 and 7 (Differentiation)

REFERENCES

Clamp, H. (1993) *The Shorter Forms of Building Contract* (3rd edn), London: Granada.

Clamp, H. (1995) *Landscape Contract Manual* (2nd edn), London: Spons.

Cobham, R. (ed.) (1990) *Amenity Landscape Management*, London: Spons.

Construction Industry Advisory Council (1995) *Designing for Health and Safety in Construction*, London: HMSO.

Cooling, P., Shacklock, V. and Scarrett, D. (1993) *Legislation for the Built Environment*, Wimbledon: Donhead Publishing.

Health and Safety Executive (1994), *Managing Construction and Approved Code of Practice (CDM)*, London: HMSO.

Heap, D. (1991) *An Outline of Planning Law* (10th edn), London: Sweet and Maxwell.

Institute of Environment Assessment and Landscape Institute (1995) *Guidelines for Landscape and Visual Impact Assessment*, London: Sweet and Maxwell.

Joint Council for Landscape Industries (1989) *Tree and Shrubs List for Landscape Planting*, London: Landscape Institute.

Joint Council for Landscape Industries (1994) *Herbaceous Plant List for Landscape Planting*, Reading: Horticultural Trades Association.

Keating, D. (1995) *The Law and Practice of Building Contracts* (6th edn), London: Sweet and Maxwell.

Landscape Institute (1996) *Engaging a Landscape Consultant: Guidance for Clients on Fees*, London: LI.

Landscape Institute (1996) *Housing Grant, Construction and Regeneration Act Seminar Delegate Pack*, London: LI.

Landscape Institute (1996) *Regulations for Practice Regulation*, London : LI.

Landscape Institute (1996) *Technical Bulletin Watering Restrictions and Watering Specification*, London: LI.

Landscape Institute (1997) *CDM Seminar Delegate Pack*, London: LI.

Landscape Institute (1997) *NBS Landscape and HTA Plant Specification Seminar Delegate Pack*, London: LI.

Speight, A. and Stone, G. (1990) *The Architect's Legal Handbook* (5th edn), London: Butterworth.

Telling, A.F. and Duxbury, R. (1993) *Planning Law and Procedure* (9th edn), London: Butterworth.

Uff, J. (1991) *Construction Law* (5th edn), London: Sweet and Maxwell.

APPENDICES

Many of the codes of professional conduct, forms of contract and subcontract, and government guidance on landscape work previously referred to in the main text are covered in the following Appendices, and include:

1   The Landscape Institute Code of Professional Conduct

2   The Landscape Consultant's Appointment

3   The JCLI Standard Form of Agreement for Landscape Works

4   The JCLI Standard Form of Tender and Conditions of Subcontract

5   The JCT 80 Standard Form of Tender for Nominated Sub-Contracts

6   The JCLI Supplement to the JCT Intermediate Form IFC 84

7   List of Recent Statutory Acts, Statutory Instruments – Regulations/Orders – DETR Circulars and Planning Policy Guidance Notes relating to the Environment

Appendices 1–4 and 6 are reproduced by permission of the Landscape Institute and Appendix 5 by permission of the Joint Contracts Tribunal.

APPENDIX 1

THE LANDSCAPE INSTITUTE

12 Carlton House Terrace, London, SW1Y 5AH
tel: 01·839·4044
Registrar Peter Bird

CODE OF PROFESSIONAL CONDUCT OF THE LANDSCAPE
INSTITUTE

19TH MAY 1986

1. The object of this Code is to promote the standard of professional
    conduct and self-discipline required by members of the Landscape
    Institute. Members of the Institute are governed by its Constitution,
    By-Laws and Code of Professional Conduct; they shall conduct
    themselves in such a manner as will not prejudice the objects of
    the Institute as set out in the Constitution and repeated below:

    OBJECTS

    The objects of the Institute are the advancement of the art of
    landscape architecture; the theory and practice of landscape
    design; the promotion of research and education therein; the
    creation and maintenance of a high standard of professional
    qualification; and the promotion of the highest standard of
    professional service in the application of the arts and sciences of
    landscape architecture and management.

2. Members appointed to control the professional work of a public
    or private undertaking shall inform their employers of this Code
    and shall advise that the business of such an undertaking insofar
    as it relates to landscape is conducted in accordance with this
    Code.

The Professional Institute for Landscape Architects, Landscape Managers and Landscape Scientists

3. Members shall act impartially in all cases in which they are acting between parties and shall interpret the conditions of contract with fairness as between their client or employer and contractor.

4. Members may be principals, partners, directors and employees of any trade or undertaking, including those connected with landscape architecture, sciences or management, provided always that they inform their client in writing at the outset of the full extent of their interest in any undertakings connected with landscape.

5. Members shall agree with their client, in writing, at the outset of a commission, the terms and conditions for the professional services to be supplied.

6. Members may promote and advertise their services provided always that the information presented is factual, relevant, and neither misleading nor discreditable to the profession.

7. Members shall not have in partnership or other direct association any person who is suspended or expelled from membership. Members shall not disregard the professional obligations or qualifications of those from whom they receive or to whom they give authority, responsibility or employment nor of those with whom they are professionally associated.

8. Members on being approached to proceed with professional work on which to their knowledge another member is employed shall notify the fact to that member. Members of one division or grade of membership shall not misrepresent themselves as being qualified to perform the work of another.

9. This Code of Professional Conduct may only be amended by resolution passed by a two-thirds majority of the professional members present in person or by proxy who are entitled to vote and do vote at a specially convened General Meeting of the Institute of which due notice to the members, containing the proposed amendments, shall have been given.

APPENDIX 2

The Landscape Consultant's Appointment

The Landscape Institute
6-8 Barnard Mews London SW11 1QU

FOREWORD

This document has been designed to advise Landscape Consultants and their Clients in the execution of landscape commissions. It has been registered with the Office of Fair Trading under the terms of the Restrictive Trade Practices Act 1976.

The Landscape Institute is the Chartered Institute in the UK for Landscape Architects, incorporating Designers, Managers and Scientists. One of its objects is to promote the highest standard of professional service in the application of the arts and sciences of landscape architecture and management. All members of the Institute, collectively referred to in this document as Landscape Consultants, are governed by the Institute's Code of Professional Conduct, but the roles of the members of the three different landscape disciplines vary in accordance with their education and experience.

Landscape Architects (Design) identify and solve problems using design techniques based on an understanding of the external environment, knowledge of the functional and aesthetic characteristics of landscape materials, and of the organisation of landscape elements, external spaces and activities.

Landscape Architects (Management) are concerned with the long term care and development of new and existing landscapes and also with policy and planning for future management and use. This involves them in the organisation of manpower, machinery and materials and requires a working knowledge of statutory measures and Grant Aid Schemes in order to preserve and enhance the quality of the landscape.

Landscape Architects (Science) are specialists in the physical and biological aspects of landscape design and management. Relating scientific expertise to the practical problems of designers and managers, they may work in any of the many scientific subjects that are relevant to landscape, especially botany, ecology and soil surveys.

The Landscape Institute has produced three inter-related documents which assist clients and landscape consultants to reach clear agreement on the terms and conditions of an appointment. The documents are:

- **The Landscape Consultant's Appointment** which sets out the Memorandum of Agreement as well as the standard and additional services provided, conditions of service which apply and a schedule of services and fees.

- **Engaging a Landscape Consultant - Guidance to Clients on Fees** which shows the various bases on which fees are calculated, and the fees typically charged for the Standard services for projects of a range of sizes and complexity. It provides a basis against which the fee for a particular project can be compared or a starting point for negotiation.

- **Guide to Procedure for Competitive Tendering** which guides clients through the initial considerations and the procedures needed to obtain comparable and valid fee tenders for projects.

Any question on or arising out of the information contained herein may be referred to the Director General, The Landscape Institute, 6/8 Barnard Mews, London SW11 1QU. Tel: 0171 738 9166. Fax: 0171 738 9134.

0   INTRODUCTION

0.1   The Landscape Consultant's professional responsibility is to act as the Client's adviser based upon a clear understanding of the Client's requirements and to administer any contract between Client and Contractor impartially and fairly. A good working relationship between the Client and the Landscape Consultant is therefore essential when proceeding with a commission. The Clients also have an important role. They must provide adequate information on the project, site and budget and fully understand and approve the Landscape Consultant's proposals at various stages of the work as it proceeds.

0.2   The most successful relationships are those which proceed in an atmosphere of mutual trust and goodwill. An understanding of the Client's and the Consultant's respective obligations by both parties is fundamental to the creation of such an atmosphere. The Landscape Institute therefore advises its members that before accepting a commission for professional services, they should agree with the Client the terms of the commission, including the scope of the services; the allocation of responsibilities and any limitation of liability; the payment of fees including the rates and methods of calculation and the provision for termination.

0.3   This document consists of the following parts:

0.3.1   **Memorandum of Agreement**
The Institute advises its members to use the Memorandum of Agreement and Schedule of Services and Fees (Appendix II). Alternatively, letters of appointment could also serve the purpose, provided that the services, responsibilities and fee basis are fully defined. If the agreement is not comprehensive it is likely to create uncertainties for either of both parties as the commission progresses.

0.3.2   **The Landscape Consultant's Appointment** (Appendix I) in three parts:
Part 1 - Landscape Consultant's Services. The work which a Landscape Consultant normally undertakes after accepting a commission is primarily concerned with landscape design, construction (including planting), and management. It comprises Preliminary Services and Standard Services, sub-divided into work stages as follows:

- Preliminary Services	Work Stage A - Inception
	Work Stage B - Feasibility
- Standard Services	Work Stage C - Outline Proposals
	Work Stage D - Sketch Scheme Proposals
	Work Stage E - Detailed Proposals
	Work Stage F - Production Information
	Work Stage G - Bills of Quantities
	Work Stage H - Tender Action
	Work Stage J - Contract Preparation
	Work Stage K - Operations on site
	Work Stage L - Completion

The Landscape Consultant may also provide services outside the design, construction and management process, for example public inquiry commissions, landscape planning issues, environmental impact assessment, landscape appraisal and evaluation.

Part 2 - Other Services. Many commissions will require Other Services additional to the Preliminary and Standard Services, and it may be necessary to obtain and incorporate advice from various different consultants.

Part 3 - Conditions of Appointment. This part describes conditions which normally apply when a Landscape Consultant is commissioned.

0.3.3   **Schedule of Services and Fees**
See 0.3.1 above.

MEMORANDUM OF AGREEMENT

Between Client and Landscape Consultant for use with the Landscape Consultant's Appointment.

This Agreement

is made on the ....day of ....(month and year)

Between ....
(insert name of Client)

Of ....

....
(hereinafter called the Client)

And ....
(insert name of Landscape Consultant or firm of Landscape Consultants)

Of ....

....
(hereinafter called the Consultant)

NOW IT IS HEREBY AGREED

that upon the Conditions of the Landscape Consultant's Appointment (Parts 1,2 and 3) (......Revision) attached hereto as **Appendix I**

save as excepted or varied by the parties hereto in the Schedule of Services and Fees, hereinafter called the 'Schedule', attached hereto as **Appendix II**

and subject to any special conditions set out or referred to in the Schedule:

1. The Consultant will perform for the Client the services listed on the Schedule in respect of

    ....
    (insert general description of the Project)

    at ....
    (insert location of the Project)

2. The Client will pay the Consultant on demand for the services, fees and expenses as indicated in the Schedule; in accordance with the following provisions:

2.1 The Consultant shall deliver invoices in the instalments and on the dates or in the circumstances specified in the Schedule. Fees so invoiced shall be due to the Consultant on the date of receipt by the Client of the invoice. If sent by post, the invoice shall be deemed to have been received two working days after posting.

2.2 Not later than 5 days after the date of receipt of an invoice in accordance with clause 2.1 hereof, the client shall acknowledge receipt of the invoice and give notice to the Consultant specifying the amount (if any) of the payment to be made and the basis on which that amount is calculated.

2.3   The Final Date for Payment of any sum due from the Client to the
        Consultant shall be 17 days* [.........] after the sum becomes due.

        insert other period if required

2.4   Any notice given by the Client of intention to withhold payment pursuant to
        section 111(1) of the Housing Grants, Construction and Regeneration Act
        1996 shall be given not later than 7 days before the Final Date for Payment
        of any sum due to the Consultant.

        AS WITNESS the hands of the parties the day and year first above written

Signatures: Client...

                     Landscape Consultant....................................

Witnesses: Name......................................   Name.......................................

                     Address.................................   Address..................................

                     ....

                     ....

                     Description..............................   Description..............................

APPENDIX I

PART 1	**1**	**LANDSCAPE CONSULTANT'S SERVICES**

1.1   This Part describes the Preliminary and Standard Services which a Landscape Consultant will normally provide. These services are common to large and small commissions and none should be omitted if the commission is to be completed successfully. However, it may be prudent to vary the sequence of the Work Stages or to combine two or more stages to suit the particular circumstances. Where, for any reason, partial services only are to be provided, the agreement between the Client and the Consultant should indicate precisely the extent of those services. Preliminary Services comprise Work Stages A and B; Standard Services comprise Work Stages C to L inclusive. Other Services are described in Part 2.

Work Stage A   1.2   **Preliminary Services - Work Stage A: Inception**

Brief   1.2.1   Discuss and assess the Client's requirements including the timescale and financial limits; advise the Client on how to proceed; advise the Client of the Employer's duties under the Construction (Design and Management) Regulations 1994 ("the CDM Regulations"); agree the Landscape Consultant's services and the terms of engagement and fee payment basis, confirming these in writing with the Client.

Information which may be provided by the Client   1.2.2   Obtain from the Client information on ownership, other legal interests in the site, existing features, including underground services, and any other matters which may influence the development or management requirements.

Site Appraisal   1.2.3   Visit the site and carry out an initial appraisal.

Advice on other Consultants, Specialist Firms and Site Staff   1.2.4   Advise on the need for other consultants' services and the extent of these services; advise on the need for specialist contractors or suppliers to execute the works; advise on the need for site staff.

Programme   1.2.5   Advise on outline programme and fee basis for further services, and obtain the Client's agreement thereto.

Work Stage B   1.3   **Preliminary Services - Work Stage B: Feasibility**

Feasibility Studies   1.3.1   Undertake such studies as are necessary to determine the feasibility of the Client's requirements; discuss with the Client alternative solutions and their technical and financial implications, advise on the need to obtain planning permissions and other statutory requirements.

Landscape Consultant's Range of Services   1.3.2   In the light of the feasibility studies, agree with the Client the detailed extent of Standard and Other Services as required.

Work Stage C   1.4   **Standard Services - Work Stage C: Outline Proposals**

Outline Proposals   1.4.1   Broadly analyse the Client's requirements, prepare outline proposals and approximate estimate of the cost of executing the proposals for the Client's approval with other Consultants where appointed.

CDM Designer's Duties	1.4.2	Perform the following duties of the Designer as defined in the CDM Regulations at the appropriate stages of the commission: - co-operate with the Planning Supervisor, if appointed; - pass relevant information to the Planning Supervisor, if appointed, for incorporation in the initial Health and Safety File.
Work Stage D	**1.5**	**Standard Services - Work Stage D: Sketch Scheme Proposals**
Sketch Scheme Proposals	1.5.1	Develop the sketch scheme proposals from those agreed in outline, taking into account any changes requested by the Client, prepare cost estimates and programme for implementation with other Consultants where appointed. The sketch scheme proposals should indicate the size and character of the project in sufficient detail to enable the Client to agree the spatial arrangements, materials and appearance.
Changes in Scheme Proposals	1.5.2	Advise the Client of the implications of any changes in the cost and timing for executing the proposals and obtain approval for such changes.
Outline Planning Application	1.5.3	If appropriate, consult with the Planning Authority and submit any necessary application for outline planning permission using sketch scheme proposals. See also 2.2.8.
Other Approvals	1.5.4	Similarly, make application for any other approvals from statutory bodies, using sketch scheme proposals, where these approvals are not dependent on detailed proposals being available. See also 2.2.8.
Work Stage E	**1.6**	**Standard Services - Work Stage E: Detailed Proposals**
Detailed Proposals	1.6.1	Develop the proposals in sufficient detail to obtain the Client's approval of the proposed materials, techniques and standards of workmanship. When acting as design team leader, co-ordinate the proposals made by other consultants, specialist contractors or suppliers; obtain quotations and other information in relation to specialist work.
Cost Checks and Changes in Detailed Proposals	1.6.2	Carry out cost checks where necessary and advise the Client of the consequences of any changes to the estimated cost and programme. Obtain the Client's consent to proceed.
Detailed Statutory Approvals	1.6.3	Make detailed applications for approvals under planning and building legislation where necessary, using detailed scheme proposals. See also 2.2.8.
Work Stages F & G	**1.7**	**Standard Services - Work Stages F and G: Production Information and Bills of Quantities**
Production Information	1.7.1	Prepare all production drawings, schedules and specification of materials and workmanship required for the execution of the work
Bills of Quantities	1.7.2	Provide information for bills of quantities to be prepared by others. All information to be supplied in sufficient detail to enable a contract to be negotiated or competitive tenders to be invited. See also 2.6.1.

Work Stages H & J	**1.8**	**Standard Services - Work Stages H and J: Tender Action and Contract Preparation**
Other Contracts	1.8.1	Where necessary, arrange for other contracts to be let in advance of the Main Contractor starting work.
Tender Lists	1.8.2	With the Client's participation advise on suitable contractors and obtain approval of a final list of tenderers.
Tender Action or Negotiation	1.8.3	Invite tenders from approved contractors; appraise and advise on tenders submitted. Alternatively, arrange for a price to be negotiated with a contractor by the Quantity Surveyor. See also 2.6.1.
Contract Document Preparation	1.8.4	Advise the Client on the appointment of the Contractor and on the responsibilities of the Client, the Contractor and the Landscape Consultant under the terms of the contract document; prepare the contract and arrange for it to be signed by the Client and the Contractor; provide production information as required by the contract.
Work Stage K	**1.9**	**Standard Services - Work Stage K: Operations on Site During Construction and 12 Months' Maintenance**
Contract Administration	1.9.1	Administer the contract during operations on site including control of the Clerk of Works where appointed.
Inspections	1.9.2	Visit the site at intervals appropriate to the Contractor's programmed activities to inspect the progress and quality of the works. Frequency of the inspections shall be agreed with the Client.
Accounts	1.9.3	Check and certify the authenticity of accounts.
Financial Appraisal and Programme	1.9.4	Make periodic financial reports to the Client; with other Consultants where appointed identify any variation in the cost of the works or in the expected duration of the contract.
Work Stage L	**1.10**	**Standard Services - Work Stage L: Completion**
Completion of Works	1.10.1	Administer the terms of the contract relating to the completion of the works and give general guidance on activities after completion of contract.

PART 2   **2**   **OTHER SERVICES**

2.1   This part describes services which may be provided by the Landscape Consultant by prior agreement with the Client to augment the Preliminary and Standard Services described in Part 1 or which may be the subject of a separate appointment. The list of services is not exhaustive.

2.2   **Surveys and Investigations**

Site Evaluation   2.2.1   Advise on the selection and suitability of sites; conduct negotiations concerned with sites and their features.

Measured Surveys   2.2.2   Make measured surveys, take levels and prepare plans of sites and their features, including any existing buildings.

Site Investigation   2.2.3   Undertake investigations into, prepare reports and schedules, and give advice on the nature and condition of the vegetation, soil or other features of the site. Investigate failures, arrange and supervise exploratory work by contractors or specialists.

Maintenance and Management Cost in Use   2.2.4   Survey and analyse the usage, management and maintenance of a site, undertake cost in use studies, and analyse the need for additional design work.

Environmental Assessment   2.2.5   Undertake environmental assessment studies of the impact of development proposals and land use changes.

Development Plans   2.2.6   Prepare development plans for sites, where development of part of the whole site will not be immediate. Prepare Masterplans showing general scheme principles and layout, and integration with surrounding land uses or proposals.

Demolition and Clearance   2.2.7   Provide services in connection with demolition and clearance works.

Special Drawings and Models   2.2.8   Prepare special drawings, models or technical information for the use of the Client for applications under planning or building regulations, or other statutory requirements, or for negotiations with ground landlords, adjoining owners, public authorities, licensing authorities, mortgagees and others; prepare plans for conveyancing, Land Registry and other legal or record purposes.

Prototype   2.2.9   Develop prototype proposals for repetitive use by the client, but only when such repetitive use is specifically agreed by the Landscape Consultant and Client as appropriate.

Site Furniture and Equipment   2.2.10   Design or advise on the selection of site furniture and equipment; arrange and inspect the fabrication of site furniture, arrange trials and training in use of equipment.

Multi-Disciplinary Meetings   2.2.11   Attendance at multi-disciplinary meetings held to discuss projects or elements outside the Landscape Consultant's appointment or fee basis (where attendance would not otherwise be required for whole or part of meeting).

Public Meetings   2.2.12   Prepare and organise material for public consultation and liaison; attend public meetings.

Works of Art	2.2.13	Advise on the commissioning or selection of works of art in connection with landscape commissions.
Scientific Developments	2.2.14	Undertake research and conduct trials if necessary; especially where technical problems indicate that traditional solutions are inadequate. It is recommended that a full brief, fee basis and funding be separately agreed.
Visits to Nurseries	2.2.15	Visit horticultural nurseries to ascertain the quantity, quality and cost of stock available for purchase.

2.3   Cost Estimating and Financial Advisory Services

Cost Plans and Cash Flow Requirements	2.3.1	Carry out cost planning for a project, including the cost of professional fees; advise on cash flow requirements for fees, works and cost in use.
Schedules of Rates and Quantities	2.3.2	Prepare schedules of rates or bills of quantities for tendering purposes; measure work executed.
Cost of Replacement and Reinstatement of Damaged Landscape	2.3.3	Carry out inspections and surveys, prepare estimates for the replacement and reinstatement of damaged landscapes; submit and negotiate claims for compensation.
Grant Applications	2.3.4	Provide information; make applications for and conduct negotiations for grants.

2.4   Planning Negotiations

Planning Applications; Exceptional Negotiations	2.4.1	Conduct detailed negotiations with a planning authority that become prolonged because of complexity.
Planning Appeals and Public Inquiries	2.4.2	Prepare and submit an appeal under planning acts; advise on other work in connection with planning appeals. Prepare and submit a proof of evidence for a public inquiry, appear as an expert witness at a public inquiry.
Royal Fine Art Commission	2.4.3	Make submissions to the Royal Fine Art Commission.
Building Regulations; Exceptional Negotiations	2.4.4	Conduct detailed negotiations for approvals under the building regulations; negotiate waivers or relaxations; all of which may become prolonged because of complexity.
Landlords' Approvals	2.4.5	Submit plans of proposed works for the approval of landlords, mortgagees, freeholders or others.
Rights of Owners and Lessees	2.4.6	Advise on the rights and responsibilities of owners or lessees including right of ways, rights of support, boundary, drainage and wayleave responsibilities etc.; such advice shall always be subject to confirmation by the Client's legal adviser.

| Statutory Bodies | 2.4.7 | Liaise with, submit plans or technical information and conduct negotiations with statutory bodies eg. Environment Agency, highway authority, statutory undertakers. |

2.5   Additional Administration of Projects

| Site Staff | 2.5.1 | Provide or recruit site staff with the Client's agreement, for frequent or constant inspection of the works. |

| Extended Administration | 2.5.2 | Administer and inspect contract aftercare and maintenance works extending beyond 12 months from completion of the capital works. |

| Suspension | 2.5.3 | Suspend and recommence work on projects where progress is unexpectedly delayed by more than 3 months due to financial constraints, delayed approvals or other reasons. |

| Project Management | 2.5.4 | Provide management from inception to completion; prepare briefs, appoint and co-ordinate consultants, implementation managers, agents, suppliers and contractors; monitor time cost and agreed targets; monitor progress of the works; handover projects on completion. |

| Record Drawings | 2.5.5 | Provide the Client with a set of drawings showing the main elements of the scheme; arrange for drawings of other services to be provided as appropriate. |

| Landscape Management Plans | 2.5.6 | Prepare management plans and maintenance schedules; prepare drawings, schedules and operational manuals, assess cost and staffing implications of proposals. |

| Contract Claims | 2.5.7 | Carry out the administration, evaluation and settlement of contract claims. |

| Litigation and Arbitration | 2.5.8 | Prepare and give evidence, settle proofs, confer with solicitors and counsel; attend court and arbitration hearings; appear before tribunals; act as arbitrator or adjudicator. |

| Health and Safety Plan | 2.5.9 | Prepare pre-tender Health and Safety Plan; notify the Health and Safety Executive of the project; assemble the Health and Safety File; prepare 'as built' drawings for the Health and Safety File. |

| Planning Supervisor | 2.5.10 | Provide the services of Planning Supervisor under the CDM Regulations. The terms and fee for this service should be agreed under a separate appointment. |

2.6   Services normally provided by other Consultants

| Other Consultants' Services | 2.6.1 | Where services such as quantity surveying, architecture, civil, structural, mechanical or electrical engineering, town planning or graphic design are provided from within the Landscape Consultant's own office or by other Consultants in association with the Landscape Consultant, it is recommended that the fees be separately agreed. |

2.7   Additional Design Services

| | 2.7.1 | Alter or modify any design, specification, drawing or other document as a result of new or modified instructions from the Client or for other reasons which could not reasonably have been foreseen. Make and issue reproductions of such altered documents. |

PART 3	3	**CONDITIONS OF APPOINTMENT**
	3.1	This Part describes the conditions which apply to a Landscape Consultant's appointment. If different or additional services are required they should be set out in the Schedule of Services, Memorandum of Agreement or letter of appointment.
Duty of Care	3.2	The Landscape Consultant will use reasonable skill, care and diligence in accordance with the normal standards of the profession
Contamination or Pollution	3.3	Unless this clause is expressly stated not to apply, nothing in the agreement shall require the Consultant to provide advice or services in connection with the presence of or risk of contamination or pollution by harmful substances. The Client shall retain sole responsibility for determining what, if any, investigations and actions shall be taken in relation to such substances, and shall commission such professional advice as he considers necessary.
Landscape Consultant's Authority	3.4	The Landscape Consultant will act on behalf of the Client in the matters set out or implied in the Landscape Consultant's appointment. The Landscape Consultant will obtain the authority of the Client before initiating any service or Work Stage.
Modifications	3.5	The Landscape Consultant shall not significantly alter an approved proposal without Client approval. Should changes be found to be necessary during implementation, the Client shall be informed and consent obtained without delay.
Terms for Payment	3.6	The Client shall pay the Landscape Consultant for his services in accordance with paragraph 2 of the Memorandum of Agreement, save that in the event of termination or suspension of the commission the Consultant shall be entitled to payment of a reasonable proportion of the interim payment or at the agreed hourly rate, whichever is applicable, for all work carried out to the date of termination or suspension and not previously the subject of an invoice for interim payment.
Revisions to the Conditions of Appointment	3.7	The agreement between a Client and a Landscape Consultant is deemed to allow for revisions due to changing circumstances. In long-term commissions such changes will probably be due to unforeseen factors or matters beyond the control of the Landscape Consultant at the date of the appointment.
Project Control	3.8	The Landscape Consultant will report any significant variations in authorised expenditure or contract period.
Impartiality	3.9	The Landscape Consultant will be impartial in administering the terms of a contract between Client and Contractor.
Appointment of other Consultants	3.10	Consultants may be appointed either by the Client direct or by the Landscape Consultant subject to acceptance by each party.
Sub-contracting	3.11	The Landscape Consultant shall not sub-contract any part of the commission without notifying the Client and receiving formal agreement on the division of responsibilities that will apply.

Liability of other Consultants	3.12	Where a Consultant is appointed under clause 3.10, the Landscape Consultant shall not be held liable for the other Consultant's work, provided that in relation to the execution of such work under a contract between Client and Contractor nothing in this clause shall affect any responsibility of the Landscape Consultant to perform his duties under the terms of that contract.
Consultant Co-ordination	3.13	The Landscape Consultant will have the responsibility to co-ordinate and integrate into the overall design the services provided by any consultant, however employed.
Design work by Contractors/ Suppliers	3.14	A specialist contractor, sub-contractor or supplier who is employed by the Client and who supplies design drawings to the Landscape Consultant for incorporation in the works may be appointed by agreement. The Landscape Consultant shall not be held liable for the execution and performance of this work. The Landscape Consultant will have the authority to integrate and co-ordinate this design information into the overall design.
Contractor Responsibility	3.15	The Client will employ a contractor under a separate agreement to undertake construction or other works not undertaken by the Landscape Consultant. The Client will hold the contractor, and not the Landscape Consultant, responsible for the contractor's operational methods and for the proper execution of the works.
Site Inspections	3.16	The Landscape Consultant will visit the site at intervals appropriate to the progress of the works. As these intervals will vary depending on the nature of the work, the Landscape Consultant will explain to the Client at the outset when inspections will be made and agree these with the Client. If more inspections/visits to the site are required by the Client, details, as an extension to the Standard Services, will be agreed in writing with the Client.
Site Staff and Resident Landscape Staff	3.17	Where frequent or constant professional inspection is agreed to be required, a resident professional shall be appointed on a full or part-time basis by the Consultant under specific terms of appointment and remuneration.
Site Staff/Clerk of Works	3.18	Where frequent or constant inspection of the works is required a Clerk of Works suitably qualified in the supervision of landscape operations shall be employed. The Clerk of Works may be employed by the Client, or the Landscape Consultant, but in either case will be under the control and direction of the Landscape Consultant
Information from Client	3.19	The Client is required to provide the Landscape Consultant with such information and make such decisions as are necessary for the proper performance of the agreed service. The requirement and reasons for such timely action shall be explained to the Client by the Landscape Consultant so that the implications of delay are clearly understood by both parties.
Client Representative	3.20	The Client, if a firm or other body of persons, will, when requested by the Landscape Consultant, nominate a responsible representative through whom all instructions will be given.
Copyright	3.21	Copyright in all documents and drawings prepared by the Landscape Consultant shall unless otherwise agreed remain the property of the Consultant. Where so agreed, copyright shall be passed to the Client only after all fees due to the Landscape Consultant have been paid.

Copyright Entitlement	3.22	The Client will be entitled to use documents and drawings in executing the works for which they were prepared by the Landscape Consultant provided that: a) All fees due to the Landscape Consultant have been submitted or paid. b) The entitlement relates only to that site or part of the site for which the design was prepared. This entitlement applies to the design, maintenance and management of the works.
Assignment	3.23	Neither the Client nor the Landscape Consultant shall assign the appointment in whole or in part without prior written agreement as to the division of responsibilities that apply.
Suspension	3.24	The length of notice for suspension should be agreed in writing at the outset. The Client may suspend the Landscape Consultant's appointment in whole or in part, the notice given being in accordance with the agreed timing and in writing.
Suspension by Consultant	3.25	The Landscape Consultant will give immediate notice in writing to the Client of any situation arising from force majeure which makes it impractical to carry out any of the agreed services, and agree with the Client a suitable course of action.
Resumption of Service	3.26	Following the notice in accordance with clause 3.24 if no instruction has been received within 6 months, the Landscape Consultant shall make a written request for instructions. If no instruction is received within 30 days, the appointment shall be treated as terminated.
Suspension of Obligations	3.27	If the Client fails to make payment in accordance with Clause 2 of the Memorandum of Agreement and no effective notice to withhold payment has been given, the Landscape Consultant may, following 7 days' notice setting out the grounds for suspension, suspend the performance of his obligations under the agreement until payment is received.
Termination	3.28	The Landscape Consultant's appointment may be terminated by either party by following the procedure in clause 3.24, where this is permitted by the appointment.
Death or Incapacity	3.29	If death or incapacity of a sole practitioner stops the Landscape Consultant from carrying out the agreed duties under this appointment, it shall be terminated. As soon as all outstanding fees have been submitted or paid, the Client will be entitled to use all data prepared on the project subject to the provisions in respect of copyright in accordance with clause 3.21 and 3.22.
Adjudication	3.30	In the event of a dispute arising under the agreement, either party may give notice at any time to the other of his intention to refer the dispute to adjudication.

Appointment of Adjudicator	3.31	An adjudicator shall be appointed by agreement between the parties within 2 working days of receipt of notice under 3.30 or, failing agreement, within 7 days of the said notice by the President or a Vice-President of the Landscape Institute. The adjudicator shall conduct the adjudication in such manner as he considers fit, having regard to the Construction Industry Council's Model Adjudication Procedure, and subject to the following matters:

- within 7 working days of notice under 3.30 the parties shall agree and provide to the adjudicator a joint statement of undisputed facts (so as to reduce the area of dispute to a minimum);
- the adjudicator shall act impartially and shall reach a decision within 28 days of referral of the dispute to him or such longer period as the parties may agree;
- the adjudicator shall be entitled to extend the period of 28 days by up to 14 days with the consent of the party giving notice under 3.30;
- the adjudicator shall be entitled to take the initiative in ascertaining the facts and the law;
- the parties shall accept the adjudicator's decision as binding upon them until such time as the dispute is finally resolved in accordance with a ruling under 3.32, arbitration under 3.33 or by agreement; alternatively the parties may agree to accept the decision of the adjudicator as finally determining the dispute;
- the adjudicator, or any employee or agent of his, shall not be liable to the parties for anything done or omitted in the discharge or purported discharge of his functions as adjudicator unless the act or omission is in bad faith.

Ruling on a Joint Statement 3.32 Any difference or dispute arising from a written appointment under this document may, by agreement, be referred to the Landscape Institute for a ruling by the President. The parties must agree:
to prepare and submit with their submission a joint statement of undisputed facts to reduce the area of dispute to a minimum; and
to accept the ruling as final and binding.

Arbitration 3.33 Subject to the parties' rights under 3.30 to 3.32, any difference or dispute arising out of the appointment shall be referred to arbitration by a person to be agreed between the parties or, failing agreement within 21 days after either party has given to the other a written request to concur in the appointment of an arbitrator, a person to be appointed at the request of either party by the President or a Vice-President for the time being of the Chartered Institute of Arbitrators.

Alternative for Scotland 3.34 In Scotland, any difference or dispute arising out of the appointment which cannot be resolved in accordance with clause 3.32 or 3.33 shall be referred to arbitration by a person to be agreed between the parties or, failing agreement within 21 days after either party has given to the other a written request to concur in the appointment of an arbiter, a person to be nominated at the request of either party by the Chairman for the time being of the Scottish Branch of the Chartered Institute of Arbitrators.

Settlement of Disputes by Agreement 3.35 Nothing herein shall prevent the parties agreeing to settle any difference or dispute arising out of the appointment without recourse to arbitration or adjudication.

Governing laws England and Wales	3.36	The application of these conditions shall be governed by the laws of England and Wales.
		or
Alternative for Scotland		The application of these conditions shall be governed by the laws of Scotland.
		or
Alternative for Northern Ireland		The application of these conditions shall be governed by the laws of Northern Ireland.
CDM Regulations 1994	3.37	Where the Client is required under the CDM Regulations to appoint a Planning Supervisor, the following Additional Conditions CDM.1 - CDM.6 shall apply to this agreement.
	CDM1	The Landscape Consultant shall, where the Client is required by CDM Regulations to appoint a Planning Supervisor, co-operate with and pass relevant information to the Planning Supervisor (whether within the same firm of landscape consultants or otherwise).
	CDM2	The Client shall, where required by the CDM Regulations, appoint as soon as reasonably practicable a competent Planning Supervisor. The Client shall procure that the appointment remains filled at all times until construction is completed.
	CDM3	The Landscape Consultant shall, where the Client is required by the CDM Regulations to have appointed a Planning Supervisor and where after the design information is complete the Client orders changes necessitating re-work, continue to co-operate with and pass relevant information to the Planning Supervisor.
	CDM4	The Client shall, where required by the CDM Regulations, appoint as soon as reasonably practicable a competent Principal Contractor.
	CDM5	The Client shall, where required by the CDM Regulations to appoint a Planning Supervisor, and where consultants are appointed, procure the consultants' co-operation in the exchange of information relating to health and safety aspects of their work, and shall co-operate with the Planning Supervisor.
	CDM6	The Client shall, where required by the CDM Regulations to appoint a Planning Supervisor, and where specialists are appointed, procure the specialists' co-operation in the exchange of information relating to health and safety aspects of their work, and shall co-operate with the Planning Supervisor.

APPENDIX II

SCHEDULE OF SERVICES AND FEES

Referred to in the Memorandum of Agreement dated ....

Between   ....
                 (insert name of Client)

And   ....
                 (insert name of Landscape Consultant)

For   ....
                 (insert description of project)

Unless otherwise stated the services listed in the conditions of
appointment will be as described in The Landscape Consultant's
Appointment (Parts 1,2 and 3) (..................... Revision), issued by
The Landscape Institute. Clause references relate to that document.

S1 SERVICES

Service	Clause	Fee basis (State whether percentage, time or lump sum)
Preliminary Services		
Standard Services		
Other Services		

S2 SPECIAL CONDITIONS

CONDITIONS WHICH SHALL APPLY	Insert any special conditions which are to apply to the appointment.
CONDITIONS NOT TO APPLY	Insert any clauses which are not to apply to this appointment.

FEES

PERCENTAGE FEES	Fees based on a percentage of the total construction cost shall be calculated as follows:

LUMP SUM FEES	The total fee for all services shown under S1 Services to be on a lump sum basis shall be £..

TIME CHARGE FEES	Rates for fees charged on a time basis shall be:

.1 for Principals   £................/hour

.2 for other staff grade............................ £................/hour

.3 for other staff grade............................ £................/hour

.4 for other staff grade............................ £................/hour

.5 for other staff grade............................ £................/hour

INTERIM PAYMENTS	The Consultant shall be entitled to (and shall render invoices for) interim payment of fees: .1 for work on a percentage or lump sum basis, at the completion of work stages and / or additional interim stages, as follows:

Work stage	Proportion of percentage or lump sum fee	Cumulative total

* insert stages and proportions to cover all interim payments

* delete where not applicable and insert commencement date

.2 for work on a time-charge basis *monthly / quarterly / half-yearly

from the commencement of work on ....

EXPENSES AND DISBURSEMENTS * delete where not applicable and insert location of rates schedule.	* The fees charged are inclusive of all expenses and disbursements or * Expenses and disbursements shall be charged in addition, in accordance with rates specified ....

Signed:

....

Client   Consultant

Date:

....

APPENDIX 3 – THE JCLI STANDARD FORM OF AGREEMENT FOR LANDSCAPE WORKS

Dated _____ 19/20_____

**Agreement for
Landscape Works
1998 Edition**

Between   _____

_____

and   _____

_____

JCLI

Issued by the
Joint Council for Landscape Industries
comprising:-

Arboricultural Association
British Association Landscape Industries
Horticultural Trades Association
Institute of Leisure and Amenity Management
Landscape Institute
National Farmers' Union

JCLI Practice Note 5 (December 1998) and JCLI.AMD98 (Revisions in the 1998 Edition of the JCLI Agreement for Landscape Works relative to the June 1996 revision and Differences between the JCTMW1998 and the JCLI Agreement for Landscape Works 1998) are supplied with this Agreement.

Published for the Joint Council for Landscape Industries by the Landscape Institute
6-8 Barnard Mews, London SW11 1QU.
Available from the Landscape Institute

© JCLI December 1998

Printed by ID Print, Hull

JCLI Agreement for Landscape Works

1998 Edition

This Agreement is made the _____ day of _____ 19 / 20 _____

between _____

of _____
(hereinafter called 'the Employer')

of the one part AND _____

of (or whose registered office is at) _____

_____

(hereinafter called 'the Contractor') of the other part.

Whereas

Recitals 1st   the Employer wishes the following work _____

_____

_____

to be carried out under the direction of

_____

(hereinafter called 'the Contract Administrator')

and has caused
     drawings numbered _____
     (hereinafter called 'the Contract Drawings') [a]
     and/or a Specification (hereinafter called 'the Contract Specification') [a]
     and/or schedules [a] and/or schedule of rates [a] and/or Bills of Quantities [a]
     (which documents are together with the Conditions and the Supplemental Conditions
     A to E annexed hereto hereinafter called 'the Contract Documents' [b])
     showing and describing the work
to be prepared and which are attached to this Agreement;

2nd   the Contractor has stated the sum he will require for carrying out such work, which sum is that stated in article 2 and has priced the Specification [a] or the schedules [a] or Bills of Quantities [a] or provided a schedule of rates [a];

3rd   the Contract Documents have been signed by or on behalf of the parties hereto;

4th   [a] the quantity surveyor appointed in connection with this Agreement shall mean

_____

or in the event of his death or ceasing to be the quantity surveyor for this purpose such other person as the Employer nominates for that purpose;

---

[a]   Delete as appropriate.
[b]   Where a Contract Document has been priced by the Contractor it is this document that should be attached to this Agreement.

5th   A   The Construction (Design and Management) Regulations 1994 (the 'CDM Regulations') do not apply to the work referred to in the 1st recital. **[c]**

      B   The Construction (Design and Management) Regulations 1994 (the 'CDM Regulations') apply to the work referred to in the 1st recital to the extent stated below; and the Employer has instructed the Contract Administrator that the design of the Works is to comply with the provisions of regulation 13 of the CDM Regulations **[c]**

         1   All the CDM Regulations apply **[d] [e]**

         2   Regulations 4,6,8 to 12 and 14 to 19 of the CDM Regulations do not apply **[d]**

         3   Regulations 4 to 12 and 14 to 19 of the CDM Regulations do not apply **[d]**

Now it is hereby agreed as follows

Article 1

Contractors obligations

For the consideration hereinafter mentioned the Contractor will in accordance with the Contract Documents carry out and complete the work referred to in the 1st recital together with any changes made to that work in accordance with this Agreement (hereinafter called 'the Works').

Article 2

Contract Sum

The Employer will pay the Contractor for the Works the sum of

_____

_____ (£ _____)

exclusive of VAT (hereinafter called 'the Contract Sum') or such other sum as shall become payable hereunder at the times and in the manner specified in the Contract Documents.

Article 3

Contract Administrator

The term 'the Contract Administrator' in the said Conditions shall mean

_____

or in the event of his death or ceasing to be the Contract Administrator for the purpose of this Agreement such other person as the Employer shall within 14 days of the death or cessation as aforesaid nominate for that purpose, provided that no person subsequently appointed to be the Contract Administrator under this Agreement shall be entitled to disregard or overrule any certificate or instruction given by the Contract Administrator for the time being.

---

[c]   Delete either A or B (including 1, 2 and 3).
[d]   If B is not deleted, delete two of the three alternatives 1, 2 and 3.
[e]   Where alternative B1 applies, see the notes on the JCT 80 Fifth recital in Practice Note 27 'The application of the Construction (Design and Management) Regulations 1994 to Contracts on JCT Standard Forms of Contract' for the statutory obligations which must have been fulfilled before the Contractor can begin carrying out the Works.

Article 4 [f]

Planning Supervisor

A　The term 'the Planning Supervisor' in the Conditions shall mean the Contract Administrator **[g]**

B　The term 'the Planning Supervisor' in the Conditions shall mean

_____

of　_____ **[g]**

or, in the event of the death of the Planning Supervisor or his ceasing to be the Planning Supervisor, such other person as the Employer shall appoint as the Planning Supervisor pursuant to regulation 6(5) of the CDM Regulations.

Article 5 [f]

Principal Contractor

A　The term 'the Principal Contractor' in the Conditions shall mean the Contractor **[g]**

B　The term 'the Principal Contractor' in the Conditions shall mean

_____

of　_____ **[g]**

or, in the event of his ceasing to be the Principal Contractor, such other contractor as the Employer shall appoint as the Principal Contractor pursuant to regulation 6(5) of the CDM Regulations.

Article 6

Dispute or difference – adjudication

If any dispute or difference arises under this Agreement either party may refer it to adjudication in accordance with the procedures set out in Supplemental Condition D. If, under clause D2, the parties have not agreed a person as the Adjudicator the nominator of the Adjudicator shall be the President or a Vice President for the time being of the Landscape Institute or their nominee.

Article 7A [h]

Dispute or difference – arbitration

Subject to article 6 if any dispute or difference as to any matter or thing of whatsoever nature arising under this Agreement or in connection therewith, except in connection with the enforcement of any decision of an Adjudicator appointed to determine a dispute or difference arising thereunder, shall arise between the Parties either during the progress or after the completion or abandonment of the Works or after the determination of the employment of the Contractor except under the Supplemental Condition B clause B6 (*Value added tax)* or under Supplemental Condition C (*Statutory tax deduction scheme)* to the extent provided in clause C8 it shall be referred to arbitration in accordance with the procedures set out in Supplemental Condition E. If, under clause E2.1, the parties have not agreed a person as the Arbitrator the appointor of the Arbitrator shall be the President or a Vice President for the time being of the Landscape Institute or their nominee.

Article 7B [h]

Dispute or difference – legal proceedings

Subject to article 6, if any dispute or difference as to any matter or thing of whatsoever nature arising under this Agreement or in connection therewith shall arise between the parties either during the progress or after the completion or abandonment of the Works or after the determination of the employment of the Contractor it shall be determined by legal proceedings.

---

[f]　Delete articles 4 and 5 when alternative A or alternative B2 or alternative B3 applies in the 5th recital.
[g]　Delete alternative A or alternative B as appropriate (retaining the final paragraph)
[h]　If disputes are to be decided by arbitration delete article 7B. If disputes are to be decided by legal proceedings delete article 7A.

As witness the hands of the parties hereto

Signed by or on behalf of the Employer   _____

in the presence of
(signature, name and address)   _____

_____

_____

Signed by or on behalf of the Contractor   _____

in the presence of
(signature, name and address)   _____

_____

_____

Contents

Conditions hereinbefore referred to

1.0 Intentions of the parties

Contractor's obligations

1.1 The Contractor shall with due diligence and in a good and workmanlike manner and, where alternative B1 in the 5th recital applies, in accordance with the Health and Safety Plan of the Principal Contractor carry out and complete the Works in accordance with the Contract Documents using materials and workmanship of the quality and standards therein specified provided that where and to the extent that approval of the quality of materials or of the standards of workmanship is a matter for the opinion of the Contract Administrator such quality and standards shall be to the reasonable satisfaction of the Contract Administrator.

Contract Administrator's duties

1.2 The Contract Administrator shall issue any further information necessary for the proper carrying out of the Works, issue all certificates and confirm all instructions in writing in accordance with these Conditions.

Reappointment of Planning Supervisor or Principal Contractor - notification to Contractor

1.3 Where alternative B1 in the 5th recital applies, if the Employer pursuant to article 4 or article 5 by a further appointment replaces the Planning Supervisor referred to in, or appointed pursuant to, article 4 or replaces the Contractor or any other contractor appointed as the Principal Contractor, the Employer shall immediately upon such further appointment notify the Contractor in writing of the name and address of the new appointee.

Alternative B2 in the 5th recital - notification by Contractor - regulation 7(5) of the CDM Regulations

1.4 Where alternative B2 in the 5th recital applies the Contractor shall, if applicable, give the notice to the Health and Safety Executive required by regulation 7(5) of the CDM Regulations and such notice shall be in accordance with regulations 7(6)(a) and (b) of the CDM Regulations. The notice shall be given (with a copy to the Employer and to the Contract Administrator) before the Contractor or any person under his control starts to carry out any construction work.

Giving or service of notices or other documents

1.5 Where this Agreement does not specifically state the manner of giving or service of any notice or other document required or authorised in pursuance of this Agreement such notice or other document shall be given or served by any effective means to any agreed address. If no address has been agreed then if given or served by being addressed pre-paid and delivered by post to the addressee's last known principal business address or, where the addressee is a body corporate, to the body's registered or principal office it shall be treated as having been effectively given or served.

Reckoning periods of days

1.6 .1 Where under this Agreement an act is required to be done within a specified period of days after or from a specified date, the period shall begin immediately after that date. Where the period would include a day which is a Public Holiday that day shall be excluded.

.2 A 'Public Holiday' shall mean Christmas Day, Good Friday or a day which under the Banking and Financial Dealings Act 1971 is a bank holiday [I]

Applicable law

1.7 Whatever the nationality, residence or domicile of the Employer, the Contractor or any sub-contractor or supplier and wherever the Works are situated the law of England shall be the law applicable to this Agreement [J].

Bills of Quantities and SMM

†1.8 Where the Contract Documents include Bills of Quantities, the Bills of Quantities unless otherwise expressly stated therein in respect of any specified item or items are to have been prepared in accordance with the Standard Method of Measurement of Building Works, 7th Edition, published by the Royal Institution of Chartered Surveyors and the Building Employers Confederation (formerly National Federation of Building Trades Employers).

[I]   Amend as necessary if different Public Holidays are applicable.

[J]   Where the parties do not wish the law applicable to this Agreement to be the law of England appropriate amendments to clause 1.7 should be made.

2.0   Commencement and completion

Commencement and completion
2.1   The Works may be commenced on

....

and shall be completed by

....

Extension of contract period
2.2   If it becomes apparent that the Works will not be completed by the date for completion inserted in clause 2.1 hereof (or any later date fixed in accordance with the provisions of this clause 2.2) for reasons beyond the control of the Contractor, including compliance with any instruction of the Contract Administrator under this Agreement whose issue is not due to a default of the Contractor, then the Contractor shall thereupon in writing so notify the Contract Administrator who shall make, in writing, such extension of time for completion as may be reasonable. Reasons within the control of the Contractor include any default of the Contractor or of others employed or engaged by or under him for or in connection with the Works and of any supplier of goods or materials for the Works.

Damages for non-completion
2.3   If the Works are not completed by the completion date inserted in clause 2.1 hereof or by any later completion date fixed under clause 2.2 hereof the Contractor shall pay or allow to the Employer liquidated damages at the rate of £...................per..............**[k]** between the aforesaid completion date and the date of practical completion.

The Employer may

either recover the liquidated damages from the Contractor as a debt

or deduct the liquidated damages from any monies due to the Contractor under this Agreement provided that a notice of deduction pursuant to clause 4.4.2 or clause 4.5.1.3 has been given. If the Employer intends to deduct such damages from the sum stated as due in the final certificate, he shall additionally inform the Contractor, in writing, of that intention not later than the date of issue of the final certificate.

Practical completion
2.4   The Contract Administrator shall certify the date when in his opinion the Works have reached practical completion and, where alternative B1 in the 5th recital applies, the Contractor has complied sufficiently with clause 5.9.

Defects liability
2.5   Any defects, excessive shrinkages or other faults to the Works, other than tree, shrub, grass and other plant failures, which appear within 6 **[l]** .... months of the date of practical completion and are due to materials or workmanship not in accordance with this Agreement or frost occurring before practical completion shall be made good by the Contractor entirely at his own cost unless the Contract Administrator shall otherwise instruct.

The Contract Administrator shall certify the date when in his opinion the Contractor's obligations under this clause 2.5 have been discharged.

Partial possession by Employer
†2.6   If before practical completion of the Works the Employer with the consent of the Contractor (such consent shall not be unreasonably withheld) shall take possession of any part of the Works (hereinafter called 'the Relevant Part') then:

The date of possession of the Relevant Part shall be the date for practical completion of the Relevant Part and clause 4.3 shall apply to the Relevant Part;

Any sum due from the Contractor to the Employer under Clause 2.3 shall be reduced by a percentage equal to the value of the Relevant Part as a percentage of the Contract Sum.

Before the Contractor shall give his consent to the Employer taking possession of the Relevant Part the Contractor or the Employer shall notify the insurers under clause 6.3A or clause 6.3B and obtain confirmation that such possession will not prejudice the insurance.

Failures of plants (pre-practical completion)
†2.7   Any trees, shrubs, grass or other plants, other than those found to be missing or not in accordance with the Contract Documents as a result of theft or malicious damage and which shall be replaced as set out in clause 2.9 A or B of these conditions, which are found not to be or not to have been in

---

[k]   Insert 'day', 'week' or 'other period.

[l]   If a different period is required delete '6' and insert the appropriate period.

accordance with the Contract Documents at practical completion of the Works shall be replaced by the Contractor entirely at his own cost unless the Contract Administrator shall otherwise instruct. The Contract Administrator shall certify the dates when in his opinion the Contractor's obligations under this clause have been discharged.

Plants defects liability and post practical completion care by Contractor **[m]**

†2.8A .1 Any grass which is found to be defective within .... months, any shrubs, ordinary nursery stock trees or other plants found to be defective within .... months and any semi-mature advanced or extra large nursery stock trees found to be defective within .... months of the date of practical completion due to materials or workmanship not in accordance with the Contract Documents shall be replaced by the Contractor entirely at his own cost unless the Contract Administrator shall otherwise instruct. The Contract Administrator shall certify the dates when in his opinion the Contractor's obligations under this clause have been discharged.

    .2 The care of trees, shrubs, grass and other plants after the date of practical completion is excluded from this Agreement.

Plants defects liability and post practical completion care by Employer **[m]**

†2.8B The care of the trees, shrubs, grass and other plants after the date of practical completion shall be undertaken by the Employer who will further be responsible for and bear the cost of the replacement of any trees, shrubs, grass or other plants which are subsequently defective.

Malicious damage or theft (before practical completion) **[n]**

†2.9A All loss or damage arising from any theft or malicious damage prior to practical completion shall be made good by the Contractor at his own expense.

†2.9B The Contract Sum shall include the provisional sum of £ .... **[n]** to be expended as instructed by the Contract Administrator in respect of the cost of all work

---

[m]   Delete 2.8A or 2.8B as appropriate.
[n]   Delete 2.9A or 2.9B as appropriate. The amount to be inserted in clause 2.9B (if applicable) should take account of the Works and the place where they are carried out.

arising from any theft or malicious damage to the Works beyond the control of the Contractor prior to practical completion of the Works.

3.0 Control of the Works

Assignment

3.1 Neither the Employer nor the Contractor shall, without the written consent of the other, assign this Agreement.

Sub-contracting

3.2 .1 The Contractor shall not sub-contract the Works or any part thereof without the written consent of the Contract Administrator whose consent shall not be unreasonably delayed or withheld.

    .2 A sub-contract for the Works or any part thereof shall provide that if the Contractor fails properly to pay the amount, or any part thereof, due to the sub-contractor by the final date for its payment stated in the sub-contract, the Contractor shall pay to the sub-contractor in addition to the amount not properly paid simple interest thereon for the period until such payment is made; that the payment of such simple interest shall be treated as a debt due to the sub-contractor by the Contractor; that the rate of interest payable shall be five per cent (5%) over the Base Rate of the Bank of England which is current at the date the payment by the Contractor became overdue; and that any payment of simple interest shall not in any circumstances be construed as a waiver by the sub-contractor of his right to proper payment of the principal amount due from the Contractor to the sub-contractor in accordance with, and within the time stated in, the sub-contract or of any rights of the sub-contractor under the sub-contract in regard to suspension of the performance of his obligations to the Contractor under the sub-contract or determination of his employment for the failure by the Contractor properly to pay any amount due under the sub-contract to the sub-contractor.

Contractor's representative

3.3 The Contractor shall at all reasonable times keep upon the Works a competent person in charge and any instructions given to him by the Contract Administrator shall be deemed to have been issued to the Contractor.

Exclusion from the Works

3.4 The Contract Administrator may (but not unreasonably or vexatiously) issue instructions requiring the exclusion from the Works of any person employed thereon.

Contract Administrator's instructions

3.5 The Contract Administrator may issue written instructions which the Contractor shall forthwith carry out. If instructions are given orally they shall, within 2 days, be confirmed in writing by the Contract Administrator.

If within 7 days after receipt of a written notice from the Contract Administrator requiring compliance with an instruction the Contractor does not comply therewith then the Employer may employ and pay other persons to carry out the work and all costs incurred thereby may be deducted by him from any monies due or to become due to the Contractor under this Agreement or shall be recoverable from the Contractor by the Employer as a debt.

Variations

3.6 The Contract Administrator may, without invalidating this Agreement, order an addition to or omission from or other change in the Works or the order or period in which they are to be carried out and any such instruction shall be valued by the Contract Administrator on a fair and reasonable basis, using where relevant prices in the priced Specification/ schedules/Bills of Quantities/schedule of rates [o] and such valuation shall include any direct loss and/or expense incurred by the Contractor due to the regular progress of the Works being affected by compliance with such instruction or, where alternative B1 in the 5th recital applies, due to the compliance or non-compliance by the Employer with clause 5.6.

Instead of the valuation referred to above, the price may be agreed between the Contract Administrator and the Contractor prior to the Contractor carrying out any such instruction.

P.C. and Provisional sums

3.7 The Contract Administrator shall issue instructions as to the expenditure of any P.C. and provisional sums and such instructions shall be valued or the price agreed in accordance with clause 3.6 hereof.

Objections to a Nomination

†3.8 The Contract Administrator shall not nominate any person as a nominated sub-contractor against whom the Contractor shall make reasonable objection or who will not enter into a sub-contract that applies the appropriate provisions of these Conditions.

4.0 Payment

Correction of inconsistencies

4.1 Any inconsistency in or between the Contract Drawings [o] and the Contract Specification [o] and the schedules [o] and the Bills of Quantities [o] and the schedule of rates [o] shall be corrected and any such correction which results in an addition, omission or other change shall be treated as a variation under clause 3.6 hereof. Nothing contained in the Contract Drawings [o] or the Contract Specification [o] or the schedules [o] or the Bills of Quantities [o] or the schedule of rates [o] shall override, modify or affect in any way whatsoever the application or interpretation of that which is contained in these Conditions.

Progress payments and retention

4.2 .1 The Contract Administrator shall, at intervals of not less than 4 weeks calculated from the date for commencement, certify progress payments as amounts due to the Contractor in respect of the value of the Works properly executed, including any amounts either ascertained or agreed under clauses 3.6 and 3.7 hereof, and the value of any materials and goods which have been reasonably and properly brought upon the site for the purpose of the Works and which are adequately stored and protected against the weather and other casualties, less a retention of 5% / ....% [p] and less the total amounts due to the Contractor in certificates of progress payment previously issued. The certificate shall state to what the progress payment relates and the basis on which the amount of the progress payment was calculated. The final date for payment by the Employer of the amount so certified shall be 14 days from the date of issue of the certificate. The provisions of clause 4.4 shall apply to any certificate issued pursuant to this clause 4.2.1.

.2 If the Employer fails properly to pay the amount, or any part thereof, due to the Contractor by the final date for its

---

[o] Delete as appropriate to follow any deletions in the recitals on page 1.

[p] If a different retention is required delete 5% and insert the appropriate percentage.

payment the Employer shall pay to the Contractor in addition to the amount not properly paid simple interest thereon for the period until such payment is made. Payment of such simple interest shall be treated as a debt due to the Contractor by the Employer. The rate of interest payable shall be five per cent (5%) over the Base Rate of the Bank of England which is current at the date the payment by the Employer became overdue. Any payment of simple interest under this clause 4.2.2 shall not in any circumstances be construed as a waiver by the Contractor of his right to proper payment of the principal amount due from the Employer to the Contractor in accordance with, and within the time stated in, the Conditions or of the rights of the Contractor in regard to suspension of performance of his obligations under this Agreement to the Employer pursuant to clause 4.8 or to determination of his employment pursuant to the default referred to in clause 7.3.1.1.

Penultimate certificate
4.3   The Contract Administrator shall within 14 days after the date of practical completion certified under clause 2.4 hereof certify payment as an amount due to the Contractor of 97½%/.............% **[q]** of the value of the Works properly executed including any amounts either ascertained or agreed under clauses 3.6 and 3.7 hereof less the total amounts due to the Contractor in certificates of progress payments previously issued. The penultimate certificate shall state to what the progress payment relates and the basis on which the amount of the certificate was calculated. The final date for payment by the Employer of the amount so certified shall be 14 days from the date of issue of that certificate. If the Employer fails properly to pay the amount, or any part thereof, due to the Contractor by the final date for its payment the provisions of clause 4.2.2 shall apply. The provisions of clause 4.4 shall apply to the certificate issued pursuant to this clause 4.3.

Notices of amounts to be paid and deductions
4.4   .1   Not later than 5 days after the issue of a certificate of payment pursuant to clauses 4.2.1 and 4.3 the Employer shall give a written notice to the Contractor

which shall specify the amount of the payment proposed to be made in respect of the amount stated as due in that certificate.

.2   Not later than 5 days before the final date for payment of the amount notified pursuant to clause 4.4.1 the Employer may give a written notice to the Contractor which shall specify any amount proposed to be withheld and/or deducted from that notified amount, the ground or grounds for such withholding and/or deduction and the amount of the withholding and/or deduction attributable to each ground.

.3   Where the Employer does not give a written notice pursuant to clause 4.4.1 and/or to clause 4.4.2 the Employer shall pay the amount stated as due in the certificate.

Final certificate
4.5   .1   .1   The Contractor shall supply within 6 **[r]** .... months from the date of practical completion all documentation reasonably required for the computation of the amount to be finally certified by the Contract Administrator and the Contract Administrator shall within 28 days of receipt of such documentation, provided that the Contract Administrator has issued the certificates under clauses 2.5 and 2.7 hereof, issue a final certificate certifying the amount remaining due to the Contractor, less only retention which the Employer will continue to hold pending expiry of the defects liability periods set out in clause 2.8A.1 if applicable, or due to the Employer as the case may be and shall state to what the amount relates and the basis on which that amount was calculated.

.2   Not later than 5 days after the date of issue of the final certificate the Employer shall give a written notice to the Contractor which shall specify the amount of the payment proposed to be made to the Contractor in respect of the amount certified

---

[q]   The alternative should be completed where a percentage other than 5% has been inserted in clause 4.2.1.

[r]   If a different period is required delete '6' and insert the appropriate period.

.3 The final date for payment of such amount as a debt payable as the case may be by the Employer to the Contractor or by the Contractor to the Employer shall be 14 days from the date of issue of the said certificate. Not later than 5 days before the final date for payment of the amount due to the Contractor the Employer may give a written notice to the Contractor which shall specify any amount proposed to be withheld and/or deducted therefrom, the ground or grounds for such withholding and/or deduction and the amount of the withholding and/or deduction attributable to each ground.

.4 Where the Employer does not give a written notice pursuant to clause 4.5.1.2 and/or the clause 4.5.1.3 the Employer shall pay the Contractor the amount stated as due to the Contractor in the final certificate.

.5† Concurrently with the notice under clause 4.5.1.2 the Employer shall give a further notice setting out the sums the Employer continues to withhold in respect of each of the defects liability periods under clause 2.8A.1 and reiterating the expiry date of each such defects liability period.

.2 If the Employer or the Contractor fails properly to pay the debt, or any part thereof, by the final date for its payment the Employer or the Contractor as the case may be shall pay to the other in addition to the debt not properly paid simple interest thereon for the period until such payment is made. The rate of interest payable shall be five per cent (5%) over the Base Rate of the Bank of England which is current at the date the payment by the Employer or by the Contractor as the case may be became overdue. Any payment of simple interest under this clause 4.5.2 shall not in any circumstances be construed as a waiver by the Contractor or by the Employer as the case may be of his right to proper payment of the aforesaid debt due from the Employer to the Contractor or from the Contractor to the Employer in accordance with clause 4.5.1.

Contribution, levy and tax changes [s]

4.6 Contribution, levy and tax changes shall be dealt with by the application of Supplemental Condition A. The percentage addition under clause A5 is ....% [t].

Fixed price

4.7 No account shall be taken in any payment to the Contractor under this Agreement of any change in the cost to the Contractor of the labour, materials, plant and other resources employed in carrying out the Works except as provided in clause 4.6, if applicable.

Right of suspension by Contractor

4.8 If, subject to any notice issued pursuant to clause 4.4.2, the Employer shall fail to pay the amount due certified under either clause 4.2.1 or clause 4.3 in full by the final date for payment as required by this Agreement and such failure shall continue for 7 days after the Contractor has given to the Employer, with a copy to the Contract Administrator, written notice of his intention to suspend performance of his obligations under this Agreement to the Employer and the ground or grounds on which it is intended to suspend performance, then the Contractor may suspend such performance of his obligations under this Agreement until payment in full occurs.

5.0 Statutory obligations

Statutory obligations, notices, fees and charges

5.1 The Contractor shall comply with, and give all notices required by, any statute, any statutory instrument, rule or order or any regulation or byelaw applicable to the Works (hereinafter called 'the statutory requirements') and shall pay all fees and charges in respect of the Works legally recoverable from him.

If the Contractor finds any divergence between the statutory requirements and the Contract Documents or between the statutory requirements and any instruction of the Contract Administrator he shall immediately give to the Contract Administrator a written notice specifying the divergence.

Subject to this latter obligation, the Contractor shall not be liable to the Employer under this

---

[s] Delete clause 4.6 if the contract period is of such limited duration as to make the provisions of Supplemental Condition A inapplicable.

[t] Percentage to be inserted.

Agreement if the Works do not comply with the statutory requirements where and to the extent that such non-compliance of the Work results from the Contractor having carried out work in accordance with the Contract Documents or any instruction of the Contract Administrator.

Value added tax

5.2 The sum or sums due to the Contractor under article 2 of this Agreement shall be exclusive of any value added tax and the Employer shall pay to the Contractor any value added tax properly chargeable by the Commissioners of Custom and Excise on the supply to the Employer of any goods and services by the Contractor under this Agreement in the manner set out in Supplemental Condition B. Clause B1.1 applies/does not apply **[u]**.

Statutory tax deduction scheme

5.3 Supplemental Condition C shall apply where at the date of tender the Employer was a 'contractor', or where at any time up to the issue and payment of the final certificate the Employer becomes a 'contractor', for the purposes of the statutory tax deduction scheme referred to in Supplemental Condition C.

5.4 [Number not used]

Prevention of corruption

5.5 The Employer shall be entitled to cancel this Agreement and to recover from the Contractor the amount of any loss resulting from such cancellation if the Contractor shall have offered or given or agreed to give to any person any gift or consideration of any kind or if the Contractor shall have committed any offence under the Prevention of Corruption Acts 1889 to 1916 or, if the Employer is a local authority, shall have given any fee or

reward the receipt of which is an offence under sub-section (2) of section 117 of the Local Government Act 1972 or any re-enactment thereof.

Provisions for use where alternative B1 in the 5th recital applies

Employer's obligation - Planning Supervisor - Principal Contractor

5.6 The Employer shall ensure:

that the Planning Supervisor carries out all the duties of a planning supervisor under the CDM Regulations; and

where the Contractor is not the Principal Contractor, that the Principal Contractor carries out all the duties of a principal contractor under the CDM Regulations.

Contractor is Principal Contractor

5.7 Where the Contractor is and while he remains the Principal Contractor, the Contractor shall comply with all the duties of a principal contractor set out in the CDM Regulations. Without prejudice to this obligation the Principal Contractor shall ensure that the health and safety plan of the Planning Supervisor provided to him is developed by him to comply with regulation 15(4) of the CDM Regulations (the 'Health and Safety Plan') and is supplied to the Employer before the Contractor or any person under his control starts to carry out any construction work; and that this Health and Safety Plan continues during the progress of the Works to have the features required by regulation 15(4) of the CDM Regulations. Any amendment by the Principal Contractor to the Health and Safety Plan shall be notified to the Employer who shall where relevant thereupon notify the Planning Supervisor and the Contract Administrator.

Contractor is not Principal Contractor

5.8 Where the Contractor is not the Principal Contractor or where the Employer appoints a successor to the Contractor as the Principal Contractor, the Contractor shall comply at no cost to the Employer with all the reasonable requirements of the Principal Contractor to the extent that such requirements are necessary for compliance with the CDM Regulations; and, notwithstanding clause 2.2, no extension of time shall be given in respect of such compliance.

Health and safety file

5.9 Within the time reasonably required in writing by the Planning Supervisor to the Contractor, the Contractor shall provide, and shall ensure that any sub-contractor, through the

---

[u] Delete as required. Clause B1.1 can only apply where the Contractor is satisfied at the date this Agreement is entered into that his output tax on all supplies to the Employer under this Agreement will be at either a positive or a zero rate of tax.
On and from 1 April 1989 the supply in respect of a building designed for a 'relevant residential purpose' or for a 'relevant charitable purpose' (as defined in the legislation which gives statutory effect to the VAT changes operative from 1 April 1989) is only zero rated if the person to whom the supply is made has given to the Contractor a certificate in statutory form: see the VAT leaflet 708 revised 1989. Where a contract supply is zero rated by certificate only the person holding the certificate (usually the Contractor) may zero rate his supply.

Contractor, provides, such information to the Planning Supervisor or, if the Contractor is not the Principal Contractor, to the Principal Contractor as the Planning Supervisor reasonably requires for the preparation, pursuant to regulations 14(d), 14(e) and 14(f) of the CDM Regulations, of the health and safety file required by the CDM Regulations.

6.0   Injury, damage and insurance

Injury to or death of persons

6.1   The Contractor shall be liable for and shall indemnify the Employer against any expense, liability, loss, claim or proceedings whatsoever arising under any statute or at common law in respect of personal injury to or death of any person whomsoever arising out of or in the course of or caused by the carrying out of the Works, except to the extent that the same is due to any act or neglect of the Employer or of any person for whom the Employer is responsible.

Without prejudice to his liability to indemnify the Employer the Contractor shall take out and maintain and shall cause any sub-contractor to take out and maintain insurance which in respect of claims for personal injury to or the death of any person under a contract of service or apprenticeship with the Contractor, and arising out of and in the course of such person's employment, shall comply with all relevant legislation and, in respect of any other liability for personal injury or death, shall be such as is necessary to cover the liability of the Contractor or, as the case may be, of such sub-contractor.

Injury or damage to property

6.2   The Contractor shall be liable for, and shall indemnify the Employer against, any expense, liability, loss, claim or proceedings in respect of any loss, injury or damage whatsoever to any property real or personal (other than loss, injury or damage to the Works or to any unfixed materials and goods delivered to, placed on or adjacent to the Works and intended therefor or, where clause 6.3B is applicable, to any property required to be insured pursuant to clause 6.3B for the perils therein listed) in so far as such loss, injury or damage arises out of or in the course of or by reason of the carrying out of the Works and to the extent that the same is due to any negligence, breach of statutory duty, omission or default of the Contractor, his servants or agents, or of any person employed or engaged by the Contractor upon or in connection with the Works or any part thereof, his servants or agents.

. Without prejudice to his obligation to indemnify the Employer, the Contractor shall take out and maintain and shall cause any sub-contractor to take out and maintain insurance in respect of the liability referred to above in respect of loss, injury or damage to any property real or personal other than the Works (or where clause 6.3B is applicable other than any property required to be insured pursuant to clause 6.3B for the perils therein listed). The insurance cover to which clause 6.2 applies:

shall indemnify the Employer in like manner to the Contractor but only to the extent that the Contractor may be liable to indemnify the Employer under the terms of this Agreement; and

shall, for any one occurrence or series of occurrences arising out of one event, be not less than:

£ ....

Insurance of the Works by Contractor - Fire etc. [v] [w]

6.3A   The Contractor shall in the joint names of Employer and Contractor insure the Works and all unfixed materials and goods delivered to, placed on or adjacent to the Works and intended therefor against loss and damage by fire, lightning, explosion, storm, tempest, flood, bursting or overflowing of water tanks, apparatus or pipes, earthquake, aircraft and other aerial devices or articles dropped therefrom, riot and civil commotion, for the full reinstatement value thereof plus ....% [t] to cover professional fees.

After any inspection required by the insurers in respect of a claim under the insurance mentioned in this clause 6.3A the Contractor shall with due diligence restore or replace

---

[v]   Delete clause 6.3A where the Works are an extension to or an alteration of an existing structure and the Employer can obtain the insurance in compliance with the requirement in clause 6.3B;
Delete clause 6.3B where the Works are not an extension to or an alteration of an existing structure or where the Employer cannot obtain the insurance in compliance with the requirement in clause 6.3B.

[w]   Where the Contractor has in force an All Risks Policy which insures the Works against loss and damage by *inter alia* the perils referred to in clause 6.3A this Policy may be used to provide the insurance required by clause 6.3A provided the Policy recognises the Employer as a joint insured with the Contractor in respect of the Works and the Policy is maintained.

work or materials or goods damaged and dispose of any debris and proceed with and complete the Works. The Contractor shall not be entitled to any payment in respect of work or materials or goods damaged or the disposal of any debris other than the monies received under the said insurance (less only the amount properly incurred by the Employer in respect of professional fees but not exceeding the amount arrived at by applying the percentage to cover professional fees stated in clause 6.3A to the amount of the monies so paid excluding any amount included therein for professional fees) and such monies shall be paid to the Contractor under certificates of the Contract Administrator at the periods stated in clause 4.

Insurance of the Works and any existing structures by Employer - Fire etc. **[v]**

6.3B The Employer shall in the joint names of Employer and Contractor insure against loss or damage to any existing structures (together with any contents owned by him or for which he is responsible) and to the Works and all unfixed materials and goods delivered to, placed on or adjacent to the Works and intended therefor by fire, lightning, explosion, storm, tempest, flood, bursting or overflowing of water tanks, apparatus or pipes, earthquake, aircraft and other aerial devices or articles dropped therefrom, riot and civil commotion.

If any loss or damage as referred to in this clause occurs to the Works or to any unfixed materials and goods delivered to, placed on or adjacent to the Works and intended therefor then the Contract Administrator shall issue instructions for the reinstatement and making good of such loss or damage in accordance with clause 3.5 hereof and such instructions shall be valued under clause 3.6 hereof.

Evidence of insurance

6.4 The Contractor shall produce, and shall cause any sub-contractor to produce, such evidence as the Employer may reasonably require that the insurances referred to in clauses 6.1 and 6.2 and, where applicable, 6.3A hereof have been taken out and are in force at all material times. Where clause 6.3B hereof is applicable the Employer shall produce such evidence as the Contractor may reasonably require that the insurance referred to therein has been taken out and is in force at all material times.

7.0 Determination

Notices

7.1 Any notice or further notice to which clauses 7.2.1, 7.2.2, 7.3.1 and 7.3.2 refer shall be in writing and given by actual delivery, or by special delivery or by recorded delivery. If sent by special delivery or recorded delivery the notice or further notice shall, subject to proof to the contrary, be deemed to have been received 48 hours after the date of posting (excluding Saturday and Sunday and Public Holidays).

Determination by Employer

7.2 .1 If the Contractor without reasonable cause makes default by failing to proceed diligently with the Works or by wholly or substantially suspending the carrying out of the Works before practical completion or by failing, pursuant to the Conditions, to comply with the requirements of the CDM Regulations, the Contract Administrator may give notice to the Contractor which specifies the default and requires it to be ended. If the default is not ended within 7 days of receipt of the notice the Employer may by further notice to the Contractor determine the employment of the Contractor under this Agreement. Such determination shall take effect on the date of receipt of the further notice. A notice of determination under clause 7.2.1 shall not be given unreasonably or vexatiously.

.2 If the Contractor

makes a composition or arrangement with his creditors, or becomes bankrupt, or

being a company,

makes a proposal for a voluntary arrangement for a composition of debts or scheme of arrangement to be approved in accordance with the Companies Act 1985 or the Insolvency Act 1986 as the case may be or any amendment or re-enactment thereof, or

has a provisional liquidator appointed, or

has a winding-up order made, or

passes a resolution for voluntary winding-up (except for the purposes of amalgamation or reconstruction), or under the Insolvency Act 1986 or any amendment or re-enactment thereof has an administrator or an administrative receiver appointed

the Employer may by notice to the Contractor determine the employment of the Contractor under this Agreement. Such determination shall take effect on the date of receipt of such notice.

.3 Upon determination of the employment of the Contractor under clause 7.2.1 or clause 7.2.2 the Contractor shall immediately cease to occupy the site of the Works and the Employer shall not be bound to make any further payment to the Contractor that may be due under this Agreement until after completion of the Works and the making good of any defects therein. The Employer may recover from the Contractor the additional cost to him of completing the Works, any expenses properly incurred by the Employer as a result of, and any direct loss and/or damage caused to the Employer by, the determination.

.4 The provisions of clauses 7.2.1 to 7.2.3 are without prejudice to any other rights and remedies which the Employer may possess.

Determination by Contractor

7.3 .1 If the Employer makes default in any one or more of the following respects:

.1 he does not pay by the final date for payment the amount properly due to the Contractor in respect of any certificate or pay any VAT due on that amount pursuant to clause 5.2 and Supplemental Condition B;

.2 he, or any person for whom he is responsible, interferes with or obstructs the issue of any certificate due under this Agreement or interferes with or obstructs the carrying out of the Works or fails to make the premises available for the Contractor in accordance with clause 2.1 hereof;

.3 he suspends the carrying out of the whole or substantially the whole of the Works for a continuous period of one month or more;

.4 he fails, pursuant to the Conditions, to comply with the requirements of

the CDM Regulations,

the Contractor may give notice to the Employer which specifies the default and requires it to be ended. If the default is not ended within 7 days of receipt of the notice the Contractor may by further notice to the Employer determine the employment of the Contractor under this Agreement. Such determination shall take effect on the date of receipt of the further notice. A notice of determination under clause 7.3.1 shall not be given unreasonably or vexatiously.

.2 If the Employer

makes a composition or arrangement with his creditors, or becomes bankrupt, or

being a company,

makes a proposal for a voluntary arrangement for a composition of debts or scheme of arrangement to be approved in accordance with the Companies Act 1985 or the Insolvency Act 1986 as the case may be or any amendment or re-enactment thereof, or

has a provisional liquidator appointed, or

has a winding-up order made, or

passes a resolution for voluntary winding-up (except for the purposes of amalgamation or reconstruction), or

under the Insolvency Act 1986 or any amendment or re-enactment thereof has an administrator or an administrative receiver appointed

the Contractor may by notice to the Employer determine the employment of the Contractor under this Agreement. Such determination shall take effect on the date of receipt of such notice.

.3 Upon determination of the employment of the Contractor under clause 7.3.1 or clause 7.3.2 the Contractor shall prepare an account setting out:

the total value of work properly executed and of materials and goods properly brought on the site for the purpose of the Works, such value to be ascertained in accordance with this Agreement as if the employment of the Contractor had not been determined, together with any amounts due to the Contractor under the Conditions not included in such total value; and

the cost to the Contractor of removing or having removed from the site all temporary buildings, plant, tools and equipment; and

any direct loss and/or damage caused to the Contractor by the determination.

After taking into account amounts previously paid to the Contractor under this Agreement, the Employer shall pay to the Contractor the full amount properly due in respect of this account within 28 days of its submission by the Contractor.

.4 The provisions of clauses 7.3.1 to 7.3.3 are without prejudice to any other rights and remedies which the Contractor may possess.

8.0 Settlement of disputes [x]

Adjudication
8.1 Pursuant to article 6 the procedures for adjudication are set out in Supplemental Condition D.

Arbitration
8.2 Pursuant to article 7A the procedures for Arbitration are set out in Supplemental Condition E.

Legal Proceedings
8.3 Where article 7B applies, any dispute or difference shall be determined by legal proceedings pursuant to article 7B.

---

[x]   It is open to the Employer and the Contractor to resolve disputes by the process of Mediation: see JCT Practice Note 28 'Mediation on a Building Contract or Sub-Contract Dispute'.

Supplemental Conditions

A: CONTRIBUTION, LEVY AND TAX CHANGES
Clause 4.6

Deemed calculation of Contract Sum - rates of contribution etc.

A1   The sum referred to in article 2 (in this Supplemental Condition called 'the Contract Sum') shall be deemed to have been calculated in the manner set out below and shall be subject to adjustment in the events specified hereunder:

A1.1   The prices used or set out by the Contractor in the Contract Documents are based upon the types and rates of contribution, levy and tax payable by a person in his capacity as an employer and which at the date of this Agreement are payable by the Contractor. A type and rate so payable are in clause A1.2 referred to as a 'tender type' and a 'tender rate'.

Increases or decreases in rates of contribution etc. - payment or allowance

A1.2   If any of the tender rates, other than a rate of levy payable by virtue of the Industrial Training Act 1964, is increased or decreased, or if a tender type ceases to be payable, or if a new type of contribution, levy or tax which is payable by a person in his capacity as an employer becomes payable after the date of tender, [y] then in any such case the net amount of the difference between what the Contractor actually pays or will pay in respect of

.1   workpeople [y] engaged upon or in connection with the Works either on or adjacent to the site of the Works and

.2   workpeople [y] directly employed by the Contractor who are engaged upon the production of materials or goods [y] for use in or in connection with the Works and who operate neither on nor adjacent to the site of the Works and to the extent that they are so engaged

or because of his employment of such workpeople and what he would have paid had the alteration, cessation or new type of contribution, levy or tax not become effective shall, as the case may be, be paid to or allowed by the Contractor.

Persons employed on site other than 'workpeople'

A1.3   There shall be added to the net amount paid to or allowed by the Contractor under clause A1.2 in respect of each person employed on the site by the Contractor for the Works and who is not within the definition of 'workpeople' in clause A4.6.3 the same amount as is payable or allowable in respect of a craftsman under clause A1.2 or such proportion of that amount as reflects the time (measured in whole working days) that each such person is so employed.

A1.4   For the purposes of clause A1.3

no period less than 2 whole working days in any week shall be taken into account and periods less than a whole working day shall not be aggregated to amount to a whole working day;

the phrase 'the same amount as is payable or allowable in respect of a craftsman' shall refer to the amount in respect of a craftsman employed by the Contractor (or by any sub-contractor under a sub-contract to which clause A3 refers) under the rules or decisions or agreements of the National Joint Council for the Building Industry or other wage-fixing body [y] and, where the aforesaid rules or decisions or agreements provide for more than one rate of wage emolument or other expense for a craftsman, shall refer to the amount in respect of a craftsman employed as aforesaid to whom the highest rate is applicable; and

the phrase 'employed ... by the Contractor' shall mean an employment to which the Income Tax (Employment)

---

[y]   See Clause A4.6.

Regulations 1993 (the PAYE Regulations) under section 203 of the Income and Corporation Taxes Act, 1988, apply.

Refunds and premiums

A1.5   The prices used or set out by the Contractor in the Contract Documents are based upon the types and rates of refund of the contributions, levies and taxes payable by a person in his capacity as an employer and upon the types and rates of premium receivable by a person in his capacity as an employer being in each case types and rates which at the date of tender are receivable by the Contractor. Such a type and such a rate are in clause A1.6 referred to as a 'tender type' and a 'tender rate'.

A1.6   If any of the tender rates is increased or decreased or if a tender type ceases to be payable or if a new type of refund of any contribution, levy or tax payable by a person in his capacity as an employer becomes receivable or if a new type of premium receivable by a person in his capacity as an employer becomes receivable after the date of tender, then in any such case the net amount of the difference between what the Contractor actually receives or will receive in respect of workpeople as referred to in clauses A1.2.1 and A1.2.2 or because of his employment of such workpeople and what he would have received had the alteration, cessation or new type of refund or premium not become effective shall, as the case may be, be allowed by or paid to the Contractor.

A1.7   The references in clauses A1.5 and A1.6 to premiums shall be construed as meaning all payments howsoever they are described which are made under or by virtue of an Act of Parliament to a person in his capacity as an employer and which affect the cost to an employer of having persons in his employment.

Contracted-out employment

A1.8   Where employer's contributions are payable by the Contractor in respect of workpeople as referred to in clauses A1.2.1 and A1.2.2 whose employment is contracted-out employment within the meaning of the Social Security Pensions Act 1975 the Contractor shall for the purpose of recovery or allowance under this clause be deemed to pay employer's contributions as if that employment were not contracted-out employment.

Meaning of contribution etc.

A1.9   The references in clause A1 to contribution, levies and taxes shall be construed as meaning all impositions payable by a person in his capacity as an employer howsoever they are described and whoever the recipient which are imposed under or by virtue of an Act of Parliament and which affect the cost to an employer of having persons in his employment.

Materials - duties and taxes

A2.1   The prices used or set out by the Contractor in the Contract Documents are based upon the types and rates of duty if any and tax if any (other than any value added tax which is treated, or is capable of being treated, as input tax (as referred to in the Finance Act 1972) by the Contractor) by whomsoever payable which at the date of tender are payable on the import, purchase, sale, appropriation, processing or use of the materials, goods, electricity and, where so specifically stated in the Contract Documents, fuels specified in the list attached thereto under or by virtue of any Act of Parliament. A type and a rate so payable are in clause A2.2 referred to as a 'tender type' and a 'tender rate'.

A2.2   If, after the date of tender, in relation to any materials or goods [y] specified as aforesaid, or any electricity or fuels specified as aforesaid and consumed on site for the execution of the Works including temporary site installations for those Works, a tender rate is increased or decreased or a tender type ceases to be payable or a new type of duty or tax (other than value added tax which is treated, or is capable of being treated, as input tax as referred to in the Finance Act 1972) by the Contractor) becomes payable on the import, purchase, sale, appropriation, processing or use of those materials, goods, electricity or fuels, then in any such case the net amount of the difference between what the Contractor actually pays in respect of those materials, goods, electricity or fuels and what he would have paid in respect of them had the alteration, cessation or imposition not occurred, shall, as the case may be, be paid to or allowed by the Contractor. In clause A2 the expression 'a new type of duty or tax' includes an additional duty or tax imposed in regard to specific materials, goods, electricity or fuels in respect of which no duty or tax whatever was previously payable (other than any value added tax which is treated, or is capable of being treated, as input tax (as referred to in the Finance Act 1972) by the Contractor).

Landfill tax

A2.3   .1 The prices used or set out by the Contractor in the Contract Documents are based upon the incidence and rate of landfill tax (as referred to in the Finance Act 1996) on waste deposited on a licensed landfill site and for which at the date of tender the landfill site operator is accountable to HM Customs and Excise.

.2 If in respect of waste arising out of the carrying out and completion of the Works which the Contractor after the date of tender deposits on a licensed landfill site the price charged by the operator of that site to the Contractor for such deposit is increased or decreased by reason only of a change in the incidence or rate of landfill tax effective after the date of tender from what would have been charged before that effective date, the net amount of that increase or decrease shall, as the case may be, be paid to or allowed by the Contractor.

.3 No payment pursuant to clause A2.3.2 shall be made if the Contractor could reasonably be expected to have disposed of the waste other than to a licensed landfill site.

Fluctuations - work sublet

A3.1   If the Contractor shall decide to sublet any portion of the Works, he shall incorporate in the sub-contract provisions to the like effect as the provisions of

clauses A1, A4 and A5 including the percentage stated in clause 4.6 pursuant to clause A5

which are applicable for the purposes of this Agreement.

A3.2   If the price payable under such a sub-contract as aforesaid is decreased below or increased above the price in such sub-contract by reason of the operation of the said incorporated provisions, then the net amount of such decrease or increase shall, as the case may be, be allowed by or paid to the Contractor under this Agreement.

Provisions relating to clauses A1, A3 and A5

Written notice by Contractor

A4.1   The Contractor shall give a written notice to the Contract Administrator of the occurrence of any of the events referred to in such of the following provisions as are applicable for the purposes of this Agreement:

.1 clause A1.2
.2 clause A1.6
.3 clause A2.2
.4 clause A2.3
.5 clause A3.2

Timing and effect of written notices

A4.2   Any notice required to be given by the preceding sub-clause shall be given within a reasonable time after the occurrence of the event to which the notice relates, and the giving of a written notice in that time shall be a condition precedent to any payment being made to the Contractor in respect of the event in question.

Agreement - Contract Administrator and Contractor

A4.3   The Contract Administrator and the Contractor may agree what shall be deemed for all the purposes of this Agreement to be the net amount payable to or allowable by the Contractor in respect of the occurrence of any event such as is referred to in any of the provisions listed in clause A4.1.

Fluctuations added to or deducted from Contract Sum - provisions setting out conditions etc. to be fulfilled before such addition or deduction

A4.4   Any amount which from time to time becomes payable to or allowable by the Contractor by virtue of clause A1 or clause A3 shall, as the case may be, be added to or deducted from the Contract Sum:

Provided:

- evidence by Contractor -
.1 As soon as is reasonably practicable the Contractor shall provide such evidence as the Contract Administrator may reasonably require to enable the amount payable to or allowable by the Contractor by virtue of clause A1 or clause A3 to be ascertained; and in the case of amounts payable to or allowable by the sub-contractor under clause A4.1.3 (or clause A3 for amounts payable to or allowable by the sub-contractor under provisions in the sub-contract to the like effect as clauses A1.3 and A1.4) - employees other than workpeople - such evidence shall include a certificate signed by or on behalf of the Contractor each week certifying the validity of the evidence reasonably required to ascertain such amounts.

- actual payment by Contractor -
.2 No amount shall be included in or deducted from the amount which would otherwise be stated as due in progress payments by virtue of this clause unless on or before the date as at which the total value of work, materials and goods is ascertained for the purposes of any progress payment the Contractor shall have actually paid or received the sum which is payable by or to him in consequence of the event in respect of which the payment or allowance arises.

- no alteration to Contractor's profit -
.3 No addition to or subtraction from the Contract Sum made by virtue of this clause shall alter in any way the amount of profit of the Contractor included in that Sum.

- position where Contractor in default over completion
.4.1 No amount shall be included in or deducted from the amount which would otherwise be stated as due in progress payments or in the final certificate in respect of amounts otherwise payable to or allowable by the Contractor by virtue of clause A1 or clause A3 if the event (as referred to in the provisions listed in clause A4.1) in respect of which the payment or allowance would be made occurs after the completion date fixed under clause 2.

.4.2 Clause A4.4.4.1 shall not operate unless:
    .1 the printed text of clause 2 is unamended; and
    .2 the Contract Administrator has, in respect of every written notification by the Contractor under clause 2 of the Agreement, fixed such completion date as he considered to be in accordance with that clause.

Work etc. to which clauses A1 and A3 not applicable

A4.5   Clause A1 and clause A3 shall not apply in respect of:

.1 work for which the Contractor is allowed daywork rates in accordance with any such rates included in the Contract Documents;

.2 changes in the rate of value added tax charged on the supply of goods or services by the Contractor to the Employer under this Agreement.

Definitions for use with clause A1

A4.6   In clause A1:

.1 the expression 'the date of tender' means the date 10 days before the date of this Agreement;

.2 the expressions 'materials' and 'goods' include timber used in formwork but do not include other consumable stores, plant and machinery except electricity and, where specifically so stated in the Contract Documents, fuels;

.3 the expression 'workpeople' means persons whose rates of wages and other emoluments (including holiday credits) are governed by the rules or decisions or agreements of the National Joint Council for the Building Industry or some other wage-fixing body for trades associated with the building industry;

.4 the expression 'wage-fixing body' means a body which lays down recognised terms and conditions of workers within the meaning of the Employment Protection Act 1975, Schedule II, paragraph 2(a).

Percentage addition to fluctuation payments or allowances

A5 There shall be added to the amount paid to or allowed by the Contractor under:
.1 clause A1.2
.2 clause A1.3
.3 clause A1.6
.4 clause A2.2
the percentage stated in clause 4.6

B: VALUE ADDED TAX
Clause 5.2

B1 In this Supplemental Condition 'VAT' means the value added tax introduced by the Finance Act 1972 which is under the care and management of the Commissioners of Customs and Excise (hereinafter called 'the Commissioners').

B1.1 .1 Where in clause 5.2 it is stated that clause B1.1 applies, clauses B2.1 and B2.2 hereof shall not apply unless and until any notice issued under clause B1.1.4 hereof becomes effective or unless the Contractor fails to give the written notice required under clause B1.1.2. Where clause B1.1 applies clauses B1 and B3.1 to B10 inclusive remain in full force and effect.

.2 Not later than 7 days before the date for the issue of the first certificate under clause 4.2 the Contractor shall give written notice to the Employer, with a copy to the Contract Administrator, of the rate of tax chargeable on the supply of goods and services for which certificates under clauses 4.2 and 4.3 and the final certificate under clause 4.5 are to be issued. If the rate of tax so notified is varied under statute the Contractor shall, not later than 7 days after the date when such varied rate comes into effect, send to the Employer, with a copy to the Contract Administrator, the necessary amendment to the rate given in his written notice and that notice shall then take effect as so amended.

.3 For the purpose of complying with clause 5.2 for the payment by the Employer to the Contractor of tax properly chargeable by the Commissioners on the Contractor, an amount calculated at the rate given in the aforesaid written notice (or, where relevant, amended written notice) shall be shown on each certificate issued by the Contract Administrator under clauses 4.2 and 4.3 and, unless the procedure set out in clause B3 hereof shall have been completed, on the final certificate issued by the Contract Administrator under clause 4.5. Such amount shall be paid by the Employer to the Contractor or by the Contractor to the Employer as the case may be within the period for payment of certificates given in clauses 4.2, 4.3 and 4.5.

.4 Either the Employer or the Contractor may give written notice to the other, with a copy to the Contract Administrator, stating that with effect from the date of the notice clause B1.1 shall no longer apply. From that date the provisions of clauses B2.1 and B2.2 shall apply in place of clause B1.1 hereof.

B2.1 Unless clause B1.1 applies, the Contract Administrator shall inform the Contractor of the amount certified under clause 4.2 and immediately the Contractor shall give to the Employer a written provisional assessment of the respective values of those supplies of goods and services for which the certificate is being issued and which will be chargeable at the relevant times of supply on the Contractor at any rate or rates of VAT (including zero). The Contractor shall also specify the rate or rates of VAT which are chargeable on those supplies.

B2.2 Upon receipt of the Contractor's written provisional assessment the Employer shall calculate the amount of VAT due by applying the rate or rates of VAT specified by the Contractor to the amount of the supplies included in his assessment, and shall remit the calculated amount of such VAT to the Contractor when making payment to him of the amount certified by the Contract Administrator under clause 4.2

B3.1 Where clause B1.1 is operated clause B3 only applies if no amount of tax pursuant to clause B1.1.3 has been shown on the final certificate issued by the Contract Administrator. After the issue by the Contract Administrator of his certificate of making good defects under clause 2.5 of the Agreement the Contractor shall, as soon as he can finally so ascertain, prepare and submit to the Employer a written final statement of the value of all supplies of goods and services for which certificates have been or will be issued which are chargeable on the Contractor at any rate or rates of VAT (including zero). The Contractor shall also specify the rate or rates of VAT which are chargeable on those supplies and shall state the grounds on which he considers such supplies are so chargeable. He shall also state the total amount of VAT already received by him.

B3.2 Upon receipt of the written final statement the Employer shall calculate the amount of VAT due by applying the rate or rates of VAT specified by the Contractor to the value of the supplies included in the statement and deducting therefrom the total amount of VAT already received by the Contractor and shall pay the balance of such VAT to the Contractor within 28 days from receipt of the statement.

B3.3 If the Employer finds that the total amount of VAT specified in the final statement as already paid by him exceeds the amount of VAT calculated under clause B3.2, he shall so notify the Contractor, who shall refund such excess to the Employer within 28 days of receipt of the notification together with a receipt under clause B4 hereof showing a correction of the amounts for which a receipt or receipts have previously been issued by the Contractor.

B4 Upon receipt of any VAT properly paid under the provisions of this clause the Contractor shall issue to the Employer an authenticated receipt of the kind referred to in Regulation 12(4) of the Value Added Tax (General) Regulations 1985 or any amendment or re-enactment thereof.

B5.1 In calculating the amount of VAT to be paid to the Contractor under clauses B2 and B3 hereof, the Employer shall disregard any sums which the Contractor may be liable to pay or allow to the Employer, or which the Employer may deduct, under clause 2.3 as liquidated damages.

B5.2 The Contractor shall likewise disregard such liquidated damages when stating the value of supplies of goods or services in his written final statement under clause B3.1.

B5.3 Where clause B1.1 is operated the Employer shall pay the tax to which that clause refers notwithstanding any deduction which the Employer may be empowered to make by clause 2.3 from monies due to the Contractor under certificates for payment issued by the Contract Administrator.

B6.1 If the Employer disagrees with the final statement issued by the Contractor under clause B3.1 he may request the Contractor to obtain the decision of the Commissioners on the VAT properly chargeable on the Contractor for all supplies of goods and services under this Agreement and the Contractor shall forthwith request the Commissioners for such decision.

B6.2 If the Employer disagrees with such decision, then, provided he secures the Contractor against all costs and other expenses, the Contractor shall in accordance with the instructions of the Employer make all such appeals against the decision of the Commissioners as the Employer may request.

B6.3 Within 28 days of the date of the decision of the Commissioners (or of the final adjudication of an appeal) the Employer or the Contractor, as the case may be, shall pay or refund to the other any VAT underpaid or overpaid in accordance with such decision or adjudication. The Contractor shall also account to the Employer for any costs awarded in his favour. The provisions of clause B3.3 shall apply in regard to the provision of authenticated receipts.

B7 The provisions of article 7A *(arbitration)* shall not apply to any matters to be dealt with under clause B6.

B8 If any dispute or difference between the Employer and the Contractor is referred for decision under the relevant procedures under this Agreement to the resolution of disputes or differences, then, insofar as any payment awarded by such decision varies amounts certified for payment of goods or services supplied by the Contractor to the Employer under this Agreement or is an amount which ought to have been but was not so certified, then the provisions of this Supplemental Condition B shall so far as relevant and applicable apply to any such payments.

B9 Notwithstanding any provisions to the contrary elsewhere in the Agreement the Employer shall not be obliged to make any further payment to the Contractor if the Contractor is in default in providing the receipt referred to in clause B4; provided that this clause B9 shall only apply where

the Employer can show that he requires such receipt to validate any claim for credit for tax paid or payable under this Supplemental Condition B which the Employer is entitled to make to the Commissioners and

the Employer has paid tax in accordance with the provisional assessment of the Contractor under clause B2.2 or paid tax in accordance with clause B1.1.

B10 The Employer shall be discharged from any further liability to pay tax to the Contractor under the clause upon payment of tax in accordance either with clause B3.2 (adjusted where relevant in accordance with the decision in any appeal to which clause B6 refers) or with clause B1.1.3 in respect of the tax shown in the final certificate. Provided always that if after the due discharge under clause B10 the Commissioners decide to correct the tax due from the Contractor on the supply to the Employer of any goods and services by the Contractor under this Agreement the amount of such correction shall be an additional payment by the Employer to the Contractor or by the Contractor to the Employer as the case may be. The provisions of clause B6 in regard to disagreement with any decision of the Commissioners shall apply to any decision referred to in this proviso.

C: STATUTORY TAX DEDUCTION SCHEME [z]
Clause 5.3

C1 In this clause: 'the Act' means the Income and Corporation Taxes Act 1988; 'the Regulations' means the Income Tax (Sub-Contractors in the Construction Industry) Regulations 1993 S.I. No. 743 or any re-enactment or amendment or remaking thereof; 'contractor' means a person who is a contractor for the proposes of the Act and the Regulations; 'evidence' means such evidence as is required by the Regulations to be produced to a 'contractor' for the verification of a 'sub-contractor's' tax certificate; 'statutory deduction' means the deduction referred to in S.559(4) of the Act or such other deduction as may be in force at the relevant time; 'sub-contractor' means a person who is a sub-contractor for the purposes of the Act and the Regulations; 'tax certificate' is a certificate issuable under S.561 of the Act.

Provision of evidence - tax certificate
C2.1 Not later than 21 days before the first payment becomes due under clause 4 or after the Employer becomes a 'contractor' as referred to in clause 5.3 the Contractor shall:

either

.1 provide the Employer with the evidence that the Contractor is entitled to be paid without the statutory deduction;

or

.2 inform the Employer in writing, and send a duplicate copy to the Contract Administrator, that he is not entitled to be paid without the statutory deduction.

C2.2 If the Employer is not satisfied with the validity of the evidence submitted in accordance with clause C2.1.1 hereof, he shall within 14 days of the Contractor submitting such evidence notify the Contractor in writing that he intends to make the statutory deduction from payments due under this Agreement to the Contractor who is a 'sub-contractor' and give his reasons for that decision. The Employer shall at the same time comply with clause C5.1.

Uncertificated Contractor obtains tax certificate
C3.1 Where clause C2.1.2 applies, the Contractor shall immediately inform the Employer if he obtains a tax certificate and thereupon clause C2.1.1 shall apply.

Expiry of tax certificate
C3.2 If the period for which the tax certificate has been issued to the Contractor expires before the final payment is made to the Contractor under this Agreement the Contractor shall, not later than 28 days before the date of expiry:

either

.1 provide the Employer with evidence that the Contractor from the said date of expiry is entitled to be paid for a further period without the statutory deduction in which case the provisions of clause C2.2 hereof shall apply if the Employer is not satisfied with the evidence;

or

.2 inform the Employer in writing that he will not be entitled to be paid without the statutory deduction after the said date of expiry.

Cancellation of tax certificate
C3.3 The Contractor shall immediately inform the Employer in writing if his current tax certificate is cancelled and give the date of such cancellation.

---

[z] The application of the Tax Deduction Scheme and these provisions is explained in JCT Practice Note 8.

Vouchers

C4 The Employer shall, as a 'contractor', in accordance with the Regulations, send promptly to the Inland Revenue any voucher which, in compliance with the Contractor's obligations as a 'sub-contractor' under the Regulations, the Contractor gives to the Employer.

Statutory deduction - direct cost of materials

C5.1 If at any time the Employer is of the opinion (whether because of the information given under clause C2.1.2 or of the expiry or cancellation of the Contractor's tax certificate or otherwise) that he will be required by the Act to make a statutory deduction from any payment due to be made the Employer shall immediately so notify the Contractor in writing and require the Contractor to state not later than 7 days before each future payment becomes due (or within 10 days of such notification if that is later) the amount to be included in such payment which represents the direct cost to the Contractor and any other person of materials used or to be used in carrying out the Works.

C5.2 Where the Contractor complies with clause C5.1, he shall indemnify the Employer against loss or expense caused to the Employer by any incorrect statement of the amount of direct cost referred to in that clause.

C5.3 Where the Contractor does not comply with clause C5.1 the Employer shall be entitled to make a fair estimate of the amount of direct cost referred to in that clause.

Correction of errors

C6 Where any error or omission has occurred in calculating or making the statutory deduction the Employer shall correct that error or omission by repayment to, or by deduction from payments to, the Contractor as the case may be subject only to any statutory obligation on the Employer not to make such correction.

Relation to other clauses of Agreement

C7 If compliance with this clause involves the Employer or the Contractor in not complying with any other provisions of the Agreement, then the provisions of this clause shall prevail.

Disputes or differences – application of relevant procedures

C8 The procedures under the Agreement relevant to the resolution of disputes or differences shall apply to any dispute or difference between the Employer and the Contractor as to the operation of this clause except where the Act or the Regulations or any other Act of Parliament provide for some other method of resolving such dispute or difference.

D: ADJUDICATION
Clause 8.1

Application of Supplemental Condition D

D1 Supplemental Condition D applies where, pursuant to article 6, either party (i.e. the Employer or the Contractor) refers any dispute or difference arising under this Agreement to adjudication.

Identity of Adjudicator

D2 The Adjudicator to decide the dispute or difference shall be either an individual agreed by the parties or, on the application of either party, an individual to be nominated as the Adjudicator by the person named in article 6 ("the nominator") **[aa]**. Provided that

D2.1 no Adjudicator shall be agreed or nominated under clause D2.2 or clause D3 who will not execute the Standard Agreement for the appointment of an Adjudicator issued by the Joint Contracts Tribunal (the 'JCT Adjudication Agreement' **[bb]**) with the parties **[aa]** and

D2.2 where either party has given notice of his intention to refer a dispute to adjudication then

-    any agreement by the parties on the appointment of an Adjudicator must be reached with the object of securing the appointment of, and the referral of the dispute or difference to, the Adjudicator within 7 days of the date of the notice of intention to refer (see clause D4.1);

-    any application to the nominator must be made with the object of securing the appointment of, and the referral of the dispute or difference to, the Adjudicator within 7 days of the date of the notice of intention to refer.

Upon agreement by the parties on the appointment of the Adjudicator or upon receipt by the parties from the nominator of the name of the nominated Adjudicator the parties shall thereupon execute with the Adjudicator the JCT Adjudication Agreement.

Death of Adjudicator - inability to adjudicate

D3 If the Adjudicator dies or becomes ill or is unavailable for some other cause and is thus unable to adjudicate on a dispute or difference referred to him, then either the parties may agree upon an individual to replace the Adjudicator or either party may apply to the nominator for the nomination of an adjudicator to adjudicate that dispute or difference; and the parties shall execute the JCT Adjudication Agreement with the agreed or nominated Adjudicator.

Dispute or difference - notice of intention to refer to Adjudication - referral

D4.1 When pursuant to article 6 a party requires a dispute or difference to be referred to adjudication then that party

[aa] The nominators named in article 6 have agreed with the JCLI that they will comply with the requirements of Supplemental Condition D on the nomination of an adjudicator including the requirement in clause D2.2 for the nomination to be made with the object of securing the appointment of, and the referral of the dispute or difference to, the Adjudicator within 7 days of the date of the notice of intention to refer; and will only nominate adjudicators who will enter into the JCT Adjudication Agreement.

[bb] The JCT Adjudication Agreement is available from the retailers of JCT Forms.
A version of this Agreement is also available for use if the parties have named an Adjudicator in their agreement.

shall give notice to the other party of his intention to refer the dispute or difference, briefly identified in the notice, to adjudication. If an Adjudicator is agreed or appointed within 7 days of the notice then the party giving the notice shall refer the dispute or difference to the Adjudicator ('the referral') within 7 days of the notice. If an Adjudicator is not agreed or appointed within 7 days of the notice the referral shall be made immediately on such agreement or appointment. The said party shall include with that referral particulars of the dispute or difference together with a summary of the contentions on which he relies, a statement of the relief or remedy which is sought and any material he wishes the Adjudicator to consider. The referral and its accompanying documentation shall be copied simultaneously to the other party.

D4.2   The referral by a party with its accompanying documentation to the Adjudicator and the copies thereof to be provided to the other party shall be given by actual delivery or by FAX or by special delivery or recorded delivery. If given by FAX then, for record purposes, the referral and its accompanying documentation must forthwith be sent by first class post or given by actual delivery. If sent by special delivery or recorded delivery the referral and its accompanying documentation shall, subject to proof to the contrary, be deemed to have been received 48 hours after the date of posting subject to the exclusion of Sundays and any Public Holiday.

Conduct of the Adjudication

D5.1   The Adjudicator shall immediately upon receipt of the referral and its accompanying documentation confirm that receipt to the Parties.

D5.2   The party not making the referral may, by the same means stated in clause D4.2 send to the Adjudicator within 7 days of the date of the referral, with a copy to the other party, a written statement of the contentions on which he relies and any material he wishes the Adjudicator to consider.

D5.3   The Adjudicator shall within 28 days of the referral under clause D4.1, and acting as an Adjudicator for the purposes of S.108 of the Housing Grants, Construction and Regeneration Act 1996 and not as an expert or an arbitrator, reach his decision and forthwith send that decision in writing to the parties. Provided that the party who has made the referral may consent to allowing the Adjudicator to extend the period of 28 days by up to 14 days; and that by agreement between the parties after the referral has been made a longer period than 28 days may be notified jointly by the parties to the Adjudicator within which to reach his decision.

D5.4   The Adjudicator shall not be obliged to give reasons for his decision.

D5.5   In reaching his decision the Adjudicator shall act impartially and set his own procedure; and at his absolute discretion may take the initiative in ascertaining the facts and the law as he considers necessary in respect of the referral which may include the following:

.1   using his own knowledge and/or experience;

.2   opening up, reviewing and revising any certificate, opinion, decision, requirement or notice issued, given or made under the Agreement as if no such certificate opinion, decision, requirement or notice had been issued, given or made;

.3   requiring from the parties further information than that contained in the notice of referral and its accompanying documentation or in any written statement provided by the parties including the results of any test that have been made or of any opening up;

.4   requiring the parties to carry out tests or additional tests or to open up work or further open up work;

.5   visiting the site of the Works or any workshop where work is being or has been prepared for this Agreement;

.6   obtaining such information as he considers necessary from any employee or representative of the parties provided that before obtaining information from an employee of a party he has given prior notice to that party;

.7   obtaining from others such information and advice as he considers necessary on technical and on legal matters subject to giving prior notice to the parties together with a statement or estimate of the cost involved;

.8   having regard to any term of this Agreement relating to the payment of interest deciding the circumstance in which or the period for which a simple rate of interest shall be paid.

D5.6   Any failure by either party to enter into the JCT Adjudication Agreement or to comply with any requirement of the Adjudicator under clause D5.5 or with any provision in or requirement under Supplemental Condition D shall not invalidate the decision of the Adjudicator.

D5.7   The Parties shall meet their own costs of the Adjudication except that the Adjudicator may direct as to who should pay the cost of any test or opening up if required pursuant to clause D5.5.4.

Adjudicator's fee and reasonable expenses - payment

D6.1   The Adjudicator in his decision shall state how payment of his fee and reasonable expenses is to be apportioned as between the parties. In default of such statement the parties shall bear the cost of the Adjudicator's fee and reasonable expenses in equal proportions.

D6.2   The parties shall be jointly and severally liable to the Adjudicator for his fee and for all expenses reasonably incurred by the Adjudicator pursuant to the adjudication.

Effect of Adjudicator's decision

D7.1   The decision of the Adjudicator shall be binding on the parties until the dispute or difference is finally determined by arbitration or by legal proceedings or by an agreement in writing between the parties made after the decision of the Adjudicator has been given. [cc]

D7.2   The parties shall, without prejudice to their other rights under this Agreement, comply with the decision of the Adjudicator; and the Employer and the Contractor shall ensure that the decision of the Adjudicator is given effect.

D7.3   If either party does not comply with the decision of the Adjudicator the other party shall be entitled to take legal proceedings to secure such compliance pending any final determination of the referred dispute or difference pursuant to clause D7.1.

Immunity

D8   The Adjudicator shall not be liable for anything done or omitted in the discharge or purported discharge of his functions as Adjudicator unless the act or omission is in bad faith and this protection from liability shall similarly extend to any employee or agent of the Adjudicator.

[cc]   The arbitration or legal proceedings are not an appeal against the decision of the Adjudicator but are a consideration of the dispute or difference as if no decision had been made by an Adjudicator.

E: ARBITRATION
Clause 8.2

E1   Any reference in Supplemental Condition E to a Rule or Rules is a reference to the JCT 1998 edition of the Construction Industry Model Arbitration Rules (CIMAR) current at the date of this Agreement.

E2.1   Where pursuant to article 7A either party requires a dispute or difference to be referred to arbitration then that party shall serve on the other party a notice of arbitration to such effect in accordance with Rule 2.1 which states:

> "Arbitral proceedings are begun in respect of a dispute when one party serves on the other a written notice of arbitration identifying the dispute and requiring him to agree to the appointment of an arbitrator";

and an arbitrator shall be an individual agreed by the parties or appointed by the person named in article 7A in accordance with Rule 2.3 which states:

> "If the parties fail to agree on the name of an arbitrator within 14 days (or any agreed extension) after:
> (i)   the notice of arbitration is served, or
> (ii) a previously appointed arbitrator ceases to hold office for any reason,
> either party may apply for the appointment of an arbitrator to the person so empowered."

By Rule 2.5:

> "the arbitrator's appointment takes effect upon his agreement to act or his appointment under Rule 2.3, whether or not his terms have been accepted."

E2.2   Where two or more related arbitral proceedings in respect of the Works fall under separate arbitration agreements, Rules 2.6, 2.7 and 2.8 shall apply thereto.

E2.3   After an arbitrator has been appointed either party may give a further notice of arbitration to the other party and to the Arbitrator referring any other dispute which falls under article 7A to be decided in the arbitral proceedings and Rule 3.3 shall apply thereto.

E3   Subject to the provisions of article 7A the Arbitrator shall, without prejudice to the generality of his powers, have power to rectify this Agreement so that it accurately reflects the true agreement made by the parties, to direct such measurements and/or valuations as may in his opinion be desirable in order to determine the rights of the parties and to ascertain and award any sum which ought to have been the subject of or included in any certificate and to open up, review and revise any certificate, opinion, decision, requirement or notice and to determine all matters in dispute which shall be submitted to him in the same manner as if no such certificate, opinion, decision, requirement or notice had been given.

E4   Subject to clause E5 the award of such Arbitrator shall be final and binding on the Parties.

E5   The parties hereby agree pursuant to Section 45(2)(a) and Section 69(2)(a) of the Arbitration Act 1996 that either party may (upon notice to the other party and to the Arbitrator):

.1   apply to the courts to determine any question of law arising in the course of the reference; and

.2   appeal to the courts on any question of law arising out of an award made in an arbitration under this Agreement.

E6   The provisions of the Arbitration Act 1996 shall apply to any arbitration under this Agreement wherever the same, or any part of it, shall be conducted. **[dd]**

E7   The arbitration shall be conducted in accordance with the JCT 1998 edition of the Construction Industry Model Arbitration Rules (CIMAR) current at the date of this Agreement. Provided that if any amendments to the Rules so current at the date of this Agreement have been issued by the JCT after the date of this Agreement the parties may, by a joint notice in writing to the Arbitrator, state that they wish the arbitration to be conducted in accordance with the Rules as so amended.

[dd]   It should be noted that the provisions of the Arbitration Act 1996 do not extend to Scotland. Where the site of the Works is situated in Scotland then the forms issued by the Scottish Building Contract Committee which contain Scots proper law and adjudication and arbitration provisions are the appropriate documents. The SBCC issues guidance in this respect.

JCLI PRACTICE NOTE No. 5   December 1998

Explanatory Notes regarding the JCLI Agreement for Landscape Works

Note: This JCLI Practice Note No 5 supersedes No 1 issued April 1978, No 2 issued April 1982 and No 3 issued April 1985 (and all subsequent revisions).
First issued June 1996, revised December 1998 (revised as indicated in JCLI.AMD98)
For use with the 1998 Edition of the JCLI Agreement for Landscape Works

1. **1st Recital: Schedules**
Schedules means a list of items giving quantities, as necessary, and descriptions of work required, prepared in accordance with an appropriate method of measurement, which will be priced by tenderers and subsequently be a contract document. Detailed information on materials and workmanship shall be contained in the Specification.

2. **1st Recital and Clause 1.8: Bills of Quantities**
Provision is made for the option of including in the contract documents Bills prepared in accordance with SMM.

3. **4th Recital**
This provides for the naming of a quantity surveyor; neither the articles nor the Conditions mention him but the Employer or the Contract Administrator on his behalf may wish to appoint a quantity surveyor in connection with the project, for example, to assist with valuations.

4. **5th Recital: CDM Regulations**
The provisions in the JCLI Agreement for Landscape Works to accommodate the CDM Regulations essentially follow those in the JCT Minor Works Agreement. The main difference is that the JCLI Agreement for Landscape Works includes 4 alternatives in the 5th recital whereas the JCTMW Agreement only includes two.

   a. Alternative A, the CDM Regulations do not apply, is for projects where none of the work is "construction work" as defined in the CDM Regulations. Current advice is that topsoiling, grading, amelioration, planting, grassing, agricultural and rabbit proof fencing, soft landscape maintenance, tree work and preparation for these works (including site clearance and excavation) are not within the definition of "construction work" in the Regulations. If soft landscape work (as listed above) is carried out as a separate main contract after practical completion of a building/engineering contract then the CDM Regulations do not apply to the soft landscape work. The borderline between earthworks (which is "construction work") and topsoiling (which is not "construction work") is unclear. The CDM Regulations also do not apply when the Local Authority are the Health and Safety enforcing authority, but this is never the case for external works

(although it may be for interior landscape works which involve hard landscape).

   b. Alternative B, the CDM Regulations apply, is for projects which include "construction work" as defined in the Regulations. Current advice is that "construction work" in relation to landscape works includes earthworks, all hard landscaping, drainage, demolition/ dismantling, temporary works, maintenance of "construction works" and preparation for such works (including site clearance and excavation). Regulation 13 (Requirements on the Designer) applies to all 3 alternatives below.

   i) Alternative B1, all the Regulations apply, is for projects involving "construction work" and where alternative B2 and B3 do not apply.

   ii) Alternative B2, Regulations 4, 6, 8 to 12 and 14 to 19 do not apply, is for projects where "construction work" is for a domestic householder having work carried out on their own residence except where Regulation 5 applies (where a domestic client enters an arrangement with a developer). A Planning Supervisor, Principal Contractor, Health and Safety Plan and a Health and Safety File are not therefore required for these projects, but the Contractor has to notify HSE (if the project involves more than 30 days or 500 person days of "construction work") - see clause 1.4 in the Conditions.

   iii) Alternative B3, Regulations 4 to 12 and 14 to 19 do not apply, is for projects which:

   - are not notifiable to HSE (i.e. will not involve more than 30 days or more than 500 person days of "construction work"), and

   - do not include demolition or dismantling, and

   - will always involve less than 5 persons on site carrying out "construction work" at any one time.

Therefore, a Planning Supervisor, Principal Contractor, Health and Safety Plan and a Health and Safety File are not required for these small projects.

5. Articles 4 and 5
Articles 4 and 5 only apply when alternative B1 in the 5th recital applies. Article 4 names the Contract Administrator as the Planning Supervisor with the option for someone else to be named. Article 5 names the Contractor as the Principal Contractor with the option for someone else to be named, but in most circumstances the Contractor should be the Principal Contractor.

6. Article 7
Article 7 includes option A: arbitration and option B: legal proceedings. Where the Employer is a consumer (i.e. "a natural person who in making a contract is acting for purposes outside his business") legal proceedings in place of arbitration should be considered by the Employer. This is necessary to avoid a potential breach of the Unfair Terms in Consumer Contracts Regulations 1994. Those Regulations set out in Schedule 3 an "indicative and illustrative list of terms which may be regarded as unfair". One of these terms (Schedule 3(q)) states: "excluding or hindering the consumer's rights to take legal action or exercise any other legal remedy, particularly by requiring the consumer to take disputes exclusively to arbitration not covered by legal provisions."

7. Clauses 1.3 and 1.4
Both clauses are qualified by the relevant alternative of the 5th recital. In both cases if the alternative stated is not relevant the clause can be deleted.

8. Clause 2.3
Liquidated Damages
Liquidated damages should be calculated prior to tender and the tenderers advised of the amount. The calculation should be the sum of three figures, an amount for the weekly cost of administering the contract during the period of delay (i.e. professional fees), an amount for notional interest lost, and any expected loss flowing from late completion.

It is not possible to estimate accurately the loss of interest an Employer will suffer when a contract is delayed, but a reasonable estimate can be made by multiplying the estimated contract value by the bank Base Rate plus 2% and dividing by 52 to give a weekly rate.

e.g. Estimated Contract Value   £75,000
Base Rate + 2%   9%
Interest = $\frac{£75,000 \times 9\%}{52}$ = £129.80

Liquidated and ascertained damages in this case would be £129.80 plus a pre-estimate of the weekly cost of professional fees, plus any expected loss per week.

9. Clause 2.4: Date of Practical Completion
The date of practical completion is that date when the Contract Administrator certifies that the Contractor has fulfilled his obligations under the terms of the contract. This does not preclude partial possession (dealt with under Clause 2.6) but simply determines the commencement of the defects liability period(s) for that part of the work.

Where the Contract Administrator is unable to certify practical completion due say to seasonal planting requirements, he may nevertheless certify practical completion on receiving the Contractor's written undertaking to complete the planting within an agreed time and, if clause 2.8A applies to extend the periods within clause 2.8A.1 by that agreed time for the planting concerned. See also item 12 below.

10. Clause 2.5: Defects Liability
Except for plants which are dealt with separately the Contractor is responsible for making good all defects which appear after practical completion within a period inserted in clause 2.5. The Conditions allow for different liability periods for hard landscape, grass, shrubs and trees. It is recommended that for hard landscape this period should normally be 6 months. In all cases the period should begin on the date of practical completion. See also item 12 below.

11. Clause 2.7: Plant Failures - at Practical Completion
All plants which have failed or which are not in accordance with the Contract Documents at practical completion shall be replaced by the Contractor entirely at his own expense (except for malicious damage or theft if clause 2.9B applies). The Contract Administrator will prepare a schedule of these defects and the Contractor will inform the Contract Administrator when the work has been rectified.

12. Clause 2.8A or B: Plant Failures - after Practical Completion
At the time of preparing the tender documents a decision must be made as to whether the Contractor or the Employer is to be responsible for the care of trees, shrubs and grass after practical completion. If a defects period (or periods) is required for the plants, a separate agreement between the Contractor and Employer will be needed to cover the care of the plants after practical completion. The JCLI Agreement for Landscape Maintenance Works is recommended for such an agreement. The construction and maintenance agreements should be separate but tendered together, accepted together and signed at the same time. The maintenance works should commence at practical completion of the construction works. A consequence of partial possession by the Employer will be the staggered

commencement of the maintenance works (but staggered completion of the maintenance works should be avoided).

A programme should be included in the tender documents stating: dates for commencement, completion, end of defects period(s); periods for operations like soiling, planting, grassing; and identifying periods for planting oddities (which may be after practical completion) e.g. bulbs, aquatic plants and wildflower plugs.

i)   If the Employer is to be responsible for care following practical completion then 2.8A.1 and 2.8A.2 are deleted and 2.8B is used, the Contractor is then relieved of all further obligations to replace defective plants other than those arising before practical completion. This option is not generally recommended because of the lack of a plant guarantee and due to the difficulty in assessing plant failures at practical completion particularly when practical completion follows just after planting in the dormant season.

ii)   If care post practical completion is to be carried out by the Contractor under a separate maintenance agreement as described above, 2.8B is deleted and 2.8A.1 and 2.8A.2 are used and the Contractor is then responsible for replacing all plants proving defective due to materials and workmanship not in accordance with the Contract Documents during the period(s) stated.

When the Contractor is responsible for care post practical completion the defects liability periods should not exceed the duration of the maintenance contract. In most cases it is ideal to have defects liability periods equal for all plants - 1 year, 2 years or more. However, minimum defects liability periods of 6 months for grass, 12 months for shrubs and trees and 2 years for semi mature and ELNS trees are recommended.

It is recommended that where varying defects liability periods are required by the Agreement, the work associated with each liability period is kept separate in the schedules/Bills of Quantities.

In all cases the defects liability periods begin at Practical Completion.

13. Clause 2.9: Malicious Damage
When the risk of malicious damage or theft prior to practical completion is considered small clause 2.9A should be used and tenderers will make their own assessments of the likely cost and include it in their tenders.

If it is preferred to reimburse the Contractor only for the actual cost of such damage which arises prior to practical completion then a provisional sum should be included in the tender documents and Clause 2.9B used.

If Clause 2.9B applies, the Contractor shall report losses from malicious damage or theft as they occur, for verification by the Contract Administrator. The Contract Administrator may issue the necessary instructions for their replacement.

14. Clause 3.7: PC Sums
Particular attention is drawn to clause 3.6 where it will be noted that no cash discount is allowable by sub-contractors or suppliers arising out of instructions issued by the Contract Administrator in respect of prime cost sums. As such quotations are accepted nett Contractors are deemed to have included for the lack of cash discount elsewhere in the Contract Sum.

15. Clause 4.1: Correction of inconsistencies
This does not provide that every correction is to be treated as a variation.

Where there are priced schedules/Bills of Quantities any correction which results in a revision to the quantities and/or rates in the schedules/Bills will result in a variation.

Where there are no priced schedules/Bills of Quantities it may be necessary for the Contract Administrator to determine which of two inconsistent documents is the ruling document or which of two inconsistent statements prevails and such determination shall be treated as a variation under clause 3.6 if the ruling document/statement is changed.

16. Clause 4.5: Final Certificate

The following procedure does **not** apply if either:

- the defects periods for hard and all types of soft landscape are the same (i.e. the periods in clauses 2.5 and 2.8A.1 are the same); or

- the Contractor will not be responsible for plant defects after practical completion (i.e. clause 2.8B applies rather than clause 2.8A).

When the Contractor is responsible for maintenance under a separate agreement (i.e. clause 2.8A applies rather then 2.8B) there are potentially 4 defects liability periods varying from 6 months to perhaps 5 years. This causes the problem of accommodating a staggered release of retention. The 1998 Edition includes modifications which aim to strike a fair balance between the interests of the Contractor and those of the Employer by releasing retention on work with short defects liability periods and retaining money on work with long defects liability periods.

When clause 2.8A applies and there are different defects liability periods in clauses 2.5 and 2.8A.1, the procedure is:

- The final certificate is issued when the relevant information has been received and the certificates have been issued under clauses 2.5 and 2.7. (The final certificate is not delayed until all the certificates have been issued under clause 2.8A.1);

- The final certificate sum is the full Contract Sum adjusted for variations less retentions associated with the unexpired defects liability periods in clause 2.8A.1. (Note: instructions for additional work like the replacement of vandalised plants or for additional plants, etc. will not be possible under the Agreement once the final certificate has been issued – they will need to be agreed and paid separately, or possibly instructed as part of the maintenance agreement);

- The Employer issues a notice (under clause 4.5.1.2) within five days of the date of issue of the final certificate stating the sum that will be paid. At the same time he also issues a notice (under clause 4.5.1.5) stating the amounts that continue to be withheld and why (pending receipt of certificates under clause 2.8A.1), including a schedule of amounts to be released when the certificates are received and the expiry date of each such defects period.

17. Supplemental Conditions A to E
The Supplemental Conditions correspond to those in the JCT Agreement for Minor Building Works.

18. Temporary Protection
Temporary protective measures prior to practical completion are the responsibility of the Contractor but any requirements and details should be specified in the preliminaries; for example, the risk and requirements for segregation of the public from the site for health and safety reasons should be specified.

If protective fencing is required and is to be retained after practical completion, it must be clearly stated and quantified at tender stage. It will be part of the Works and owned by the Employer and not 'temporary works' (owned by the Contractor).

19. Watering
Watering prior to practical completion is the responsibility of the Contractor. The Specification (preliminaries) should include details of watering points, irrigation system, who pays for water including during periods when restrictions on watering apply and any other relevant information. Watering and liability for losses due to lack of water after practical completion does not form part of this contract but will form part of any subsequent maintenance contract.

20. Frost Damage
Severe winter weather conditions can cause considerable damage to plant material. The Contractor is entirely responsible for the replacement of plants which fail before practical completion due to weather conditions. Protection from frost and liability for losses due to frost after practical completion do not form part of this contract but will form part of any subsequent maintenance contract.

21. Plants / Specification
Several initiatives to improve performance, quality and standardisation within the Landscape Industry were implemented in 1997/8. The JCLI recommends that plants should be specified in accordance with the National Plant Specification (available from the Landscape Institute, tel. 0171 738 9166) and supplied by a nursery (nurseries) in the HTA Nursery Certification Scheme (list of such nurseries and details of the scheme are available from HTA, tel. 0118 9303132)

NBS Landscape has also been developed (in conjunction with LI Technical Committee) to improve standardisation of specification for landscape works and it supports the JCLI Agreement for Landscape Works (as well as JCTIFC 84 with the JCLI Supplement). JCLI would like to see NBS used widely for specifications in the Landscape Industry and particularly when the JCLI Agreements are used (NBS, tel. 0191 232 9594).

22. Housing Grants Construction and Regeneration Act
The 1998 Edition of the JCLI Agreement for Landscape Works incorporates the requirements of the Housing Grants Construction and Regeneration Act (i.e. payment and adjudication provisions) in the same way as the 1998 Edition of the JCT Minor Works Agreement does. These revisions are explained in JCT Amendment MW11.

JCLI

This Practice Note is issued by the Joint Council for Landscape Industries

This document is for issue with the JCLI Agreement for Landscape Works 1998 Edition.

Published for the Joint Council for Landscape Industries by the Landscape Institute

© JCLI December 1998

APPENDIX 4 – THE JCLI STANDARD FORM OF TENDER AND SUBCONTRACT CONDITIONS

Form of Tender and Conditions of Subcontract

For use with the JCLI Agreement for Landscape Works.

Information for Tenderers

1. Contract name and location: ....

2. Employer: ....

3. Contractor: ....

4. Landscape Architect: ....

5. The Form of Contract is the JCLI Agreement for Landscape Works, completed as follows:

   Clause 2·1: The Works may be commenced on .... and shall be completed by ....

   Clause 2·3: Liquidated damages: £ .... per week or part of a week.

   Clause 2·5: Defects Liability Period: .... months

   Clause 2·7: Plant Failures grass .... months after Practical Completion

   　　　　　　　shrubs and trees .... months after Practical Completion

   　　　　　　　semi mature and ELNS trees .... months after Practical Completion

   Clause 4·4　　Documents for Final Valuation ....

   Clause 4·5　　Contributions levy and tax changes ....

   Clause 6·3 A/B Insurance against fire .... clause A/B deleted.

   Clause 6·3A　Percentage to cover professional fees ....

   Clause 6·5B　Provisional sum for malicious damage ....

   *Clause 6·3A will be deleted.
   *Clause 6·3B will be deleted, the insurance under clause 6·3A being the full value plus ....%

6. The Subcontractor shall, before tendering, visit the Site or otherwise make himself familiar with the extent of the Subcontract Works, the Site Conditions, and all local conditions and restrictions likely to affect the execution of the work. The Subcontractor may have access to any available drawings or work programmes relative to the preparation of his tender on request and by appointment.

7. Two copies of this Form are provided – One copy to be priced, signed by the Subcontractor and

   returned to .... the other is for his retention.

Form of Tender

1. Tender price for ....
    (The Enquirer should enter trade or brief description of Works)

    .... Total tender price

    The Tenderer should enter the amount of his tender in words and figures.

    2a The tender is to be adjusted for price fluctuations of labour only/materials only*/labour and materials* as set out in Subcontract Condition 4·4, a list of relevant basic prices being enclosed.

    2b The tender is to be adjusted for price fluctuations by use of the NEDO Price Adjustment Formula Indices (Category ....)/the Specialist Engineering Installation Indices (Category ....)*.

    *2c The tender is to be on a firm price basis.

3. **Schedule of Daywork Charges**
    The Subcontractor is requested to insert his hourly daywork rates in the space provided in the Schedule below. His rates for labour shall be deemed to include overheads and profit and all payments in connection with Holidays with Pay, Bonus and Pension Schemes, Subsistence Allowances, Fares and Travelling Time, Imported Labour Costs, Non-Productive Overtime Costs, and any other payments made under the Working Rule Agreement, any Regulation, Bye-law or Act of Parliament. The Subcontractor is also invited to insert in the space provided the percentage addition he will require for his overheads and profits on the nett cost of materials and on plant charges.

    (i) **Labour**

        Craftsmen @ ....£ .... per hour

        Labourers/Mates @ .... £ .... per hour

    (ii) **Materials and Plant**
        Materials invoice cost plus .... %

        Plant Charges plus .... %

4. Period of notice required before commencing the Subcontract Works: ....

    Time required to complete the Subcontract Works (the Subcontract Period unless agreed

    otherwise): ....

5. We, the undersigned, agree that this quotation will be open for acceptance within .... week(s) and that we have read and understand the terms and conditions printed overleaf and that should our quotation be accepted we will enter into a Subcontract in accordance with the said terms and conditions.

    For and on behalf of ....

    ....

    Signed ....Date ....

---

*Delete if not required.

This page may be torn off.

Conditions of Subcontract

1·0 Intentions

Subcontractor's Obligation

1·1 The Subcontractor shall with due diligence and in a good and workmanlike manner carry out and complete the Works in accordance with the Subcontract Documents using materials and workmanship of the quality and standards therein specified provided that where and to the extent that approval of the quality of materials or of the standards of workmanship is a matter for the opinion of the Landscape Architect such quality and standards shall be to the reasonable satisfaction of the Landscape Architect.
No approval expressed or implied by the Contractor and/or the Landscape Architect shall in any way relieve the Subcontractor of his responsibility for complying with the requirements of this Subcontract.

Principal Contract and Special Conditions

1·2 The Subcontractor is deemed to have full knowledge of, and so far as they are applicable to the Works agrees to comply with, the provisions of the Principal Contract as though the same were incorporated herein and the Main Contractor were the Employer and the Subcontractor were the Contractor. Any conditions contained in the Subcontractor's Tender shall be excluded.

Information provided by others

1·3 The Subcontractor must make written application to the Contractor for instructions, drawings, levels or other information at a date which is not unreasonably distant from nor unreasonably close to the date on which it is necessary for the Subcontractor to receive the same.

Information provided for others

1·4 Any instructions, drawings, levels or other information relating to the Works which is requested from the Subcontractor must be provided in due time and so as not to cause disruption or delay to the works to be performed under the Principal Contract.

2·0 Commencement and Completion

Progress and Completion

2·1 The Works are to be commenced within the period of notice stated on the Form of Tender and are to be completed within the Subcontract period subject only to such fair and reasonable extension of time as the Contractor shall allow. The Works are to be carried out diligently and in such order, manner and time as the Contractor may reasonably direct so as to ensure completion of the Principal Contract Works or any portion thereof by the completion date or such extended date as may be allowed under the Principal Contract. If the Subcontractor is in breach of the foregoing he shall pay or allow to the Contractor the amount of loss or damage suffered by the Contractor in consequence thereof.

Overtime

2·2 No overtime is to be worked without the Subcontractor first obtaining the consent in writing of the Contractor. No additional payment for overtime will be made unless the Subcontractor is so advised in writing by the Contractor and, if the Subcontractor is so advised, he will be reimbursed the net additional non-productive rate incurred, including any net additional cost of Employers' Liability and Third Party Insurances. The Subcontractor will be required to obtain any necessary overtime permit from the appropriate authority.

Annual Holidays

2·3 Under the Annual Holiday Agreement, the Site will be closed down for certain periods which may be whilst the Subcontractor's work is in progress. The Subcontractor will be deemed to have included in his Tender for any additional costs and time resulting from such closure.

Maintenance and Defects Liability

2·4 The Subcontractor will (1) maintain the Works at his own expense to the Contractor's and the Landscape Architect satisfaction both during the progress of the Works and until the Landscape Architect has issued a Certificate of Practical Completion including the Works and (2) make good at his own expense, and at a time to be decided by the Contractor, any defects or damage to the Works.

3·0 Control of the Works

Assignment

3·1 Neither the Contractor nor the Subcontractor shall, without the written consent of the other, assign this Contract.

Use of Site

3·2 The Site shall not be used for any purpose other than for the carrying out of the Works. Works to be executed outside the Main Contractor's Site boundary shall be carried out to suit the convenience of adjacent occupiers or Local Authorities at times to be agreed by the Contractor in writing.

Variations

3·3 No variation shall vitiate this Subcontract. The Subcontractor shall advise the Contractor in writing of all work involving a variation or extra work within 14 days of such variation or extra work becoming apparent, at the same time submiting detailed and priced calculations based upon this Subcontract showing such price adjustment, if any. Variations or extra work shall not be undertaken by the Subcontractor nor shall he receive payment for such variation or extra works without written authority from the Contractor.
Where variations or extra works cannot be valued by reference to this Subcontract then the value of such variations or extra works shall be subject to agreement between the Contractor and/or the Landscape Architect and the Subcontractor.

Dayworks

3·4 No daywork will be permitted except where in the opinion of the Contractor and/or the Landscape Architect, it would be unfair to value such work at other than daywork rates. Where the Subcontractor considers he has claim to daywork due notice must be given and valuation by daywork approved by the Contractor in writing prior to the execution of the work in question in order to facilitate checking the time and materials expended thereon. All daywork sheets shall be rendered by the end of the week during which the work is executed. All daywork will be paid for at the rates stated on the Form of Tender.

Adjustment for Provisional Sums

3·5 Instructions will be issued in respect of Provisional Sums. No loss of profit will be allowed in respect of such instructions.

4·0 Payments

Discount to the Contractor

4·1 The Subcontractor will allow for all payments to be made in full within 17 days of the date of the Landscape Architect's Certificate to the Employer without any cash discount for prompt payment. Any such discount included on the Form of Tender will be deducted from the tender sum before the order for the subcontract works is placed.

Progress Payments

4·2 Payment will, subject always to these terms and conditions, be made to the Subcontractor as and when the value of such Works under the terms of the Principal Contract is included in a Certificate to the Contractor and the Contractor receives the monies due thereunder. Applications for payment are to be rendered to the Contractor in duplicate by the Subcontractor.
Payment shall be by instalments of the rate of:
95% of the value executed as the Works proceed.
2½% upon practical complete of the Works.
2½% on satisfactory completion of making good defects under the Principal Contract or as soon as the final account for all Works executed under this Subcontract shall have been agreed, whichever may last happen.
Progress payments shall be on account only and shall not be held to signify approval by the Contractor and/or the Landscape Architect of the whole or any part of the Works executed nor shall any final payment prejudice any claim the Contractor may have in respect of any defects in the Works whenever such defects may appear.

Estimates of Loss, etc.

4·3 In addition to the Contractor' Common Law rights of set off, if the Subcontractor shall cause the Contractor loss by reason of any breach of this Contract or by any tortious act or by any breach of statutory duty giving rise to a claim for damages or indemnity or contribution by the Contractor against the Subcontractor, or the Contractor shall become entitled to payment from the Subcontractor under this Contract, then without prejudice to and pending the final determination or agreement between the parties, the Contractor shall bona fide estimate the amount of such loss, indemnity or contribution or payment, such estimate to be binding and conclusive upon the Subcontractor until such final determination or agreement.

Fluctuations (to apply only if item 2a of the Form of Tender is completed).

4·4 The sum or sums referred to in this Subcontract shall be based upon the rates of wages and such other emoluments, allowances and expenses (including the cost of Employers' Liability and Third Party Insurances) as are properly payable by the Subcontractor to work-people engaged upon or in connection with the Works in acccordance with the rules or decisions of the wage fixing body of the trade or trades concerned applicable to the Works. Such rates of wages and the prices of materials shall be as detailed in the Basic Price List as provided by the Subcontractor and attached hereto.
Should any fluctuations from the Basic Price List occur during the currency of this Subcontract, the net additional cost actually and properly incurred or saving that ought to have been made, by such fluctuations shall be added to or be deducted from the total amount payable under the terms and conditions of this Subcontract. Fluctuations in the cost of materials will be adjusted net.
Provided always that immediate notice in writing shall be given of such fluctuations, and an approved weekly return submitted to the Contractor showing the total number of men and hours and the deliveries of materials effected for detailed checking by the Contractor and Landscape Architect.

5·0 Statutory Obligations

Safety, Health and Welfare

5·1 The Subcontractor shall comply with the Contractor's requirements on matters affecting the safe conduct of work on the Site and all statutes, bye laws and regulations affecting the Works and the carrying out thereof.

Statutory Payments

5·2 The Subcontractor shall include in his quotation for any payments to be made under the Working Rule Agreement, all payments in connection with holidays with Pay, Bonus and Pension Schemes, National Insurance, Subsistence Allowances, Fares and Travelling Time, Imported Labour Costs or any payments required by Regulations, Bye-law or Act of Parliament.

6·0 Injury, Damage and Insurance

Responsibilities of the Subcontractor

6·1 The Subcontractor shall indemnify the Contractor against all claims, causes of action, costs, loss and expense whatsoever in respect of:

1. Personal injury or death of any person or injury or damage to any property real or personal arising out of or in the course of or caused by any works executed by the Subcontractor and/or the execution of such works (including but not restricted to the use of any plant, equipment or facilities whether in connection with such execution or otherwise) and/or any design undertaken by the Subcontractor and
2. Any negligence or breach of duty on the part of the Subcontractor, his Subcontractors, his or their servants or agents and
3. Any breach or non-performance or non-observance by the Subcontractor, his Subcontractors, his or their servants or agents of the provisions of the Principal Contract in so far as they relate or apply to the Works and are not inconsistent with the provisions of this Subcontract.
4. Any act, omission, default or neglect of the Subcontractor, his Subcontractors, his or their servants or agents which involves the Contractor in any liability under the Principal Contract.
5. Any damage, claim loss or expense to or involving any plant (whether of the type aforesaid or otherwise) hired or loaned or otherwise made available to the Subcontractor or operating for the Subcontractor's benefit.

Responsibilities of Others
6·2 The Subcontractor shall not be responsible for loss or damage caused by fire, storm, tempest, lightning, flood, bursting and overflowing of water tanks, apparatus or pipes, earthquake, aircraft or anything dropped therefrom, aerial objects, riot and civil commotion, to the Works or to any materials (other than temporary buildings, plant, tools, scaffolding and machinery provided by the Subcontractor, or any scaffolding or other plant which is loaned to him by the Contractor), properly upon the Site and in connection with and for the purpose of the Subcontract. In the event of any such loss or damage, the Subcontractor shall, if and when directed by the Contractor in writing, proceed immediately with the rectification or replacement of the damaged work and materials and the erection and completion of the Works in full accordance with the terms, provisions and conditions hereof, and expenses in respect of any of the matters referred to in subclause 6.1.1 and 6.1.2 above and shall on demand produce to the Contractor adequate evidence of such insurance.

Subcontractor's Work, Materials and Plant
6·3 The Works, materials, tools, plant, scaffolding, machinery and buildings of the Subcontractor, the subject of or used in connection with this Subcontract whether on Site or not, shall in every respect be at the Subcontractor's risk (except those risks for which the Subcontractor is not responsible under Clause 6·2).

Subcontractor's Insurance
6·4 The Subcontractor shall adequately insure:
1 His and the Contractor's liability in respect of any claims, causes of action, costs, losses and expenses in respect of any of the matters referred to in sub-clauses 6·1·1 and 6·1·2.

2 Against all Employers' Liability and Third Party (including Third Party Fire) risks arising out of the execution of the Works.

The Subcontractor shall produce on demand policies of such insurances, together with receipts for premiums, or other adequate evidence of such insurance.

In case of neglect by the Subcontractor to effect the insurances, the Contractor shall be at liberty to insure on behalf of the Subcontractor and to deduct the premium so paid from any monies due or becoming due to the Subcontractor.

7·0 Determination

Determination by the Contractor
7·1 The Contractor may without prejudice to any other of his rights or remedies determine the Subcontractor's employment under this Subcontract if the Subcontractor:
1. fails forthwith upon notice from the Contractor to commence remedial work to any defective workmanship and/or materials or fails to proceed with the same with due diligence or to complete such remedial work to the satisfaction of the Contractor or the Landscape Architect within a set period as the Contractor may specify in the said notice or if none is so specified within a reasonable time.
2. fails to withdraw immediately, at the request of the Contractor, any one or more of his employees to whom the Contractor objects or whose presence on the Works may contravene the conditions of this or the Principal Contract, or may cause labour disputes in the Subcontractor's or any other trade, and to replace such employees within a reasonable time by others against whom there is no such objection.
3. makes any arrangements with his creditors, has a Receiving Order made against him, executes a Bill of Sale, or commits an act of bankruptcy or, being a limited company, goes into liquidation, or has a Receiver appointed.
4. fails within seven days' notice in writing from the Contractor to comply with any of the obligations on the part of the Subcontractor herein contained.

Upon determination by the Contractor the Subcontractor shall not remove any of his equipment, materials or property from the Site and, notwithstanding anything contained in these conditions, shall be entitled to no further payment until completion of the Works by the Contractor or by others whereupon the Subcontractor shall become entitled to payment for Works executed and materials provided by the Subcontractor subject always to the right of the Contractor to set off all losses expense and damages suffered or which may be suffered by the Contractor by reason of such determination and subject further to any other right of set off which the Contractor may have. For the purposes of such completion the Contractor shall have the right to use the Subcontractor's equipment, materials and property on the Site and to any materials or fabricated work lying at the Subcontractor's works or workshop which have been bought or fabricated for the purpose of this Subcontract.

Determination by the Subcontractor

7·2 The Subcontractor may without prejudice to any other of his rights or remedies determine the Subcontractor's employment under this Subcontract if the Contractor:

1. fails to make any payments in accordance with this subcontract.

2. unreasonably attempts or obstructs the carrying out of the Subcontractor's Works

3. makes any arrangements with his creditors, has a Receiving Order made against him, executes a Bill of Sale, or commits an act of bankruptcy or, being a limited company, goes into liquidation, or has a Receiver appointed.

Upon determination by the Subcontractor the Contractor shall pay to the Subcontractor, after taking into account amounts previously paid, such sum as shall be fair and reasonable for the value of work begun and executed, materials on site and the removal of all temporary buildings, plant tools and equipment. Provided always that the right of determination shall be without prejudice to any other rights or remedies which the Subcontractor may possess.

8·0 Temporary Works and Services, Attendance, Related Works

Temporary Accommodation

8·1 The Subcontractor shall provide to the approval of the Contractor and at his own expense, any requisite temporary site office, workshop accommodation, together with the necessary equipment, lighting, power, fuel etc.

Welfare facilities

8·2 The Subcontractor shall, at his own risk have reasonable and free use of the temporary welfare accommodation and/or services (including First Aid facilities and treatment) which the Contractor or the Employer may provide on the Site in connection with the Works.

Temporary services

8·3 The Subcontractor shall, at his own risk, have reasonable and free use, in common with others engaged upon the Site, of the water supply, temporary plumbing, temporary lighting and temporary electric power. Electric power supply for small tools and equipment used on the Site shall not exceed 110V A.C. single phase. Any electrical equipment used to carry out the Works must be in good mechanical condition and suitable for the electric power supply and fittings made available and fitted with suitable plugs, sockets and connectors to BS4343 (CEE 17) or any other standard that the Contractor may direct.

Use of Scaffolding

8·4 The Subcontractor shall at his own risk and at such time(s) and for such period(s) as the Contractor may direct have free use of the Contractor's scaffolding, ladders and mechanical hoisting facilities which may be available on the Site or already in position.

Delivery and Storage of Materials

8·5 The Subcontractor shall provide all materials, package and carriage to and from the Site. He will be responsible for unloading during the progress of his Works, storing in the areas provided and moving his own materials at the Site. Any materials delivered prior to commencement on Site shall be off-loaded by the Contractor at the sole risk and cost of the Subcontractor.

Removal of Rubbish etc.

8·6 All rubbish and/or surplus materials and plant of the Subcontractor must be removed forthwith from the vicinity of the Works, paths, roads etc., to an approved position on the Site.

Cutting Away

8·7 In no circumstances whatsoever shall any cutting away be done without the prior written authority of the Contractor.

Sub-surfaces

8·8 The Subcontractor shall satisfy himself before commencing work, as to the suitability of any surfaces to which the Subcontractor is to fix, apply or lay his work.

This Form is issued by the Joint Council for Landscape Industries comprising:

Landscape Institute
Horticultural Trades Association
British Association Landscape Industries
National Farmers Unions
Institute of Leisure and Amenity Management.

Published for the Joint Council for Landscape Industries by the Landscape Institute 6/7 Barnard Mews, London SW11 1QU and available from RIBA Publications Finsbury Mission, 39 Moreland Street London EC1V 8BB
© JCLI January 1986

Printed by Codicote Press Limited.

Issued January 1986

APPENDIX 5 – THE JCT 80 STANDARD FORM OF TENDER FOR NOMINATED SUB-CONTRACTS

The Standard Form of Nominated Sub-Contract Tender NSC/T and Articles of Nominated Sub-Contract Agreement 1991 Edition

for use with the Standard Form of Building Contract 1980 Edition incorporating Amendments 1 to 9 and Amendment 10 ('SF 80')

53

NSC|T: Part 3

Particular Conditions:

to be agreed by a Contractor and a Sub-Contractor nominated under SF 80 clause 35·6

Pad of 15 sets of 4-page form

The Tender NSC/T and Agreement comprise:

NSC/T Part 1   **The Architect's/The Contract Administrator's Invitation to Tender to a Sub-Contractor**

NSC/T Part 2   **Tender by a Sub-Contractor**

NSC/T Part 3   **Particular Conditions: to be agreed by a Contractor and a Sub-Contractor nominated under SF 80 clause 35·6**

Agreement NSC/A   **The Standard Form of Articles of Nominated Sub-Contract Agreement between a Contractor and a Nominated Sub-Contractor**

Pads containing sets of NSC/T Part 1, NSC/T Part 2 and Agreement NSC/A are each available separately.

The **Standard Conditions of Nominated Sub-Contract (Conditions NSC/C) 1991 Edition** referred to in Agreement NSC/A, Article 1·1, are issued separately and are by that Article incorporated in the Nominated Sub-Contract.

JCT

Joint Contracts Tribunal for the Standard Form of Building Contract   1991 Edition

Part 3 – Particular Conditions

Note: NSC/T Part 3 must be completed by the Contractor and the Sub-Contractor forthwith after receipt by the Contractor of the Instruction of the Architect/the Contract Administrator on Nomination NSC/N nominating the Sub-Contractor under SF 80 35·6.

Upon its completion the Contractor and the Sub-Contractor must sign NSC/T Part 3 on page 4.

The agreed provisions of NSC/T Part 3 items 1, 2 and 4 supersede the entries in items 1, 2 and 3 on pages 6 and 7 of NSC/T Part 2 which entries must be deleted and the deletions initialled by or on behalf of the Contractor and the Sub-Contractor.

The identification term in column 1 is used in NSC/T Part 3 for the document whose full title is given in column 2.

Identification term	Title
SF 80 35	Clause 35 of the Standard Form of Building Contract, 1980 Edition, all versions, incorporating Amendments 1 to 9 and Amendment 10 *(Nominated Sub-Contractors).*
NSC/T	The Standard Form of Nominated Sub-Contract Tender 1991 Edition
– Part 1	Part 1: The Architect's/The Contract Administrator's Invitation to Tender to a Sub-Contractor.
– Part 2	Part 2: Tender by a Sub-Contractor.
– Part 3	Part 3: Particular Conditions: to be agreed by a Contractor and a Sub-Contractor nominated under SF 80 35·6.
Agreement NSC/A	The Standard Form of Articles of Nominated Sub-Contract Agreement between a Contractor and a Nominated Sub-Contractor, 1991 Edition.
Conditions NSC/C	The Standard Conditions of Nominated Sub-Contract incorporated by reference into Agreement NSC/A, Article 1·1, 1991 Edition.
Agreement NSC/W	The Standard Form of Employer/Nominated Sub-Contractor Agreement, 1991 Edition.
Nomination NSC/N	The Standard Form of Nomination Instruction for a Sub-Contractor nominated under SF 80 35·6.

Part 3 – Particular Conditions

Items to be completed by the Contractor and the Sub-Contractor

Notes on completion of these Particular Conditions

[a] Insert the same details as in NSC/T Part 1, pages 2 and 3.
In NSC/T Part 3 the expression 'Contract Administrator' is applicable where the Nomination Instruction on Nomination NSC/N will be issued under a Local Authorities version of the Standard Form of Building Contract and by a person who is not entitled to the use of the name 'Architect' under and in accordance with the Architects (Registration) Acts 1931 to 1969. If so, the expression 'Architect' shall be deemed to have been deleted throughout Tender NSC/T. Where the person who will issue the aforesaid Nomination Instruction is entitled to the use of the name 'Architect' the expression 'Contract Administrator' shall be deemed to have been deleted throughout NSC/T.

[b] The Sub-Contractor's entries in NSC/T Part 2, items 1 to 4 should be considered when agreeing the entries in NSC/T Part 3.

[c] Conditions NSC/C state in clause 2·1: 'The Sub-Contractor shall carry out and complete the Sub-Contract Works in accordance with the agreed programme details in NSC/T Part 3, item 1, and reasonably in accordance with the progress of the Works but subject to receipt of the notice to commence work on site as detailed in NSC/T Part 3, item 1, and to the operation of clauses 2·2 to 2·7.' *(extension of Sub-Contract time).*

[d] The period of notice must take account of any period stated for the execution of the Sub-Contract Works off-site prior to commencement on site.

56

[a] Main Contract Works and location:

[a] Sub-Contract Works:

[b]

1   (1) Period required by the Architect/the Contract Administrator to approve drawings after receipt will be that set out in NSC/T Part 1, item 14.

[c] (2) The earliest starting date and the latest starting date for the Sub-Contract Works to be carried out on site:

are   (earliest)

and   (latest)

(3) Periods required for:

(i) submission for approval of all necessary Sub-Contractor's drawings etc. *(co-ordination, installation, shop or builders' work or other as appropriate)*   weeks

(ii) the execution of the Sub-Contract Works

off-site (if any)
prior to commencement on site   weeks

on site   weeks
from expiry of **period required for notice to commence**
[d]   **work on site** which is   weeks

(4) Further details:

Part 3 – Particular Conditions

Items to be completed by the Contractor and the Sub-Contractor *continued*

1   *continued*

[e] If the Sub-Contractor and the Contractor are able to agree a programme for the Sub-Contract Works this should be set out here or on an attached sheet.

[e] (5) Other arrangements:
state whether they are additional to those in items (3) and (4) or whether they supersede the details at items (3) and (4).

57

[f] Clause 5B can only be used where the Contractor under the Value Added Tax (General) Regulations 1985, Regulations 12(3) and 26 or any amendment or re-making thereof has been allowed to prepare the tax documents in substitution for an authenticated receipt issued by the Sub-Contractor under Regulation 12(4) of the above Regulations; and the Sub-Contractor has consented to the use of this method.

2   Conditions NSC/C clause 6·5·2

Insurance cover for any one occurrence or series of occurrences arising out of one event   £

3   Conditions NSC/C clause 4·30·1·2   The Adjudicator is:

Conditions NSC/C clause 4·32·1·2   The Trustee-Stakeholder is:

[g] Clause 5A-5 or clause 5B-5 can only apply where the Sub-Contractor is satisfied at the date the Sub-Contract is entered into that his output tax on all supplies to the Contractor under the Sub-Contract will be at either a positive or a zero rate of tax. Some supplies by the Contractor to the Employer are zero rated by a certificate in statutory form. Only the person holding the certificate, usually the Contractor, may zero rate his supply. Sub-Contract supplies for a main contract zero rate by certificate are standard rated: see the VAT leaflet 708 revised 1989.

4   Conditions NSC/C clause 5A/5B

[f]   Value Added Tax – alternative VAT   clause* 5A / 5B to apply
[g]   provisions   clause 5A·5* to apply / not to apply
                                                                                clause 5B·5* to apply / not to apply

[h] The entries in item 5 must have regard to the entry in item 4 of NSC/T Part 2 and are to include any other matters in relation to safety or site security as agreed between the Contractor and the Sub-Contractor.

5   [h]   Any other matters to be set out here or on an attached sheet.

*delete as applicable   **Page 3**

Part 3 – Particular Conditions

Items to be completed by the Contractor and the Sub-Contractor *continued*

[i] If these changes or additions cause the Sub-Contractor to reconsider his Tender on NSC/T Part 2 so that agreement with the Contractor on, and the signing of, NSC/T Part 3 is delayed see SF 80 clause 35·8·2 and clause 35·9·2.

6 [i] Any changes or additions to the information given in NSC/T Part 1:
item 7: obligations or restrictions imposed by the Employer;
item 8: order of Works: Employer's requirements;
item 9: type and location of access;
as confirmed in the Nomination Instruction (Nomination NSC/N) issued by the Architect/ the Contract Administrator

7   Conditions NSC/C
Section 9

Settlement of disputes – Arbitration

Appointor (if no appointor is selected the appointor shall be the President or a Vice-President, Royal Institution of Chartered Surveyors)

President or a Vice-President of:
*Royal Institute of British Architects
*Royal Institution of Chartered Surveyors
*Chartered Institute of Arbitrators

Signed by or on behalf
of the Contractor

Date   19

Signed by or on behalf
of the Sub-Contractor

Date   19

*delete as applicable   **Page 4**

APPENDIX 6 – THE JCLI SUPPLEMENT TO THE JCT INTERMEDIATE FORM IFC 84

Practice Note No. 4 (APRIL 1985) JCLI Supplement to the JCT Intermediate Form IFC 84

The JCLI Agreement for Landscape Works was first issued in April 1978 at which time the 1968 JCT Minor Works Form on which it was based had no provision for 2·7 Plant Failures nor 6·5 Malicious Damage, neither did it cover:-

2·6   Partial possession
3·6   The valuation of variations using tender rates
3·8   P.C. Sums and objections to nominations
3·9   Direct loss and expense if progress is disturbed
4·6   Fluctuations

detailed provisions were therefore incorporated to cover these aspects.

While suitable for the majority of landscape contracts over the six years since it was first published, instances have occurred of Local Authorities expressing reluctance to use the Form on landscape contracts in excess of £75,000.

The JCT has now published an 'Intermediate' Form (IFC 84) for use on all contracts both private and public sector local authority, with or without quantities prepared in accordance with the Standard Method of Measurement (SMM6). While it still does not cover Plant Failures and Malicious Damage, the remaining aspects previously omitted are now provided for.

For those larger landscape contracts the detailed provision of the JCT Intermediate Form may be appropriate and the attached landscape supplementary clauses should be incorporated.

This introductory page may be torn off

Introductory note may be torn off

JCLI Supplement to be read in conjunction with the JCT Intermediate Form (IFC84)

Clause 2·0 Possession and Completion

Add new clause 2·11

Partial Possession by the Employer

2·11 If any at any time before Practical Completion of the Works the Employer with the consent of the Contractor shall take possession of any part or parts of the same (any such part being referred to in this clause 2·11 as 'the relevant part') then notwithstanding anything expressed or implied elsewhere in this Contract:

- for the purpose of clause 2·10 *(Defects liability)* and 4·3 *(Interim payment)* Practical Completion of the relevant part shall be deemed to have occurred and the defects liability period in respect of the relevant part shall be deemed to have commenced on the date on which the Employer shall have taken possession thereof;

- as from the date which the Employer shall have taken possession of the relevant part, the obligation of the Contractor to insure under clause 6·3A, if applicable, shall terminate in respect of the relevant part but not further or otherwise;

- in lieu of any sum to be paid or allowed by the Contractor under clause 2·7 *(Liquidated damages)* in respect of any period during which the Employer shall have taken possession of the relevant part there shall be paid or allowed such sum as bears the same ratio to the sum which would be paid or allowed apart from the provisions of this clause 2·11 as the Contract Sum, less the amount contained therein in respect of the said relevant part, bears to the Contract Sum.

Add new clause 2·12

Failures of Plants (Pre-Practical Completion)

2·12 Any trees, shrubs, grass or other plants, other than those found to be missing or defective as a result of theft or malicious damage and which shall be replaced as set out in clause 6·4 of these conditions, which are found to be defective at practical completion of the works shall be replaced by the Contractor entirely at his own cost unless the Landscape Architect shall otherwise instruct. The Landscape Architect shall certify the dates when in his opinion the Contractor's obligation under this clause have been discharged.

(Post-Practical Completion)

*A The maintenance of trees, shrubs, grass and other plants after the date of the said certificate will be carried out by the Contractor for the duration of the periods stated in accordance with the programme and in the manner specified in the Contract Documents. Any grass which is found to be defective within.......... months, any shrubs, ordinary nursery stock trees or other plants found to be defective within .... months and any trees, semi-mature advanced or extra large nursery stock found to be defective within .... months of the date of Practical Completion and are due to materials or workmanship not in accordance with the contract shall be replaced by the Contractor entirely at his own cost unless the Landscape Architect shall otherwise instruct. The Landscape Architect shall certify the dates when in his opinion the Contractor's obligations under this clause have been discharged.

Note:
Clauses marked · should be completed/deleted as appropriate

*B The maintenance of the trees, shrubs, grass and other plants after the date of the said certificate will be undertaken by the Employer who will be responsible for the replacement of any trees, shrubs, grass or other plants which are subsequently defective.

Clause 4·0 Payment

Add to clause 4·3

and unless the failures of plants as set out in clause 2·7 are in excess of 10% in which case the amount retained shall be adjusted accordingly.

Clause 6·0 Injury, damage and insurance

Add new clause 6·4

Malicious Damage or Theft (before Practical Completion)

†6·4A All loss or damage arising from any theft or malicious damage prior to practical completion shall be made good by the Contractor at his own expense.

B The Contract sum shall include the provisional sum of £.............. * to be expended as instructed by the Landscape Architect in respect of the cost of all work arising from any theft or malicious damage to the works beyond the control of the Contractor prior to practical completion of the works.

Signed .... date ....
for and on behalf of the Employer

Signed .... date ....
for and on behalf of the Contractor

These Supplementary Clauses are issued by the Joint Council for Landscape Industries comprising:-

Landscape Institute
Horticultural Trades Association
British Association Landscape Industries
National Farmers' Union
Institute of Leisure and Amenity Management

Published for the Joint Council for Landscape Industries by the Landscape Institute 6/7 Barnard Mews, London SW11 1QU and available from RIBA Publications Limited Finsbury Mission, 39 Moreland Street, London EC1V 8BB and from RIBA Bookshops
© JCLI June 1985

Printed by Duolith Ltd.
Welwyn Garden City, Hertfordshire

Revised October 1991

APPENDIX 7 – RECENT STATUTORY ACTS, STATUTORY INSTRUMENTS – REGULATIONS/ORDERS – DETR CIRCULARS AND PLANNING POLICY GUIDANCE NOTES RELATING TO THE ENVIRONMENT

STATUTORY ACTS

Alkali and Works Regulations Act 1906
Public Health Act 1936
National Parks and Access to the Countryside Act 1949
Clean Air Acts 1956 and 1968
Weeds Act 1959
Caravan and Control of Development Act 1960
Commons Registration Act 1965
The Countryside Act 1968
Control of Pollution Act 1974
Inner Urban Areas Act 1980
Local Government and Planning Act 1981
T & C Minerals Act 1981
Derelict Land Act 1982
Litter Act 1983
Food and Environment Protection Act 1985
Housing and Planning Act 1986
Forestry Act 1986
Agriculture Act 1986

STATUTORY INSTRUMENTS – REGULATIONS AND ORDERS

1981

81/14	T&CP Tree Preservation Order Amendment Regulations
246	Development in National Parks
288	Wild Life and Countryside Variation of Schedules Order (rev 89, 91, 92 and 94)
1301	Ancient Monument Consent Regulations
1302	Ancient Monument Class Orders
1742	T&CP Enforcement Notices and Appeals Regulations
1743	T&CP Enforcement Enquiries Procedure Rules

1982

82/6	Compulsory Purchase of Land Regulations
209	Commons Schemes Registration Regulations
975	T&CP Mineral Regulations

1346	Wild Life and Countryside Claims for Compensation Regulations

1983

83/21	Wild Life and Countryside Rights of Way Definitive Map Regulations
23	Public Rights of Way Orders and Extinguishing Rights
1190	T&CP Local Plans for Greater London Regulations

1984

84/6	T&CP Structure and Local Plans Amendment Regulations
222	Ancient Monuments Class Consents Amendment Order
421	T&CP Control of Advertisement Regulations
582	Control of Pollution Underground Water Regulations
1285	Operations in Areas of Archaeologial Importance Forms of Notice Order
1286	Areas of Archaeological Importance Notification of Exemption Order
1992	Control of Noise, Code of Practice for Construction Sites Order
2026	Environmentally Sensitive Areas Orders

1985

85/1182	Fees for Applications Regulations
1981	T&CP General Development Amendment No. 2 Order

1986

86/8	T&CP National Parks, AONB and Conservation Areas Order
148	Local Government Reorganisation of Property Order
183	Removal and Disposal of Vehicles Regulations
854	Local Government Inspection of Rights Order
1176	T&CP Agriculture Forestry in National Parks Order
1510	Control of Pesticides Regulations
1536	Land Registration Official Searches Rules
2249	Environmentally Sensitive Areas General Notes [Note: see also separate SIs for each of 36 Designated SSSIs]

1987

87/632	Forestry Felling of Trees Regulations
701	T&CP Written Representation Procedure Regulations
764	T&CP Use Classes Order (rev 95/297)

1730	Code of Practice for Construction and Open Site Regulations
1750	T&CP Simplified Planning Zone Regulations
1760	T&CP Structure and Local Plan Amendment Regulations
1849	T&CP Simplified Planning Zone Excluded Development Order

1988

88/424	Harbour Work Assessment of Effect on the Environment Regulations
945	T&CP Determination by Inspector Procedure Regulations
963	T&CP Tree Preservation Order Regulations (rev 69/17, 81/14)
1199	T&CP Assessment of Environmental Effects Regulations
1207	Afforestation Assessment of Effect on the Environment Regulations
1217	Land Drainage Assessment of Effect on the Environment Regulations
1218	Salmon Farming in Marine Waters Assessment of Effect on the Environment Regulations
1241	Highways Assessment of Effect on the Environment Regulations
1291	Farm Woodland Scheme
1336	Harbour Works Assessment of Effect on the Environment Regulations
1352	Set Aside Regulations (rev 89/1042, 90/1716, 91)
1541	Transport and Works Assessment of Effect on the Environment Regulations
1815	T&CP Permitted Development (rev 94/3294)

1989

89/670	Control of Advertisement Regulations

1990

90/367	T&CP Assessment of Environmental Effects Amendment Regulations
442	Electricity and Pipe Line Assessment of Effect on the Environment Regulations
703	Highways Road Humps Regulations (rev 90/1500)
1519	Listed Building and Conservation Area Regulations

1991

91/111	Street Litter Fixed Penalty Regulations
324	Control of Silage and Slurry

1324	Street Litter Control Notices
1590	Crop Residue Restrictions on Burning
1624	Registration of Waste Carriers

1992

92/666	T&CP Control of Advertisements Regulations
905	Farm Woodland Premium Scheme
1494	T&CP Assessment of Environmental Effects Amendment Regulations
3240	Public Access to Environmental Information

1993

93/10	T&CP Public Path Regulations
11	Creating, Diverting and Extinguishing Public Paths

1994

94/677	Wind Generators, MSA and Coast Protection Assessment of Effect on the Environment Regulations
1291	Habitats in Water Fringe Land (rev 96/1798)
1292	Habitats in Set Aside Land (rev 96/1478)
1293	Habitats in Salt Marsh Areas (rev 96/1479)
1381	Ancient Monuments Class Consents
1541	Trains, Railways and General Transport Assessment of Effect on the Environment Regulations
2349	Countryside Access Regulations
2351	Control of Advertisements (Site Flags)
2716	Conservation of Habitats

1995

95/419	T&CP General Development Procedures Order
1541	Transport and Works Assessment of Effect on the Environment Regulations
2195	Land Drainage Improvements Assessment of Effect on the Environment Regulations
2258	Unauthorised Development Assessment of Effect on the Environment Regulations
2825	Amendments to 1981 and 1985 Wild Life and Countryside Act for Waterways, Wild Animals and Birds

DETR CIRCULARS

1978

36/1978	Trees & Forestry – Encouragement to Tree Planting

1985
1/85	Conditions in Planning Consents
2/85	Oil and Gas Operations
5/85	Reservoirs Act – Landscaping Raised Reservoirs
25/85	Restoring Mineral Workings with a High Water Table

1986
6/86	Access of Public to Meetings and Papers
18/86	Planning Appeals by Written Representations
19/86	Planning Control of Hazardous Substances, Conservation, Advertisements

1987
11/87	Time Limits on Written Representations
12/87	Redundant Hospital Sites
21/87	Contaminated Land – Sewage Farms, Industrial and Land Fill
27/87	Nature Conservation (replacing 108/87) – Landscape and Wild Life

1988
3/88	Preparation of Unitary Development Plans
10/88	Code for Planning Enquiries and Appeals
15/88	Procedures for Environmental Assessments and Statements
88/24	EAs in Simplified Planning and Enterprise Zones

1989
89/14	Space Standards for Mobile Homes and Caravan Sites
89/17	Development Control on Landfill Sites

1990
90/7	Avoiding EC National Discrimination
90/14	EA and Energy S of S Approval Required for Electricity Stations and Overhead Lines
90/16	EC Directive on Public Works Tendering
90/17	Protection of Rights of Way of Ploughed, Field Edge and Unsurfaced Highways

1991
15/91	Compensation and Compulsory Purchase
16/91	Obligations under Planning Compensation Act 1991
18/91	Development – Planning Systems
20/91	Fees for Planning Applications

21/91   Enforcement of Planning Regulations
23/91   Costs in Planning Enquiries
24/91   Crime Prevention
26/91   Control of Development

__1992__
1/92   Planning Controls over SSSIs – Requirements for
        Temporary Uses
19/92   Planning Controls Applicable also to Local Authorities
30/92   NRA Powers for Flood Defence Work

__1993__
2/93   Managing, Altering and Extinguishing Public Rights of
        Way

__1994__
1/94   Provision for Gypsies
5/94   Planning out Crime
7/94   Further Projects Requiring Environmental Assessments

__1995__
3/95   EAs Required for Permitted Development
9/95   Consolidation of Permitted Development Orders
11/95   Conditions on Planning Permissions
13/95   EAs and Unauthorised Development

PLANNING POLICY GUIDANCE NOTES

PPG   1 (1992) General Policy and Principles
                Operation of the Planning Control System and Time
                Limits

      2 (1994) Green Belts
                Policy, Objectives, Protection and Definition of
                Boundaries

      3 (1992) Housing
                Constraints, Demand and Needs

      4 (1992) Industrial and Commercial Development – Small Firms

      5 (1992) Simplified Planning Zones
                The Purpose and Planning Procedures in SPZs

6 (1993) Town Centres and Major Retail Development

7 (1992) The Countryside and the Rural Economy

8 (1992) Telecommunications
          Planning Authorities to Co-operate to Ensure
              Economic Growth

9 (1989) Strategic Planning Guidance for the South East
          Unitary Development Plans and Land Use Objectives

10 (1988) Strategic Planning Guidance for West Midlands
          Unitary Development Plans and Land Use Objectives

11 (1988) Strategic Planning Guidance for Merseyside
          Unitary Development Plans and Land Use Objectives

12 (1992) Development Plans and Regional Planning Guidance
          Code of Practice; Content, Range and Consistency of
              Plans

13 (1995) Transport
          Reduction in the Need to Travel, inc. Tourism and
              Recreation

14 (1990) Development on Unstable Land
          Selection of Appropriate Uses, Underground, on
              Slopes, Changed Water Tables

15   Deleted

16 (1990) Archaeology and Planning
          Mapping, Preliminary Investigations and Preservation

17 (1991) Sport and Recreation
          NPFA and LPA Standards for Public Open Space

18 (1991) Enforcing Planning Control
          Powers under 1991 Planning and Compensation Act,
              revises PPG 1, 4 and Circ 22/80

19 (1992) Outdoor Advertisement Controls
          Strict Control in Conservation Areas and Open
              Countryside

20 (1992) Coastal Planning
          Needs of Tourism, Recreation, Flood Defences, Water
            and Sewage

21 (1992) Tourism
          Economics and the Effect on the Environment

22 (1993) Renewable Energy

INDEX

Addressing CDM Regulations Through Quality Management Systems

Brian Thorpe

The 1994 CDM (Construction (Design and Management)) Regulations placed new demands upon those engaged in the construction industry. The question of how these demands are to be best identified, managed and controlled has become a major issue for many organizations.

Several of the better organizations already have in place well-proven quality management systems, which help them to demonstrate their professionalism and to win and manage contracts. Can such systems be adapted to meet the additional requirements of CDM? This methodical and 'easy to follow' book demonstrates how this can be achieved and why quality systems provide such a practicable and effective framework for CDM compliance.

Part 1 concentrates on those factors which constitute a sound quality management system, and also discusses the more proactive TQM (Total Quality Management) approach and its relationship to the formal quality system. The author then describes how these mesh with the key expectancies of the CDM Regulations. Part 2 looks at the roles of each of the key parties, namely client, designer, planning supervisor, principal contractor and contractor, along with their respective duties and interface obligations under the Regulations.

Subjects such as selecting and appointing others, setting quality levels, establishing and using preferred lists, team working, project control, the use of quality plans, feedback, training, and risk assessment are all discussed. Numerous sample documents are included. Finally, the book looks at the likely effects upon the quality systems of those concerned, with particular emphasis on policy, organization, and responsibility and procedures.

Gower

An Introduction to Landscape Design and Construction

James Blake

How do you design a landscape suitable for its intended uses? How can the natural qualities of a landscape be enhanced with new features and focal points? How can you make pedestrians stay on the footpath? What kind of plant, path or wall should you put where and what sort of contract should you choose for your client's contractor? This refreshingly down-to-earth introduction to the vast subject of landscape design and construction answers all these questions, guiding new students through the many facets of professional practice and welding together the artistic, legal, financial, environmental and management issues which can seem so dauntingly disconnected.

Illustrated with original drawings by the author, photographs and sample plans and facsimiles, this readable, jargon-free book opens with an explanation of design and aesthetic principles, exploring the history of our relationship to landscape, and showing how design principles can be applied to influence reactions to the finished site. The author then considers the different elements of hard landscape and their relative merits in different situations. The soft landscape section includes coverage of the different effects of mass and form, natural and abstract planting, and the difficult subject of plant selection. A step-by-step guide through all the stages of project management, from initial discussions with clients, site inspection, surveying and quoting, through tendering, contracting, contractual agreements, development from concept design to final plans and drawings, as well as maintenance, provides readers with a plain-speaking reference on client management and contractual administration which will become their bible. The book ends with a guide to drawing and lettering techniques. A bibliography and list of useful organizations is also included.

Gower